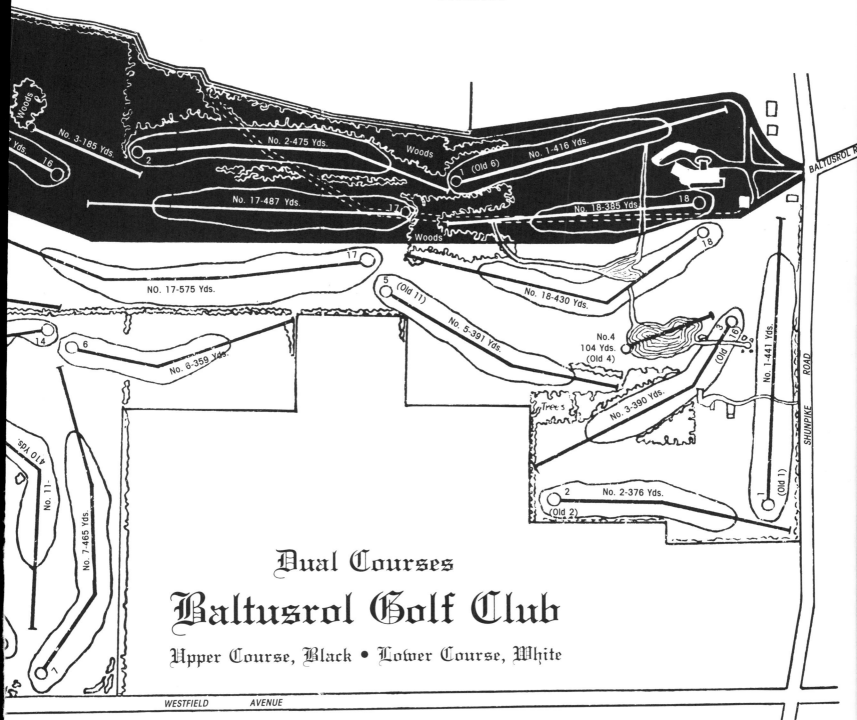

# Dual Courses
# Baltusrol Golf Club
## Upper Course, Black • Lower Course, White

# *Baltusrol*
## 100 YEARS

## *The Centennial History of Baltusrol Golf Club*

By
Robert S. Trebus and Richard C. Wolffe, Jr.

Creative and Editorial Advisor, Stephen Goodwin
Library and Pictorial Research, Stuart F. Wolffe

# Foreword

As Baltusrol's twenty-fifth President, I knew I'd have the privilege of serving as we celebrated our Centennial—but I had no idea that I still had so much to learn about the club and its golf courses. Of course I had seen plaques and photographs that adorn the clubhouse and commemorate so many special Baltusrol events, and I was familiar with the tales that have been handed down over the years, preserved and embellished in clubhouse lore.

Yet as I watched this book take shape, I was fascinated to learn more about exactly how Baltusrol had won its place as a landmark in American golf. It didn't happen by accident. Our founder, Louis Keller didn't even play golf—but it was Keller, who took the lead in making sure that our golf courses stayed ahead of the curve, and Keller who orchestrated every detail to establish our reputation as a premier site for important tournaments.

His story is only one of many told in this book. You will also read about the flamboyant A.W. Tillinghast, "Tillie the Terrible," the architect of our Dual Courses, who reported for work in a chauffeured limousine—but I don't want to give away too much of the story. Let me say that our history is filled with memorable personalities.

Virtually every great golfer of the century has left a footprint at Baltusrol and some of them, like Jack Nicklaus, have left large, indelible tracks. Both of Jack's classic Open duels with Arnold Palmer in 1967 and Isao Aoki in 1980 are recounted in vivid detail.

The Centennial Book Committee has done a tremendous job of research and writing to get so much between these covers. It's all here—the people, the championships, the parties, the challenges, the hundreds of anecdotes that convey the flavor of the past. The members of the Committee, especially Bob Trebus, Rick Wolffe, Stu Wolffe and Ken Wagner, devoted literally thousands of hours to produce a book that wouldn't be just another dry-as-dust club history but a volume that was complete, informative, entertaining, and beautiful.

I think you'll agree that they succeeded on all counts. Just browse through the wonderful photographs—many of which have never before been published—and you can watch the Baltusrol story unfold in pictures.

I'm proud to share with all of you, both members and guests, the rich panorama of Baltusrol's first century.

F. Duffield Meyercord
President

## To My Fellow Members at Baltusrol

*I am honored to preface this commemorative chronicle of Baltusrol's first 100 years, for I shall always count Baltusrol among my favorite golf courses—it is certainly one of the finest in the world. Part of its greatness is its extreme fairness, which has made the course such an accurate test of golfing ability and the perfect venue for seven U.S. Open Championships. Significant too is that throughout its years, the club's members have always respected the stature of their golf course and have sought to ensure that it has been maintained to perfection.*

*Baltusrol has been the setting for some unforgettable moments in my career. In 1967, my victory over Arnold Palmer in our fourth round match was probably one of the most exciting rounds in my career, as I won my second U.S. Open and broke Ben Hogan's U.S. Open scoring record. One of my most satisfying moments came thirteen years later, when I won my head-to-head duel with Isao Aoki in the 1980 U.S. Open. I had just turned forty that January, which didn't thrill me, and I had not won a tournament in 18 months. People were saying I was finished, and I guess I was beginning to wonder if they were right. Winning that day taught me that life doesn't end at forty—and obviously, for Baltusrol, greatness endures well past 100 years.*

*There is a wonderful affinity enjoyed among the world's golfers. Beyond a love for the game itself, we share a reverence for its history and commitment to its preservation. In a few short years, we will welcome the twenty-first century and golf will continue to be introduced to new ideas and developments. I hope the game that has given us all such tremendous pleasure will be preserved and enjoyed for generations to come, and I hope that Baltusrol will thrive and prosper for another hundred years.*

*Congratulations and best wishes.*

*Jack Nicklaus*

# Dedicated to Mr. Louis Keller

*Gratitude to Dee Trebus and Liz Wolffe for their support.*

*Thanks also for the support from Bob and Rick's
respective firms, Trelined Communications and
Deloitte & Touche LLP.*

***This book was made possible by contributions of many including:***

David Applegate, Jim Brooks, Philip W. Brown,Jr., Diane Becker, Karen Bednarski,
Ed Beimfohr, Emile Bontempo, Susan Cummings, Ted Dalziel, Frank Durnien, Bill Eldridge,
Lorene Emerson, Ken Estabrook, David Fay, Ken Estabrook, Kay Farrell, Richard Fraser, Red
Hoffman, Cheryl Ingersol, Brent Ingersol, Hilton Jervey, Rees Jones, Kenneth Kakol, Harriet
Kalendek, Larry Kelly, Leslie Linden, Joyce Manko, Barry Markowitz, Thomas McGill, Jr.,
Mark Morrison, Bunny O'Neill, Hugho Parrote, Al Reed, Richard Rumery, Angie Singletary,
Craig Smith, Jean Storey, Nancy Stulack, Neal Turtell, Les Unger, Robert Walker, Matt Ward,
Steve Weisser, and Gene Westmorland.

***Photo Credits*** (Code: T-Top, C-Center, B-Bottom, R-Right, L Left)

*American Golf* (108 L, 109 TR, BR, 109 B, 110 C); *American Golfer* (106, 118 BR, TR, TC,
119 BC, 122 LC, 126 LR, 128 UL, 129 C, 156 TL, TR, CL, CR, BR, 160 B); AP/WIDE WORLD
PHOTOS (137); Bachrach (31 C, B, 106, 45, 146-148 ); Philip W. Brown, Jr. (58 T); Michael
Cohen (83, 151 ); *Country Life* (45); *Golf* (5, 6, 14 UR, 38 TL, 58 BL, BR, 106, 108 TR, 109
CR, L, 110 T, 111 B, C, 112 T, 113 CR, T, C, 114 T, B, 115, 116, 118 C, CR, CL, 120 B, 121 C, 122
BC, TR, 154, 163 B); Marc Feldman (153 BR); *Golf Illustrated* (14 CR, LR, 15 T, B, 16 T, B, 17 T,
22 TR, 27 TL, 46, 57 T, 38 TR, 121 T, 120 T, B, CB, 123 RB, LT, RT, 125 T, 126 T); *Golf World* (30,
31, 90 B 133 BR, 134 B, 135 TR, 139 TR, BR); *Golfing* (22 BL, 128 B, 129T, BR); Robert Trent
Jones, Inc. (26 BR, 39 R, 80 L, 81 C); Leanord Kamsler (138); Levick (119 LC, 126 BR, 126
TR); Lawrence Levy (152); Dan McKean (1, 21 T, 33, 36 TL, TR, 38CR, BR, C, 63 B, 67 B, C, 75
C. 75B. 76 B, C, 81 TR, 86, 87, 88 B, 89 B, 92 B, 93  C, B, 94 C, 95 B, T, 96 B, 97 B, 98 B, 100 C,
101 T, C,, 103  TB, 104 T, B, 105 B, back cover); Jim Morrison (34 B, 37 T, B, 153 R); Bruce
Morrison (149 TL, TR, C, 150 C); Bill Nesbit (119 TR); *Newark Evening News* (131 T); *The
Golfer* (111 L, 112 B); The *Metropolitan Golfer* (22 BR, 27 TR, 107 TL, 126 CB, 125 B, C, 156
CR); New Jersey State Golf Association  (157 L); *The New York Times (*18); Lou Odor
(cover, 10 LR); John Parsekian (36 L, CR, B L); Catherine Rock (23, 24); Skyshots (35 T, 66,
68, 69 C, L, 72, 73 T, 75 T, 77 TC, 88 T, 89 T, C, 90 T, 91 T, CB, 92 T, 93 T, 94 T, B, 95 C, 96 T,
97 T, 98 T, 99 B, 100 T, B, 101 B, 102 T, B, 103 C, 105 T, C); The Sports Marketing Group
(2, 82); Peter Stackpole, *Life Magazine* C Time Warner Inc.(134 T); United States Golf
Association (13, 23, 28, 23, 30, 38 CB, B, CR, 39 C, 58, 106, 136, 137, TL, 139 TC, 139 BL);
UPI/BETTMANN (135); Vogue (2); Ken Wagner (33 BR, 35 B, 38 CR, 99 T, 107 TR, CR, BL, BC,
BR, 150 R C, 157R, (1 BR); Robert Walker (137 B); Wilson Sports (29, 137 R).

Library of Congress Catalogue Card Number: 95-077892

ISBN 0-9647398-0-1

Printed by Progress Printing, Lynchburg, Virginia, USA.

# Preface and Acknowledgements

$\mathcal{W}$hen asked to produce a book about Baltusrol's 100 years, we first thought of updating James J. Mahon's *Baltusrol: 90 Years in the Mainstream of American Golf.* We also gathered a collection of centennial books from other clubs. The more we reflected on this milestone in Baltusrol's history, the more convinced we were that our book should be broader in scope. More than an update was needed, and the other books were more limited in their approach. Our club has played a leading role in American golf, and our story isn't ours alone—it belongs to everyone interested in the game itself.

Fortunately we were blessed with documentation and photographs dating back to the day the club was founded in 1895. The Centennial Book Committee devoted many of their free evenings and weekends scouring the Clubhouse for memorabilia and researching the club's archives for photographs, facts and information. They read through minutes of every Board of Governors' meeting, scrapbooks, announcements, Open correspondence, etc. But there were still many holes to be filled.

Thanks to the efforts of Stu Wolffe, who spent hours and hours in the Library of Congress, searching every golf publication from the late 1800's through the present, we accumulated a wealth of information. In addition to the extensive press coverage of our 14 national championships and many other tournaments, we discovered a treasure trove in the writings of our course architect, A.W. Tillinghast. He liked to expound on his philosophy of golf course architecture and often illustrated his arguments with reference to holes he had designed at Baltusrol. Many fascinating stories were uncovered about Baltusrol and its members that had been lost in time, such as the contributions to early golf by James Tyng, the forgotten club champion—Craig Hamilton, and the heroic matches of Margaret Gavin.

After organizing this bountiful resource, we began writing. Bob Trebus directed the overall production and was tireless in his efforts. He also secured many of the photographs from outside sources and performed the computerized page layout.

Rick Wolffe developed the book's outline, directed much of the research and took on the bulk of the writing and editing. These duties were shared by Steve Goodwin, a contributing editor of *Golf*, who wrote and edited significant portions and added a touch of style to much of the prose.

And the pictures—well, we think they're something special. Most of the more than 200 historic photographs that compliment the story were gathered by Stu Wolffe from early issues of celebrated golf publications dating as far back as 1895. Many of these photographs were reproduced with startling clarity, while other originals, unfortunately, were of poor quality and could not be fully restored.

Special thanks go to Ken Wagner, who provided a great deal of the current club photographs and was always available to help us in laying out the book.

Thanks also go to several others for their contribution: Richard and Seena Brown researched and wrote the Women's section; Bob McCoy provided valuable input to get the project going in the right direction; Gil Zimmerman wrote the piece on the Baltusrol Invitational; Lowell Schmidt Art Services provided the creative touch for the book's design; and Progress Printing restored most of the original quality of the photographs and produced this beautiful book.

There were also many others who made notable contributions, and we hope we have recognized all of them in the credits on the preceding page.

Most of the credit, however, belongs to the hundreds of devoted club members and staff who from our very beginnings made sure Baltusrol would be in the forefront of golf. And no one worked harder to achieve this goal than our founder, Louis Keller, who never played a round of golf but loved everything about it. We therefore dedicate this book to him.

Centennial Book Committee

Robert S. Trebus, Chairman
Richard C. Wolffe, Jr.
Stuart F. Wolffe
Kenneth R. Wagner

*Bob Trebus, Chairman.*

*Rick Wolffe.*

*Stu Wolffe.*

*Ken Wagner.*

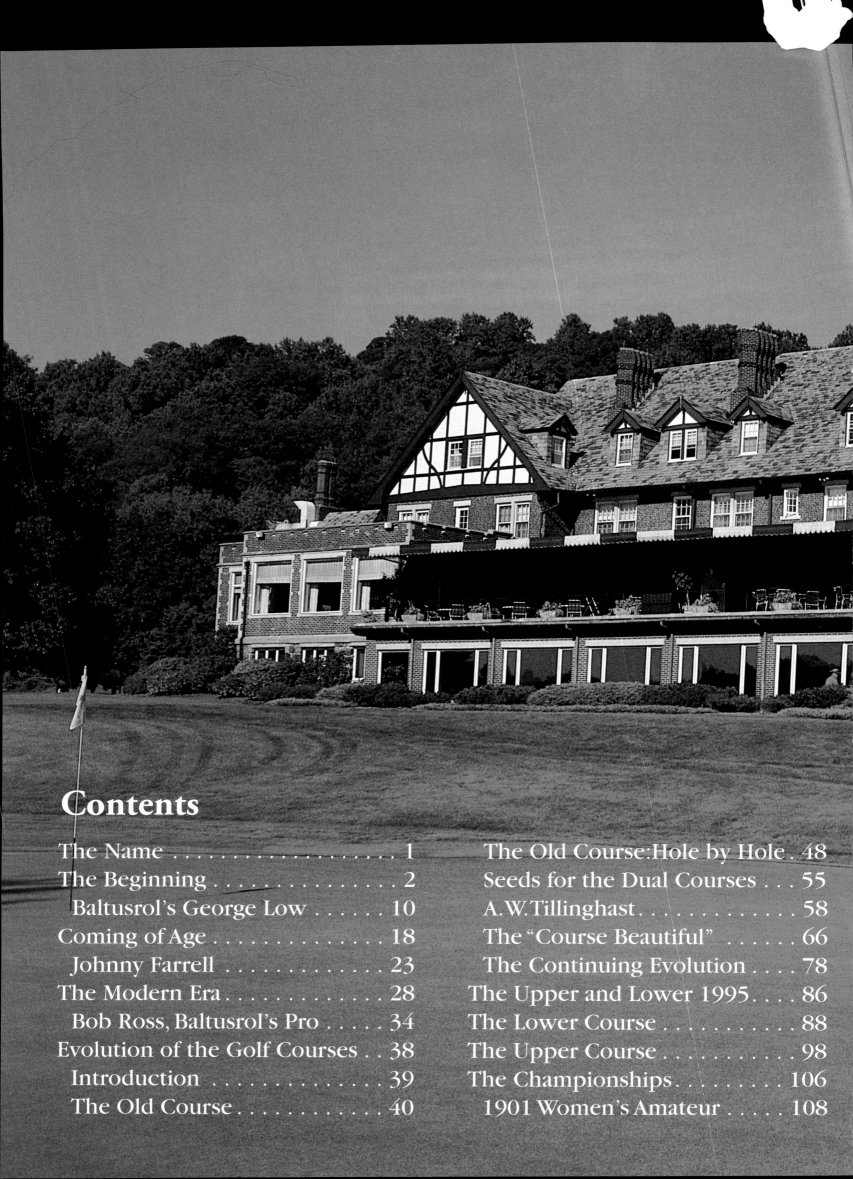

# Contents

# The Name

*Ye friends that weep around my grave*
*Compose your minds to rest*
*Prepare with me for sudden death*
*And live forever blest.*

*The naked, lifeless body lay by the gate in a puddle of icy water, bound hand and foot by heavy rope, with ugly bruises visible about the throat. The coroner fixed the time of death at approximately one hour after midnight: "There were no mortal wounds on the deceased," he would testify at the trial, "but his throat appeared to be so hard pressed as to convince me that he had been chocked to death." The date was February 22, 1831, the place a small modestly profitable farm and farmhouse on the mountain between the towns of Springfield and Summit, New Jersey.*

The victim's wife had witnessed virtually the entire brutal event. "We were awaken [sic] at about midnight by a loud pounding on the door," she testified, "and then the door burst open and two men came in and dragged my husband out of bed, punched and beat him, and took him out of the house. They seemed to ignore me, but I could see the face of the larger man—a full face with large whiskers and light blue eyes. I watched them tie my husband and choke him and throw him on the ground, and not knowing what to do, I hid myself in the woods and wandered about until daylight. Then I went for help to a neighbor's house."

Returning with three local men, she found her husband's body near the gate; the house had been thoroughly pillaged, in an apparent search for money or valuables. Two men, Peter B. Davis and Lycidias Baldwin, were obvious suspects: Davis had made no secret in the community that he was in need of money; he had been openly asking around for someone to go with him "where we can get a thousand dollars," and he had large whiskers and light blue eyes.

Davis was quickly taken into custody, but when Baldwin heard that he had been taken, he took a room in a tavern in a neighboring town and killed himself with an apparent overdose of narcotic.

At Davis' trial in Newark, despite overwhelming, albeit circumstantial, evidence, much of it ruled inadmissible by the presiding judge, the jury acquitted Davis of the crime. However, according to a footnote to the transcript of the trial, he was then indicted on four charges of forgery (of which the court documents reveal no details), convicted on all counts, and sentenced to serve a total of 24 years, during which he died in prison.

The affair somehow caught the attention of the New York metropolitan newspapers which gave it wide and sensational coverage. And the deceased farmer, one Baltus Roll by name, whose tombstone may be found in the Revolutionary Cemetery in Westfield, NJ, went to his final resting place unaware that his name – in a slightly contracted form – would be immortalized in the mountain where his home had been located and at the golf club of the same name.

by Marshall Lewis

10 OCTOBER, 1895        PRICE TEN CENTS.     FOUR DOLLARS A YEAR

VOL. VI., NO. 15 (WHOLE NUMBER 148).     PUBLICATION OFFICE, 156 FIFTH AVENUE, NEW YORK.     COPYRIGHT, 1895, BY THE FASHION COMPANY.     TRADE MARK REGISTERED.

# VOGUE

*The* year was 1895. Grover Cleveland was in the White House, the country was prospering as never before, and Americans were discovering their passion for golf.

The first rounds of golf on American soil were played on makeshift courses on a lawn in Chicago, an apple orchard in Yonkers, and a meadow in Vermont. And from there the royal and ancient game quickly spread and captured the national imagination. Newspapers began to report on this new pastime not merely as a curiosity but as a "craze." By 1895 the New York Times noted that weekend trains to the suburbs were crowded with passengers "armed with golf bags," and the Chicago Daily News published testimonials extolling the healthful benefits of the game. Fewer than eighty bona fide golf courses had

# *The Beginning 1895 - 1922*

been built by 1895; by the turn of the century, there would be nearly a thousand in play. So explosive was the growth of golf that the New York Times made this pronouncement on December 27, 1895:

"In the history of American field sport there can be found no outdoor pastime that developed and attained such popularity in such a relatively short period of time as

the game of golf."

The appeal of the new sport was not lost on Louis Keller. Indeed, Keller – the man who founded the Social Register – was perfectly situated to observe just how avidly men and women of fashion were taking up the game. The son of a patent lawyer who became Commissioner of U. S. Patents, Keller had tried his hand at gunsmithing and dairying

before coming up with the idea of the Register in 1887. Though he was only 30 years old, Keller didn't lack confidence; he set himself up as the sole arbiter of social acceptance. The only way to be included in the Register was to meet with Keller's approval, and one of his contemporaries summed up his character by saying that Keller "was a gentleman—but just."

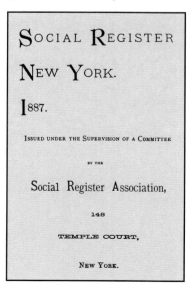

SOCIAL REGISTER

NEW YORK.

1887.

ISSUED UNDER THE SUPERVISION OF A COMMITTEE

BY THE

Social Register Association,

148

TEMPLE COURT,

NEW YORK.

*Painting of Baltusrol farmland around 1890.*

Ironically, Keller did not play golf himself, but he had many acquaintances who did. In fashionable spots like Newport, the Hamptons, and Westchester County, golf was all the rage, and Keller decided that he wanted to get in on this new trend. He tried to persuade the Short Hills Club, a racquet club to which he had belonged since 1881, to build a new clubhouse and golf course. When the club balked, he decided to go it alone.

Keller owned some 500 acres of land in Springfield Township. This was the same land farmed by Baltus Roll some 50 years earlier, and the same land that overlooked the Battle of Springfield in the revolutionary War. Some 110 years earlier, from the high ground, American soldiers traced the watchfires of

maneuvering British forces and General George Washington, himself, observed the Redcoats and Hessians from an overlook known as Washington's Rock. On this property, Keller fixed up an old farm house as his country place, his primary residence was the Calumet Club in New York City—the very club, incidentally, where in 1894, over a dinner attended by representatives of five leading golf clubs, the United States Golf Association was formed. Keller was not present at this meeting, but in April 1895 he sent a brief letter to selected friends, inviting them to become members of the new golf club he was forming. The invitation was perfectly simple and straightforward, and indicated that two essential matters had already been determined. The first was

that the golf course was ready for play. Keller had retained George Hunter, an Englishman who later became a member of Baltusrol and served on the Board of Governors, to design nine holes.

Second, Keller had already given the club a name. In an article in the New York Herald about the formation of Baltusrol, a certain Louise McAllister was given credit for choosing the name. The Herald tells us that Miss McAllister, the daughter of one of the lions of New York society, was a frequent guest at Keller's parties, and that she coined the name by running the murdered farmer's first and last names together, Baltus and Roll, and dropping off the final "l." Actually, the spelling of the man's name had always been a problem; some newspapers referred to him as Baltus Rahl, and his tombstone read Boltos Roll. The mountain had long since been known as Baltusrol, in whatever variant spelling, and the rutted road that ran near the site of the clubhouse had always been

called Baltusrol Way. Miss McAllister had only given the final orthographic form to the haunting, evocative name that had long been a part of local lore.

In any case, the Baltusrol Golf Club had been launched, and the response to Keller's letter was prompt and enthusiastic. On October 19, 1895, the Baltusrol Golf Club was formally opened. The new members and their guests arrived by bicycle, rail, and carriage to celebrate the occasion. Among those present were, as one newspaper put it, "nearly all the society people in the immediate vicinity." Keller had rallied his acquaintances to help Baltusrol make its debut, and the prominence of the original membership – about 30 strong – virtually guaranteed that the club would be in the social vanguard.

One week later, in his office in New York City, Keller sat down with three other men to organize the club. The three were Arthur D. Weeks, John DuFais, and Arthur B.

---

### BALTUSROL GOLF CLUB

*Y*OU are invited to become a member of the Baltusrol Golf Club, the grounds of which are at the foot of Baltusrol Mountain, midway between Orange, Morristown, Newark and Plainfield, about seventeen miles from New York. A course of nine holes, averaging two hundred and fifty yards and with forty-foot greens has been laid out upon sandy hills naturally adapted for the purpose, and is now ready for use.

An eight-room house on the grounds will be fitted up with a grill room and club house facilities.

The club can be reached from New York in fifty minutes by the Del., Lack, or Jersey Central Railroads, and on bicycles via the 23d street Ferry and West Orange.

Carriages will take members to the Club from Millburn, Short Hills, Summit and Westfield Stations at a charge of 25 to 50 cents each.

The course has a southern exposure and is adapted for use during the entire year.

Annual dues, Ten Dollars each.

Family membership, Twenty Dollars

**Patronesses**

| | |
|---|---|
| Mrs. Wm B. Beekman | Mrs. Wm Fellowes Morgan |
| Mrs. Oliver S. Carter | Mrs. John A. Stewart, Jr. |
| Mrs. Ed Renshaw Jones | Mrs. John C. Wilmerding |
| Mrs. Clement C. Moore | Mrs. Edward H. Wright |

George Bird, Esq.,
John L. Du Fais, Esq.,  } Golf Committee
George Hunter, Esq.,

Should you desire to become a member kindly notify

Louis Keller,

Secretary pro tem.,
35 Liberty Street, NY City

Turnure—with Keller, they were the club's first Board of Governors. Weeks was elected president, and Keller accepted the position of secretary—a position he would hold until his death in 1922. In addition to naming officers, the four appointed golf, house, constitution, and by-laws committees, and they agreed to lease the land and clubhouse from Keller for 15 years.

Their last order of business was to approve an application for Allied membership in the United States Golf Association, and Baltusrol, along with 14 other clubs, soon joined the five charter members of the USGA as the game's governing body. This was a vital step, for it meant that Baltusrol members – many of whom served as USGA officers and committee members – would have a finger on the pulse of developments in golf. It meant, too, that Baltusrol would become a favored site for the national tournaments that the USGA had been expressly created to host. Indeed, over the course of a century, Baltusrol would serve as the venue of a national championship in almost every decade, and its story would be inextricably linked with the story of American golf.

*The original Clubhouse circa 1898.*

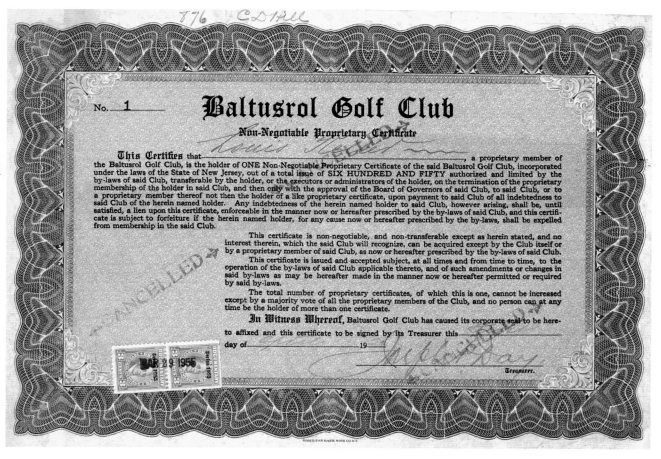

*In 1920, proprietary certificates were issued to the members to fund the new courses—the Upper and Lower. Par value was $400 and was paid in by each member over three years. At the time, this method of club finance was a new and radical idea. It would soon be followed by other clubs and has since become the norm for private equity clubs in the U.S. Appropriately, Louis Keller was issued the first certificate.*

### The Early Membership

It didn't take long for Baltusrol to spread its wings. The membership grew rapidly from the original 30 to 137 by the end of 1895, to 312 by March 1897, and to nearly 400 by February 1898. But these numbers are a bit deceptive, for each spring brought an influx of new members, and each fall was marked by wholesale resignations, with as many as 60 members leaving the club at once. These seasonal fluctuations were an inevitable result of the novelty of the game; many people joined for a season to try their hand at this new sport—and not all of them shared the enthusiasm for it. So they resigned in the fall to avoid dues for the following year.

Nevertheless, Baltusrol soon had a core of stalwart members, and it goes without saying that these early members were people of substance, talent, and accomplishment. Wall Street was well-represented by men like William Beekman, a governor of the New York Stock Exchange and treasurer of the company that made ticker tape, and Henry Pennington Toler, a successful broker who was one of the club's top golfers. Lewis P. Bayard, who served as club President from 1898 to 1919, was manager of the Phoenix Assurance Company, and William A. Larned would become a seven-time national singles tennis champion, as well as a pretty good golfer. Carroll P. Bassett was a civil engineer and utilities magnate whose family name appears twice in the Magna Carta.

Women, too, were admitted to membership.

The original invitation to join had included a list of patronesses, among them Mrs. John C. Wilmerding, who was directly descended from Commodore Vanderbilt. And Mrs. William Fellowes Morgan – one of the leading players of her day and one of the original 13 in the USGA's first Women's Amateur at the Meadow Brook Club in 1895 – was not only a founding patroness of Baltusrol, but was also a founding member of the Morris County Golf Club, where women built their own seven-hole course and conducted their own tournaments. The first single woman, Miss Marie L. Harrison, who was a noted amateur golfer of her time, joined the club in November 1895.

Given the credentials of its membership, it is worth underscoring the fact that Baltusrol was one of the least expensive golf clubs in the United States. The original initiation fee was $20 – about the price of an inexpensive man's suit – and the yearly dues for an individual were $10. Indeed, throughout the club's first two decades, the dues were kept low as a matter of policy, and there were several categories of membership based on the distance that members lived from the club. The relatively low cost of belonging to Baltusrol was emphasized in newspaper stories, as Keller and the Board of Governors never slackened their recruiting efforts. When the dues were raised 5 dollars in 1900, Keller was quoted in the paper as follows:

"We don't believe in charging a man for more than he gets. Our New York Members don't use the course often, have to pay more to get there and spend more to stay there than others. We charge them $15. Those who live within five miles we charge $30, and those more than five miles away, $20. So, you see, the scale varies according to value of the links to the players. Most clubs work the other way. The initiation fee is, however, the same for all, $25."

*James Tyng.*

These modest fees were possible because Keller had leased the club both the land and the clubhouse at a very nominal fee. Thanks to this favorable lease, Baltusrol started out free of debt, and its revenues easily covered the expenses, even though improvements to the course and clubhouse began almost as soon as the club opened.

### The Early Tournaments

The club didn't waste any time launching a schedule of tournaments, either. In January 1896, members were braving icy winds to compete for the Toler Cup in the first club championship. The cup was won by James A. Tyng, who was the first of the Baltusrol "greats." The donor of the cup, Henry P. Toler, was Tyng's closest rival, and the newspapers of the day reported their frequent duels in detail. They also played together as partners, and were the anchors of a four-man Baltusrol team, with Hugh K. Toler and Louis Bayard, Jr., that was unbeaten over a long string of matches.

Of the two, Tyng was perhaps the most talented and certainly the most dedicated, and his career as an amateur conveys some of the flavor of American golf at the turn of the century. Golf at the time was a gentleman's game—and Tyng was the model of the gentleman athlete. Though he didn't take up the game until 1895, he was absolutely smitten, and within a year he had mastered the "St. Andrew's" swing and was playing in tournaments on a monthly basis. A member both at Baltusrol and Morris County, he won cups and set course records with regularity, often managing to break 80—a phenomenal score in those days. His exploits were reported in detail, and newspaper accounts often referred to him as the former "Harvard pitcher," but he had been a catcher as well and was said to have been the first player to don a catcher's mask.

Today we would regard Tyng as a very good "club

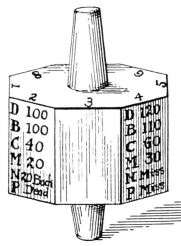

*Tyng's game of parlor golf featured an octagonal teetotum that was spun on a colored lithograph board of a nine hole course.*

player"—but in his own time Tyng was a celebrity with enough name recognition to invent and market his own game of parlor golf. Together with other leading amateurs, men like C. B. Macdonald and Walter Travis, Tyng was both a pioneer and a missionary who helped to spread the word to the growing flock. All by himself, Tyng must have been the kind of man who could light up a club with competitive fire, but he had plenty of company at Baltusrol.

The hardy golfers of a century ago did not put away their clubs for the winter. As a matter of fact, one of Baltusrol's early claims was that its sheltered position in the lee of the mountain made it "a nice little winter resort." In February 1896, the club hosted its first inter-club event – The Washington's Birthday Tourney. It was a handicap event open to all members of clubs in the USGA. A cold snap had stiffened the turf into frosty ridges and hollows, so the greens were sprinkled with sand to make them level. Although 45 contestants

representing several golf clubs played, only 31 golfers finished. Given the icy conditions, the winning score was a very respectable 96 gross, 86 net, by W. M. McCawley of the Philadelphia C. C.

In the fall of 1896, Golfing magazine reported that at Baltusrol "the full eighteen hole course will soon be ready for winter play, and a series of team matches with other leading clubs will be held every Saturday"—that is, throughout the winter. In the scene imagined by the writer, "the little red ball flies merrily in the cold and exhilarating air, while the players trudge gaily over the crisp snow and hardened ground."

That might have been poetic license, but the eagerness of Baltusrol golfers was a fact. During the first several years, it was a club boast that the course had been in use every single day. In fact, the club was already outgrowing its nine-hole course after its first year; so in the summer of 1897 the links were expanded to 18 holes. Much work also was carried out on the original nine holes to toughen them, with several steep, sod-faced bunkers added to protect the greens. In the meantime, Louis Keller, always enterprising, had a surveyor carry out a unique redesign. There would be 18 holes comprising a long course intended for better players, and within that course, several other greens and tees would provide a short course for beginners and women. This unique course opened for play in 1898.

Another sign of Baltusrol's keen interest in competition was the hiring of Willie Anderson as its profes-

*H. P. Toler (L) and Jasper Lynch at Morris County during the 1898 U.S. Amateur Championship.*

sional in 1898. Though he hadn't yet won the Open – he would win four times, a record – the young Anderson was already known as one of the most talented of the Scottish players who dominated the professional game. A restless man who worked for ten different clubs in his brief career, Anderson stayed only one year before moving on.

Baltusrol also was instrumental in creating the organizations that governed competitions, becoming a founding member of the Metropolitan Golf Association in 1897. At the MGA's inaugural meeting at Delmonico's in New York City, John DuFais, a Baltusrol member, was named the first secretary, and served five terms. Baltusrol's first "open" – a tournament sanctioned by the MGA and open to all members of clubs belonging to the USGA – was held in May 1897, and played over the

original nine. In women's golf, Baltusrol also played the lead. In October 1899, one of Baltusrol's founding patronesses and top players, Mrs. William Fellowes Morgan – her husband was one of the first Baltusrol Governors and an early secretary and later treasurer of the USGA – was one of the founders, and named the first president, of the Women's Metropolitan Golf Association. Later in 1900, in an effort to develop golf locally in New Jersey, Baltusrol and five other clubs founded the New Jersey League, forerunner of the New Jersey Golf Association, and a Baltusrol member, L. E. Graham, served as its first president.

Each of these organizations fulfilled a different need as golf took strong root in a new country. The primary function of the USGA was to conduct the national amateur and open

## TWO GOLF MATCHES ARE KEENLY FOUGHT

Both Games in the Semi-Final Round for the President's Cup in the Baltusrol Club's Open Tournament ...ied to the Nineteenth Green.

## TOLER LEADS THE GOLFE...

The Baltusrol Expert Makes a... cellent Score in the Clu... Open Tournament.

S. D. BOWERS IS SE...

Sixteen of the Forty Players for the Governors' Cu... Contest.

MANY WOMEN ON THE...

Golf of a very high order and w...

## TYNG CHAMPION OF BALTUSROL

Defeats Louis Bayard, Jr., for Club Honors at Short Hills, and Also Wins Memorial Day Handicap.

MAKES NEW RECORD FOR THE COURSE.

Returns Eighty-Two for His Firs... Round Against the Former Intercollegiate Crack.

MORRISTOWN'S TWO EVENTS

## HAMILTON LEADS CRACK GOLFERS

...altusrol Expert Wins Cup in Qualifying Round of Lakewood Club's Tournament.

...UGLAS COMES SECOND

...er Champion Finishes with Rush in Second Round and Is Two Strokes Behind.

...ER TRAVIS IS THIRD

championships—a need that had become all too clear in 1894, when competing clubs hosted "national" tournaments, and the results were bitterly disputed. The USGA also set itself up as the formulator of the

rules of golf, and it established a uniform system of handicapping. Similarly, the MGA and the WMGA were tasked with regulating the calendar of events in the metropolitan area to prevent conflicts between clubs, regulate the handicaps of club players, and to sanction tournaments that counted as legitimate championships—precisely the same role that the NJGA would come to play in New Jersey.

*Baltusrol members brave the elements in the early years.*

*King Edward VII on the Baltusrol Links in 1907.*

### The First Championships

Baltusrol quickly became noted as a tournament site and by 1899 was known as the "Club of Golf Clubs". This was no accident, for Louis Keller was determined to make his club preeminent. Not only did he oversee all the details of the first tournaments, from the applications to the catering, he also went directly into competition with other clubs.

Nearby Morris County was known as the best course in the neighborhood, but Keller scheduled tournaments head-to-head with his neighbor—and Morris County courteously changed its dates. The rivalry between Morris County and Baltusrol always remained amicable, for the two clubs enjoyed a close golfing and social affinity. Many prominent players were members of both clubs, like James Tyng, Mr. & Mrs. William Fellowes Morgan, Henry P.

Toler and others. When one club gave a big tournament it was supported by the other. Although, Baltusrol had a distinct advantage over Morris County as a place to play golf, for it was open for play on Sundays, while the Blue Laws kept Morris County closed.

When the original 18-hole course was completed, Baltusrol began to think of hosting its first national

tournament. In February of 1899, the club upgraded its USGA membership from a non-voting Allied member to an Associate member, which would give it a vote on USGA policy matters including tournament site selection. And after a very successful women's "open" tournament in 1899, which was hailed as the second playing of the USGA National (Women's Amateur) that was held on the Bala Course in Philadelphia, Baltusrol began to angle for selection by the

USGA to conduct the 1900 Women's Amateur. Keller pulled out all the stops in making the appeal to the USGA; he even succeeded in obtaining from C. B. Macdonald, one of the most influential figures in golf, an "unsolicited" letter, and more importantly a vote, supporting Baltusrol's bid. The club also highly publicized the improvements it had made to its 18-hole

course in anticipation of hosting the Amateur. In the end, however, the USGA selected Shinnecock as the site for this event—and Baltusrol went right ahead with its plans to run a major women's tournament later in the season.

Nearly all of the top women players came to Baltusrol, and they came from all over the country. Most of them were quartered either in the clubhouse or the cottages owned by the club, and

reports of the tournament make it clear that they had a grand time both on and off the golf course. The field was larger and markedly superior, and, according to the writer for the Sun, this hugely successful Baltusrol tournament "completely dwarfed" the "National event" that had been held earlier in the season at Shinnecock. For instance, Baltusrol had 113 entries

versus only 65 entries at Shinnecock.

Baltusrol had proved its point, and the next year, 1901, the club hosted its first national tournament, the U. S. Women's Amateur. The tournament was played over what we now call the "Old Course." At the time, it was barely a year old, but it had already been lengthened, and the clubhouse enlarged, for the express purpose of demonstrating to the USGA that Baltusrol was prepared to stage a major event.

*Miss Griscom driving at the Baltusrol Women's Open Golf Tournament in 1900.*

In this first test, Baltusrol came through with flying colors, and so did the women. Playing before hundreds of spectators, they broke 100 with some consistency. Some of their success can be attributed to the brand-new rubber ball that was just replacing the gutta-percha ball; the women could hit this new ball a long way. The long-drive competition was won with a poke of 193 yards! The winner of the tournament, Genevieve Hecker, was one

*Baltusrol's tennis courts can be seen in the background.*

our national titles, but in that era the Amateur enjoyed even greater prestige; it was the prize that Baltusrol truly desired. The two previous national tournaments had proven to the USGA's satisfaction that Baltusrol could successfully stage a major event, and in 1904 Baltusrol was awarded the Tenth U. S. Amateur Championship. In a little less than a decade, Baltusrol had made its mark.

of the most formidable women players of the day and the first woman to write a golf book, which she called simply, *Golf for Women.*

Now there were only a few distinctions that Baltusrol lacked, and they came soon enough. In 1903 the club hosted the Ninth U. S. Open Championship, and it was won, fittingly enough, by Willie Anderson, the former Baltusrol pro. Today the Open ranks as the most important of all

The first years of the new century were on all fronts a grand success. Not only had Baltusrol proven itself as a championship site, but the club was known for its hospitality and "royal good times." Every golf tournament was accompanied by appropriate entertainment—lunches, teas, dinners, dances. There were also extravagant masquer-

ades, and the parties at Baltusrol were reported in the New York and New Jersey society pages.

The club also flirted with several other outdoor sports. Two tennis courts were built in 1901, and more were added in 1907. At the same time the club built a pair of squash courts, and later trap shooting came strongly into vogue. Fox hunts originated from the club grounds, and in 1911 a sports committee was established to oversee these activities. But support for sports other than golf was always cautious, for the board and the membership understood that golf was Baltusrol's reason for being.

The golf course was now under the supervision of George Low, another Scotsman. He had taken the job of Club Professional in 1903, and his duties were very different from those of a professional today. Low gave lessons, but one of his most important jobs was to make clubs—or rather to insure that the lads toiling in the shop, amid hickory shafts and pots of varnish,

did their jobs properly. Low was also the greenkeeper, a job he relished; he had designed golf courses before coming to Baltusrol, and he made numerous changes to the Old Course. (When he left the club in 1925, he went into business as a golf course architect.) A fine golfer, Low played in many exhibitions and tournaments. He is credited with the oft-repeated remark, "Golf is a humblin' game."

Low was probably instrumental in designing the most famous hole on the Old Course, the "Island Green" on the tenth hole. This hole was a sensation, and it was light years ahead of its time. The next island green that would claim to be a "first" was not built until 1936, at the Ponte Vedra Club in Florida; the architect who designed this hole was Herbert Strong, the same man who went into partnership with Low in 1925. The circular green on the tenth was girdled by a moat of water, but it wasn't used in the 1904 Amateur. The hole was a par 4, and a delegation of club members had deemed the second shot unfair.

9

# *Baltusrol's Beloved George Low*

*George Low demonstrates his new rake and its furrows.*

*Low & Hughes Golf Shop at 14 East 44th Street in New York City.*

George Low was an institution at Baltusrol. He was born in Carnoustie, Scotland in 1874 and emigrated to the United States in the late 1890's. George was an accomplished player and was joint runner-up in the 1899 United States Open.

He was hired by Baltusrol in 1903 as both head professional and green keeper. In those days, it was commonplace for the golf professional to also be the green keeper. In this role, he directed many of the improvements to the Old Course.

Low was a witty and lively Scotsman. Always on hand for Club activities, he was held in high, affectionate regard by the members. His style was decidedly tongue-and-cheek; after making a hole in one on the third hole, Low said rather dolefully that "the playing of that hole has no longer any charm for him."

Low also was a leader in the golf world, hosting or playing in several international amateur matches. He also was one of the most sought after club makers in the United States. He had an active club making and repair shop in New York City that became so successful he had to expand to a second location.

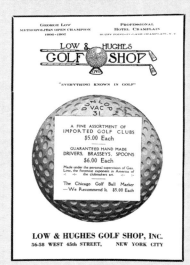

On another note, George Low also was the inventor of a rake and furrowed bunker that would gain national prominence at Oakmont. To penalize properly a ball in a bunker Low devised a rake which produced furrows in the sand about an inch and a half deep and three inches wide. The objective of the furrow was to prevent the use of a putter or other clubs to effect an escape, and reinstate the explosion shot with the mashie-niblick or the niblick (nine iron). (Note: the sand wedge had not yet been invented.) Low described his invention in a noted golf magazine:

"By raking the traps at right angles to the line of play I found that the bunkers maintained a uniform surface much better and for longer periods of time than under the old system of raking them smooth so that it was rarely possible altogether to overcome the penalty. The Green section of the United States Golf Association, which is a grand institution, is always looking for new ideas and if it would recommend it (the rake) for general use it would help solve the difficulty."

It is not known how long the furrowed bunkers were played at Baltusrol, but history does remember the tradition that Oakmont maintained with its furrowed bunkers.

George Low's extensive outside interests may have led to his early retirement from Baltusrol. We know that he considered resigning from the Club in late 1919 and took a six month leave of absence from May through November 1920 to pursue business interests in Scotland. Low finally did leave Baltusrol in 1925 to pursue golf architecture on a full time basis. For his 20 years of dedicated service to the Club, George Low was awarded honorary life membership in 1922.

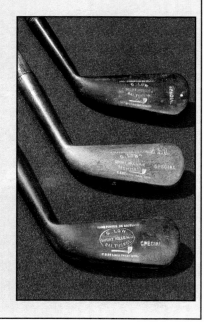

*The moat around the Island Green.*

In 1906, George Low won the Metropolitan Open and held the title for two years; there was no Met Open in 1907, when Baltusrol declined to host the event. Then, in 1908, the club reconsidered and staged its first Met Open, won by John Hobens in a field from which Willie Anderson was conspicuously absent; he declined to travel to Baltusrol because the prize money was too small. Baltusrol's other important tournament that year was the Metropolitan Amateur; a year earlier the club had hosted the New Jersey Amateur. Jerry Travers, the leading amateur of the day, had figured in the outcome of both events,

winning the New Jersey title and blowing a six hole lead to lose the Met to Charles Seely.

### Clubhouse & Railroad

One of the few problems at Baltusrol was how to get people to the club. Early transportation invariably involved horses and carriages – and for the members who didn't mind exerting themselves, bicycles. The club was equipped to provide feed for member's horses at 50 cents a day, and two horses were kept at the club to pick up members arriving at the Lackawanna Railroad Stations in Short Hills and Summit. Both stations were roughly two miles from the club.

These arrangements did not satisfy Louis Keller. To shorten the haul, the ever-enterprising Keller purchased the New York and New Orange Railroad in 1904. He reorganized the financially troubled company, changed its name to Rahway Valley Railroad, and built a passenger station and siding where the track crossed Baltusrol Way about a quarter of a mile east of the club. Club members coming from New York by ferry could now board a "through" car at Jersey City on the New Jersey Central Railroad, connecting with the Rahway Valley Railroad at Aldene and proceeding to Baltusrol. Or they could take the Lackawanna Railroad to Summit, where they had to walk only a block to catch the Baltusrol train. The 2-locomotive, 10-employee, 12-mile Rahway Valley Railroad was hardly a giant company—but how many golf clubs had a virtually private railroad?

Keller's bold strategies had paid off. By the fall of 1906, Baltusrol's membership was around 750 strong, making it one of the largest clubs in America. And by 1909, the facilities at Baltusrol were unexcelled in all respects but one—the clubhouse. While many members and guests loved the rambling, rustic club-

house, it was by no means on a par with the luxurious, elegant structures that had been erected by many other leading golf clubs. Some golf writers had muttered that, sooner or later, the old building would have to make way for a new one. And some of the people who frequented the build-

*Summit Station.*

*Short Hills Station.*

ing – including Crossmier Zizi, the chef, who lived in the clubhouse – were frankly worried that the building was a firetrap.

Zizi was right to be worried. In the middle of the night of March 27, 1909, a fire started in the kitchen. A housekeeper was the first to see the flames at about one o'clock.

Her screams awoke the clerk, who alerted the steward, who in turn sent someone to awaken the 15 others sleeping in the clubhouse, including Hugh Toler, the only member on the premises. Toler, in a sound sleep, muttered, "Don't want to be disturbed. Go away." The bartender, who had made his way to safety, became nervous about Toler and went to rescue him with a ladder.

Newspaper accounts differ on what happened next; one report has Toler coming down the ladder, while another presents him as the "hero" of the fire, with a headline proclaiming, "As Frightened Women Servants Run Screaming Through Halls He Grabs and Swings Them From Window to Ground." The only injury reported was to Crossmier Zizi. In his fear of fire, he had fashioned a rope ladder, but it gave way as he was escaping his second floor room and he broke both ankles in the fall.

The clubhouse lay in ashes. It had been completely destroyed, along with the stables and a new wing containing the squash courts. The club's trophies and artwork were lost in the fire, as were all personal belongings – including hundreds of golf club sets – in the locker rooms. The greatest loss may have been the original deed of the

NOTED GOLF CLUB HOUSE DESTROYED BY EARLY MORNING FIRE, AND ITS RUINS.

RUINS of BALTUSROL GOLF CLUB at SHORT HILLS N.J.

BALTUSROL GOLF CLUB

property that dated back to colonial days and had been held by Baltus Roll. The club's records, however, were unscathed, for they were safely locked away in Keller's Manhattan office.

The club's reaction was swift, to say the least. The very next day, Louis Keller, after meeting with the Board of Governors, announced that the garage would be immediately converted into a locker room, and that a temporary structure, with dining facilities, would be erected forthwith. Moreover, the Governors decided to build a modern clubhouse at a cost of

$50,000. The fire was a boon for George Low as he busily furnished hundreds of sets of new golf clubs to the members.

Less than two months later, on April 9th, at a general meeting of the membership held at Delmonico's roof garden, the decision of the Governors was ratified. A resolution passed unanimously empowering the Governors to raise, "at their discretion, by voluntary subscription or by bonds," the amount necessary to construct and furnish the new clubhouse. By May 19, the plans submitted by Chester H. Kirk, a member of the

club, had been approved, and contractor Charles L. Bell had been engaged to build the new clubhouse. It was to be finished within six months.

Ground was broken in early June, and by December the clubhouse – the magnificent Tudor structure that stands today – was under roof. Nearly all of the exterior work had been completed, but the interior would not be ready for use until April. Incidentally, one of the few schemes that Louis Keller did not succeed in carrying out had to do with the clubhouse; he wanted to top it off with an immense glass dome. The builder had taken a little longer than expected, and the cost was a little higher too—about $100,000 (the fire insurance on the old clubhouse was settled at just over $60,000).

After the second story of

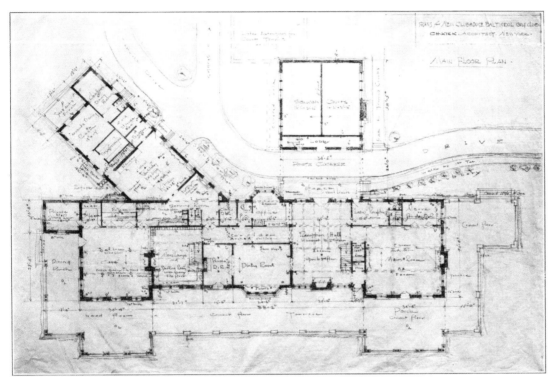

the kitchen wing was added in 1914, with the Governors' room and business offices, the clubhouse would stand for many years without major additions.

### Keller's Bold Vision

It was to this splendid and still-new clubhouse that Baltusrol welcomed for the first time a President of the United States. The date was April 1912, and the visitor was William Howard Taft, who said, "They tell me that Baltusrol is probably the best course in America." Taft played an exuberant round and lunched in a private dining room with a small group of friends. The Board of Governors decreed that the club should not have to pay for the President's lunch since he came as a private guest and not at the invitation of the club!

Other distinguished visitors came regularly to Baltusrol. In September 1911, Harold Hilton – the British and American amateur champion – played

*President Taft on the tee.*

13

an exhibition match, paired with professional George Duncan, against the team of George Low and amateur Fred Herreshoff. The following year, saw Wilfrid Reid, the young English professional, and Louis Tellier of France play a match against George Low and Max Marston. And in the week prior to the 1913 Open at Brookline, the legendary Harry Vardon, a six-time winner of the British Open, and Ted Ray, the long-hitting, pipe-smoking Englishman made Baltusrol a stop on their American tour. The team of Vardon and Ray, trounced George Low and Alex Smith, 7 and 6, in a 36-hole match followed by a crowd of nearly 2,000. A week later Vardon and Ray encountered Francis Ouimet and destiny.

Such exhibition matches were enormously popular, for they provided a rare opportunity to see the leading golfers in action—and the leading golfers, almost by definition, came from across the Atlantic. The Ryder Cup matches didn't start until 1927, but it is easy to see in the early international matches the seeds of their enormous success.

By all measures the most ambitious of the exhibition matches was the PGA War Relief Tournament, staged in August 1917, which brought together four different teams—Amateurs, Homebreds, English Pros, and Scottish Pros. The play was in foursomes and singles, and the roster of players was a veritable who's who in golf. One of the stars was "Little Bob" Jones, all of 16 years old, who won all his individual matches,

*Hilton and Duncan of England versus Low and Herreshof.*

*Harry Vardon putting on the fourteenth green at Baltusrol.*

*Harry Vardon, Ted Ray, Alex Smith and George Low.*

*Edward "Ted" Ray playing a mid-iron from the short ninth.*

and showed his stuff at Baltusrol, where his opponent made the turn in 37—and stood 2 down. The matches were sponsored by the fledgling Professional Golfers Association and put thousands of dollars into the coffers of the Red Cross.

Keller's promotional strategy for Baltusrol was straightforward—host at least one major event of some kind each year to keep Baltusrol in the spotlight. If Baltusrol couldn't get a national championship, it would host an exhibition match, or a regional tournament of some kind. During these early years, some of the important regional tournaments that Baltusrol hosted included the 1908 and 1912 Metropolitan Amateurs and New Jersey State Amateurs in 1903, 1907 and 1913. Baltusrol also was the site of the Lesley Cup matches in 1911, where teams of top amateurs representing Pennsylvania, Massachusetts and the Metropolitan area competed against each other. In virtually all of these events, the outcome was determined by the play of Jerry Travers, a four-time winner of the U. S. Amateur title who hailed from nearby Upper Montclair Country Club.

When Baltusrol hosted the U. S. Open in 1915, Travers was in the field, but no one gave him much of a chance. Though he was feared in match play, Travers had always been too inconsistent to fare well in medal events. At Baltusrol, however, he was a model of steadiness—at least on the scorecard. On the course he made one

*Travers and Nicholls leaving the first tee in the PGA War Relief Tournament.*

*Group joking with George Low (seated) at the Red Cross booth during the PGA War Relief Tournament.*

*A group of prominent contestants in the Lesley Cup matches at Baltusrol.*

miraculous save after another. It didn't hurt that he probably knew his way around Baltusrol better than most of the members, and he putted as if he owned the greens. When he held on to win the Open, after two days of 36 holes, Travers was carried off the final green on the shoulders of his fans. It was a tremendously popular victory—and if Travers wasn't a Baltusrol member, he was close enough so that it almost seemed that Baltusrol had produced its own national champion.

In the afterglow of Travers' victory, a few criticisms of the Old Course began to emerge. In addition, the club membership had climbed to 700, and the demand for tee-times, especially on the weekends, had become so acute that a lottery system had been introduced. Taking all this into consideration, Louis Keller came up with what was perhaps his most audacious and visionary proposal. In 1916 he suggested building a new course, or duplicate course, and offered Baltusrol the pick of a site

# A New Red Cross Partnership

Evans and Jones Beat Kirkby and Marston at Baltusrol, September 17, 1918

*Charles Evans, Jr., Max Marston, Oswald Kirkby, "Bobby" Jones and George Low.*
*Warren Wood was unable to partner the champion as orginally planned and "Bobby" Jones filled his place.*

*The feature of the Match, Bobby Jones' 200 yard jigger to the first green. This young player pushed his drive into the trap, but decided to try and make the green with his second, and did so.*

*Walter Hagen putting out on eighteen during the PGA War Relief Tournament in 1917.*

from the 500 acres he owned adjacent to the Old Course.

At the same time, Keller offered to sell the land which the club had been leasing from him, plus whatever additional land would be needed for the duplicate course. As always, this non-golfer was sensitive to the development of the game, noting that "within the next few years all the leading clubs in the country will find a duplicate course necessary." Thus the machinery was set in motion for the purchase of some 318 acres, for which the club paid $154,000, and for the construction of the two existing courses, the Lower and Upper, that are the twin jewels in Baltusrol's crown.

Sad to say, Louis Keller died on February 16, 1922, a few months before the official opening of the new courses. His remarkable regime at Baltusrol had lasted for 27 years, and make no mistake about it: though he never held a post other than secretary, he ran the show. The club had been

his idea. He provided the land and the first club-house. He oversaw the building of the first golf course and took the initiative in each successive revision of the links. He made sure that Baltusrol not only kept pace with competing clubs but outstripped them.

In the formative years of the club, he even supplied the membership, drawing on friends and acquaintances he had made through the Social Register. Even though, as owner of the property, he was in several potentially compromising situations in dealing with the board, the record shows that his conduct was impeccable. He could certainly be high-handed and auto-cratic – there is more than one story of members who finished a round of golf only to find that their lockers had been emptied and that Keller had dismissed them from the club – and there is no record that he had any sense of humor or that he was well liked. He never married and in his last years he seems to have grown

*Louis Keller*

rather distant and remote; he was most frequently seen lopping off branches from the small trees and shrubbery around the course and clubhouse.

Yet Keller had lavished his unstinting attention on Baltusrol. The club was his life's work and his lasting achievement. Step by painstaking step, Keller built Baltusrol into what it is today—a major American sporting institution, one of the definitive golf clubs in the world.

# The New York Times

*Bobby Jones Driving From the First Tee in Amateur Golf Play at Baltusrol.*

Times' Wide World Photos.

*George Von Elm, Winner of National Amateur Title.*

Printed with permission of the New York Times.

# COMING OF AGE
# 1922-1954

*The Golden Age* During the decade of the 1920s, the game of golf enjoyed a new surge of popularity. After World War I, the country was enjoying another era of prosperity, and more people had the time and means to pursue leisure activities; they also had an attractive set of heroes to emulate. Starting with Francis Ouimet, American golf had produced an extraordinary set of home-grown champions, including two professionals who transformed the way that Americans thought about the men who played golf for money: Gene Sarazen and Walter Hagen. And they were overshadowed, of course, by the man who didn't play golf for money and still won every title worth winning—the peerless Bobby Jones.

The 1920's have also been called the Golden Age of American golf course architecture, for it is the decade when many of the country's classic courses came into being. A group of talented architects had learned their trade the hard way, by simply plunging in and building golf courses. In effect, they had invented the profession, taking it over from the Scottish professionals who had laid out so many of the first American courses. One of the most opinionated, irrepressible, and talented of these American architects was A. W. Tillinghast, who billed himself as the "Creator of Baltusrol."

The construction of the "dual" courses at Baltusrol took four years—a long time, but Tillinghast had orders not to disrupt play entirely. The new courses had to take shape hole by hole, always leaving members some way to get in their rounds of golf.

*A. W. Tillinghast — Creator of Baltusrol.*

Naturally, the membership was less than pleased with this arrangement, and when the courses were finally opened in 1922, there were grumbles about the quality of the turf and the general difficulty of play. The golf courses had already cost the club some $130,000, far more than planned, but an additional outlay of $50,000 was required for Tillinghast to complete the work and bring the courses up to the desired standard.

Still, it must have seemed worth all the trouble when the National Amateur returned to Baltusrol in 1926. The tournament was played over the Lower Course, which had been brought into peak condition. A. W. Tillinghast was on hand throughout the tournament, receiving congratulations for his handiwork. The course was hailed for its beauty and challenge, for it had inspired golf of a high order. It also rewarded very different styles of play, for the two finalists were Bobby Jones and George Von Elm. Jones was much longer off the tee, but Von Elm was uncannily accurate with his approach shots, often played with a wood or long iron.

On the final day of play, more than 15,000 fans

turned out to follow the match. It was then the largest gallery ever gathered for a golf tournament, and the fans expected to see Bobby Jones win his third successive amateur title. But this was to be Von Elm's day. The decisive hole was the thirteenth in the afternoon round, the thirty-first of the match. Standing two down and needing to make up ground, Jones tried to carry the ditch which cross-es the fairway at its longest point—and failed. This was precisely the sort of drama that Tillinghast had imagined when he designed the hole, and Jones could not recover. The match ended on the seventeenth green, with Von Elm winning two up.

Once again Baltusrol had proven its ability to host a national championship with style and aplomb. And given the soaring popularity of golf, the championships were no longer tournaments that could be handled simply in the normal course of events; they were large affairs that called for careful planning and management. The success of the 1926 Amateur must be credited to General Tournament Chairman J.B. Monroe and club Presidents Robert Sinclair, who took the job in 1919 and oversaw the completion of the dual courses, and William G. McKnight, who took the reins in 1926.

Yet these capable men could not entirely replace Keller, who had run Baltusrol almost as if he were a highly paid professional manager. The affairs of the club demanded the full attention and energy of someone—and that someone turned out to be Major R. Avery Jones, who had been hired as green keeper in 1923.

Major Jones, who came to be known at Baltusrol as "Mr. Outside," had served as a major in the British Army in World War I, and was reputed to have served as equerry to the Prince of Wales. Though not a large man, he was every inch a boss, tough and dictatorial. He let it be known that he regarded most Americans as barbarians, though he made an exception for the members of Baltusrol. Having worked at several other golf clubs, he said at the time of his retirement, "When you leave Baltusrol, where else is there to go?"

Jones's drive and abilities did not go unnoticed, and he did not remain green keeper for long. Within months after he was hired, the board observed that the club was saving consider-

*The gallery surrounds the eighteenth green during the 1926 Amateur.*

able amounts on the cost of certain supplies simply because Jones refused to accept commissions from the supply houses he dealt

*Major Jones.*

with. Here was a man who could be trusted, and in May 1925 he was appointed general manager in charge of all departments and employees, a post he held until his retirement in 1945.

During the "Roaring 20's" the club thrived financially and socially, and the scrapbooks show a full program of tournaments, dinner-dances, and holiday festivities. The leading Baltusrol golfers of the decade were E. M. Wild and Augie Kammer. Wild, a slight man with an injured left arm, nevertheless won the Baltusrol club championship eight times in a row, from 1922-1929. Wild's chief rival was Augie Kammer, noted for his superb play on the greens. To this day Baltusrol stages an annual Augie Kammer putting contest on Labor Day. One curious feature of their rivalry was that Wild regularly beat Kammer at Baltusrol, but when they found themselves in competition at outside tournaments it was always Kammer who prevailed, notably in the New Jersey Amateurs of 1924, 1925, and 1926.

The club also consolidated its financial position in

*E. M. Wild.*

1927, paying off the balance owed on the land purchased from Keller in 1918. Recognizing the need to protect what had become a valuable and unique property, the board also acquired from the Keller estate an additional 352 acres of land along the Upper Course and over Baltusrol Mountain, for an outlay of $155,000. This expenditure was more than recouped only four months later when the club sold off 178 acres on the Summit side of the mountain for $168,845, thus turning a nice little profit on the transaction. Other, smaller

tracts were also acquired—including the purchase of a few acres to the rear of the green of two Lower to guard against the encroachments of real estate developers. And last but not least, the Men's Grill, a major addition to the clubhouse, was completed in 1928 at a cost of $180,000.

The facilities and the balance sheets showed a flourishing club—but there was trouble ahead. Fortunately for Baltusrol, an unusually strong and capable leader, J. Stewart Baker, was elected club President in 1929. A banker born and bred, Baker was the President of the Bank of Manhattan and its chairman when it merged with the Chase Bank in 1955 to form Chase Manhattan. His financial

expertise would serve Baltusrol well during its most trying years.

### The Great Depression

After the stock market collapse in October 1929, the national economy went into a tailspin. Every day the newspapers reported the collapse of banks and other businesses, and the unemployment rate soared to 25 percent. Nearly everyone felt the pinch, and golf clubs, being luxuries, were among the first to suffer.

Baltusrol was no exception. By the mid-30's the club had lost a third of its members and endured a 44 percent decrease in revenues. In a long report to the membership, dated February 1935, Baker out-

*Baltusrol Way meanders across the mountain.*

*The Clubhouse prior to adding the Men's Grill.*

*Dining room circa 1920's.*

20

lined the situation in frank terms. Despite the problems, however, Baker asserted that there was no cause for alarm since the club had maintained a sound financial policy from the outset. Throughout its history, income had always exceeded expenses, and all the repairs, replacements, and improvements to the large plant, as well as amortization of the club's indebtedness, had been paid for out of the revenues. There had never been an assessment of the membership. Except for a small amount of capital furnished by the founders in 1895, and a voluntary subscription when the new clubhouse was built in 1909, the growth of the club had been financed entirely from income.

Baker credited Major Jones with having reduced the club's operating expenses by more than 30 percent, including a 40 percent reduction in golf course maintenance, between 1930 and 1934. Jones had voluntarily taken a cut in his own pay, and he showed a keen instinct for sniffing out bargains. For instance, he had seized the opportunity to buy 1,000 evergreen trees from a failed nursery for 10 cents each and he got the WPA to plant them. These trees, mature now, have greatly enhanced the beauty of Baltusrol; they are Major Jones's living legacy.

Restoring the membership to a sufficient level was another matter. It had shrunk from 650 to a low of 450 in 1934, well below the necessary minimum. The club tried to meet this crisis by waiving the initiation fee for a while and permitting up to 50 new mem-

*Many of Major Jones' evergreens have matured to full height.*

bers to pay for their proprietary certificates over a period of three years. It also appealed to members to make efforts to interest their friends in joining the club, and even provided prospective members with a map showing how quickly and easily residents of New York City could reach the club via the new express highways. The membership

quota had been set at 650, but the drive succeeded only in maintaining the level at approximately 450—a level that persisted through World War II. Even at that level, Baltusrol remained solvent. In those hard times, that alone was an achievement.

But all was not gloom. Bowling on the green was introduced in 1938, and

*The pond on thirteen Upper was stocked with trout.*

Major Jones had another diversion for the membership—trout fishing, one of his own favorite pastimes. The pond on thirteen Upper was stocked with 550 trout, and for $15 per annum, members could try to catch them. The rules were clear and simple:

Fly fishing only.
Limit 6 fish per day.
Limit 12 fish per week.
No guests.
No fishing after dark.

There were social activities, too, including frequent football outings to Princeton, followed by dinner dances. For a time during the late '30's members could take dancing classes conducted by the Arthur Murray Studio. First-run movies were shown on the lawn and terrace, and the blowout of the decade took place in July 1935 when club member Paul Whiteman presented his full orchestra in concert on the lawn. Among the artists who performed that evening were Johnny Hauser, Helen Jepson, Ramona, and the King's Men. Whiteman had long been nationally recognized for his symphonic approach to dance music, and in 1935 he was at the height of his career. After the concert, the band moved into the men's grill and played for dancing. Later that year, Whiteman's fellow club members honored him with a stag dinner attended by stars of stage and radio.

The spectacular Whiteman party made the newspapers, but it was not reported as earlier functions at Baltusrol had been—that is, as a high society affair. It had been

anything but stuffy, and it signaled a change in Baltusrol that had occurred gradually. The club's association with the swells of New York society, so much a part of its early history, had faded almost completely. There were still plenty of captains of industry and finance, but the vast majority of the membership now lived in New Jersey, not New York, and Baltusrol's strongest credentials were in the golf world, not the social world.

Another small symbol of the change was that in 1935 the board changed the club's address from Short Hills to Springfield, even though Short Hills was a "better" address.

In 1936 the U.S. Open was played at Baltusrol for the third time, and the Upper Course got its national christening. The Upper had been selected as the site by a blue-ribbon USGA delegation consisting of Bobby Jones, Francis Ouimet, Prescott Bush and John G. Jackson. They had suggested, and Baltusrol had carried out, several changes to the Upper course, but essentially it played as Tillinghast had designed it, and wasn't in any way tricked up for the pros.

After the final round of play, radio announcers told the world that "Lighthorse"

Harry Cooper had won the Open with a record-setting total of 284. A half hour later they had to eat their words, for an unsung pro named Tony Manero had shot a 67 and finished at 282. And still the result was in doubt, for Manero had played with Gene Sarazen, and some golf writers thought that Sarazen had crossed the line, giving Manero not just encouragement but advice. A formal complaint was made to the USGA, and after an hour-long meeting, the official result was finally announced: Manero's victo-ry would stand.

This Open was conducted like a modern Open, with members expected to buy tickets, limited access to the clubhouse, tightly controlled parking, and all the other measures that are now so familiar—though gallery ropes were not used, and wildly surging crowds frequently disrupted the play. Cooper's playing partner actually had his pocket picked as he made his way to the final green!

The club netted $17,000 from the Open, no small sum in those lean days.

*Tony Manero and Harry Cooper (inset) both broke the Open record at Baltusrol.*

*Dr. Lowell, left, tells Johnny Farrell and Jack Forrester, Baltusrol Pro, about his Reddy Tee invention.*
*Below: George Low prepares a sand tee for Mrs. Gavin, the old fashioned way.*

# The Legendary Johnny Farrell

In 1934 the club hired a professional who brought with him the respect of the golf world— Johnny Farrell. The slender, raven-haired Farrell had reached the pinnacle of competitive golf. In 1927 he won eight consecutive tournaments, setting a record that would stand for nearly 20 years. Then, in 1928, Farrell accomplished what only a handful of golfers can even dream of accomplishing; he won the U. S. Open. And he did it in the most unforgettable fashion, by beating Bobby Jones in a 36-hole playoff after they had tied for the title at Olympia Fields CC.

Johnny Farrell virtually dropped out of competitive golf after taking the Baltusrol post, though he surely would have stayed on the tournament circuit had the Depression not taken such a heavy toll on the professional tour. Prize money had been drastically reduced, and Farrell had a wife and five children to consider (his three sons were all fine golfers). If Johnny Farrell ever regretted leaving the tour, it didn't show, for he was a man of many talents. He became a celebrated teacher who counted among his pupils

Edward, Duke of Windsor. The two had met when Farrell played on the Ryder Cup team and, when the Duke came to New York, he sought Johnny out for playing lessons. Years later, at a White House dinner hosted by President Richard Nixon, the Duke singled out Johnny, who was also present, as "the man who saved my golfing life."

The well-spoken, well-dressed Johnny Farrell had a knack for moving easily in any circle, and he was sought after as a performer and entertainer of sorts, a

sportsman of impeccable credentials who could hold the interest of an audience without a golf club in his hands. He made appearances in vaudeville and sports shows, appeared in golf movies and advertisements, and produced one of the first TV golf shows. He was elected to the Golf Hall of Fame in 1961 and held his position at Baltusrol until 1972.

When he retired, the club made him an honorary member and dedicated a large room on the second floor of the clubhouse to the memory of his long and distinguished service.

*The Duke and Johnny.*

ROBERT TYRE JONES, JR.
75 POPLAR STREET, N.W.
ATLANTA, GEORGIA
30303

May 13, 1970

Dear Johnny:

Here's the picture I promised. I am sorry the signing has been so awkwardly done, but I can assure you that with my hands in their crippled condition, this is the best effort I have produced in years. I wish you could appreciate how much labor went into it. Then you would know how highly I regard you and the members of Baltusrol.

Just now, I cannot think of anything else that I might send you, but if I should run across anything, it will certainly come along.

Most sincerely,

Bob

Mr. John Farrell
Baltusrol Golf Club
Springfield, New Jersey

*Johnny Farrell and his family.*

Better times were ahead, and for a few years at the end of the '30's, a brief period of normalcy prevailed. The club had ordinary matters to contend with—such as flood, drought, and Japanese beetles. Extreme weather had ravaged greens and fairways, and the beetle grubs had virtually devoured the rough. By 1940, though, Major Jones had matters in hand, and the dual courses were coming back into splendid condition. Then, in 1941, Jones had to solve a different kind of problem when the caddies went out on strike. They wanted their rate to go up from $1.00 to $1.50 per bag. The compromise negotiated by Jones split the difference, and the new rate was $1.25.

In 1938, Stewart Baker stepped down as President, and was succeeded by Caxton Brown, one of the chief officers of the Weston Electrical Instrument Company with offices in Newark. Brown faithfully dropped by the club every afternoon on his way home from work to see that everything was all right, and the highlight of his term in office was the high-

*The burning of the mortgage. L-R: Stewart Baker, former President; W.P Conway, former Governor and Caxton Brown, Club President.*

ly publicized dinner on April 12, 1941, to celebrate the final payment of the club's debt. About 200 members gathered to witness the burning of the mortgage, which Brown held aloft and then dropped into a flaming caldron.

### World War II
When the United States mobilized for war in 1941, the effects were felt immediately at golf clubs across the country. The country was engaged in a global

conflict, and golf, like all other sports, simply didn't seem very urgent. At Baltusrol, the membership dipped to its lowest level of the century, with only 403 members on the books in April 1943. Dues were waived for those in military service.

Many golf clubs closed for the duration of the war, but Baltusrol – under the guidance of Major Jones – sought ways to participate in the war effort and still keep the golf courses in

play. There were shortages in manpower, food, and gasoline. Fuel rationing had made travel to and from Baltusrol so difficult that the club purchased four teams of horses and five wagons, or tallyhos, to transport members from the Short Hills railroad station. On weekends the tallyho's were kept busy, sometimes shuttling as many as 140 members to and from the station.

Even golf balls were in short supply because of the shortage of rubber. The USGA urged members to turn in old balls for reconditioning, and a special drop rule went into effect on four Lower to prevent members from losing more than one ball on this notorious water hole.

Victory gardens were planted in 1943, and marginal land along the Upper Course was used to raise hay. Eight acres were in crops and 1 & 1/2 acres were devoted to vegetables. That same year Baltusrol embarked on an animal husbandry program, acquiring 30 steers, 13 Guernsey cows with calf, and 80 sheep. The sheep were helpful in "mowing" the grass on the fairways, but their sharp hooves cut up the greens, and they had to be sold. Nevertheless, the club took justifiable pride in these highly-publicized efforts and the example that was set for other clubs and institutions.

In 1945, the year World War II ended, Major Jones, the driving force in keeping Baltusrol in operation during the war, retired early. His departure was marked by acrimony, for he did not see eye-to-eye with the new President, Walter Hine, who assumed his duties in 1943.

*Ambulance donated by Baltusrol to the war effort.*

Not long after Jones left, Hine resigned as President and left the club as well, evidently because of the sharp criticism that was directed at him by the admirers of Major Jones.

The club celebrated its fiftieth anniversary in 1945, and then turned to the serious work of rebuilding. The golf courses needed attention, and the buildings were in urgent need of rehabilitation. In particular, the clubhouse showed signs of weariness and neglect, with peeling paint and plaster, worn carpets, rusting pipe. A major overhaul was called for, and it was initiated by Maurice Trainer, who became President in November 1945. One of his first acts as President was to write a detailed letter to the membership setting out a course of action to restore the run-down golf courses and clubhouse to their former condition.

Trainer also emphasized the need to attract new members, and in 1946 the membership did increase by 48, nearly 10 percent. Out on the golf course, the green keeping crew was expanded and new equipment was purchased.

Inside, the kitchen equipment was replaced and major repairs and improvements were made to the heating, plumbing, and electrical systems. Pretty mundane, but it was exactly what the club required at the time.

Baltusrol was in fine enough shape to win yet another national tournament, the 1946 U. S. Amateur. This was the first Amateur to be played since 1941, for the tournament had been suspended during the war years. Played on the Lower Course, the tournament was won by Ted Bishop after a tense 37-hole final with Smiley Quick. The galleries were the largest for a national championship since 1930, and the field included just about every amateur of note, including two of Baltusrol's former club champions, Max Marston and Augie Kammer, Jr.

Even though this tournament was deemed a success, the next club President – Stoddard M. Stevens – authorized the committee on structural improvements to the golf courses to seek recommendations from Francis

Ouimet and Robert Trent Jones. At the time, Jones was the foremost golf architect in the country, and he was establishing his reputation and ability to update the great championship courses while preserving the integrity of their original design. The very fact that Jones' services had been engaged showed that Baltusrol was quietly beginning to prepare itself for another U.S. Open, but Jones approached his task with two goals in mind: "To make the courses fairer for the average player and harder for the low handicapper."

Meanwhile, Stevens went methodically about the business of upgrading the club, spending a total of

$200,000 dollars between 1947 and 1952. He was succeeded as President by Hobart C. Ramsey, the chairman of Worthington Pump. Ramsey's wife, Collette, was one of the finest women golfers in the metropolitan area and the donor of the Ramsey Tournament trophy. Ramsey continued the program of improvements, and made what proved to be a decisive move when he hired Carl J. Jehlen as club manager in 1953.

Jehlen, dubbed "Mr. Inside" by club members who remembered "Mr. Outside," brought to Baltusrol an entirely new set of professional and managerial skills. The German-born Jehlen had been engaged in hotel and club work for 31 years before coming to Baltusrol, and he was elected president of the Club Managers Association of America in 1953. Even though Baltusrol had been headed by a series of high-powered executives, there was not a single one of them who had any real experience or expertise in the kind of management required to run a large club

*Men's Locker Room before renovation.*

*Golf architect, Robert Trent Jones at his drawing table.*

like Baltusrol. The club had always assumed, for instance, that food service was doomed to be unprofitable, but under Jehlen the food operation soon became a dependable source of revenue. Moreover, the Baltusrol dining room's reputation for good food and elegant service grew to such a point that it was sometimes described as the best restaurant in New Jersey.

Jehlen's importance to the club was recognized immediately, and he was invited to sit in on board meetings, where his cogent opinions and recommendations were attentively heard and often followed. Jehlen also commanded the respect of the staff and club members, and in 1962 he was given complete charge of everything about the club except the grounds. With Jehlen on board to steer the club's

internal affairs, and Robert Trent Jones directing the upgrading of the golf courses, Baltusrol was prepared to meet the challenges of the modern era.

*Jack Forrester, Baltusrol Pro, and family (1925).*

*Aerial view prior to the 1926 U.S. Amateur*

*Bobby Locke in one of the new bunkers on four Lower.*

*Drawing from "Golf Holes They Talk About," published in 1927.*

*Panoramic view taken behind sixteen Upper in 1924.*

# The Modern Era
# 1954-1995

*The Ed Sullivan Show.*

$\mathcal{I}$f the modern era is defined by a single fact, that fact is television—and the 1954 U. S. Open at Baltusrol was the first to be televised nationally. Millions were able to watch at home as Ed Furgol scrambled on the final hole, playing eighteen Lower by way of the fairway of eighteen Upper, to secure the victory. Out on the course, record crowds had followed the play, and – another Open first – they were kept at a distance from the players by the use of gallery ropes.

The Lower Course, as revised by Jones, was at 7,060 yards, the longest course in Open history. As Jones was well aware, the modern era had arrived in golf in the form of longer-flying balls, balanced steel shafts, and the perfection of course maintenance. Not only had Jones significantly lengthened the Lower Course, he had also added a significant number of fairway bunkers, consolidated or enlarged many greenside bunkers, and eliminated bunkers that no longer came into play. This was the fourth Open played at Baltusrol—and the third Baltusrol course over which the Open was played, a unique record.

The 1954 Open was an unqualified success. The Lower Course had secured its place not just in golf history but as a perennial on the lists of top American courses. It had won for Baltusrol all kinds of attention, including an appearance on the Ed Sullivan Show by club President Ramsey and Johnny Farrell, accompanied by their wives. Thanks to television, it had ushered in a new era of spectator golf. Last but not least, it had netted the club the useful sum of $78,000.

Baltusrol had always been committed to hosting national tournaments, but the 1954 Open had demonstrated just what was required in the modern era. To put it simply, national tournaments were well on the way to becoming big business, and they required more of everything—more planning, more preparation, more volunteers, more expense. The rewards were correspondingly larger in terms of prestige and revenue, but no club that wanted to retain its position as a host for USGA events could afford to rest on its laurels.

The leadership at Baltusrol understood that the golf courses and clubhouse facilities had to be maintained to meet the highest standards. Over the next several years the club was guided by a series of presidents who kept pace with needed improvements. Monroe J. Rathbone, the president of Standard Oil of New Jersey, served as President from 1955-1958; a towering man with the battered look of a retired boxer, Rathbone enjoyed great popularity with the membership. He was followed by John Smaltz (1958-1961); Walter Feldman (1961-1964), who had succeeded Hobart Ramsey as chairman of Worthington Pump; and William M. Walther (1964-1967), who also served as chairman of the NJGA Caddies Scholarship Foundation.

During these four administrations, the pro shop was enlarged, the terrace lounge was enclosed, a new parking

PRESIDENTS

MONROE J. RATHBONE
1955-1958

JOHN C. SMALTZ
1958-1961

WALTHER H. FELDMANN
1961-1964

WILLIAM M. WALTHER
1964-1967

ROBERT FINNEY
1967-1970

MATTHEW J. GLENNON
1970-1973

JOHN S. ROBERTS
1973-1976

B. P. RUSSELL
1976-1979

ROBERT J. BOUTILLIER
1979-1982

PAUL J. HANNA
1982-1985

*Mickey Wright, 1961 Women's Open Champion.*

lot and service road were added behind the garage, the men's locker room was completely refurbished, the dining room was extensively renovated, as was the kitchen, at a cost of $140,000. This was substantially more than the cost of the original clubhouse, but the price tag for everything connected with golf and golf clubs had risen steeply.

To help finance improvements, the value of proprietary certificates was increased from $500 to $1,500, and dues were regularly raised to meet the accelerating costs of operating the club in the manner to which Baltusrol members had become accustomed. They expected the best, and they didn't always welcome changes. One small innovation that failed was the installation of a Muzak system in the Dining Room. "What's that, music at Baltusrol?" roared a longtime member on hearing it for the first time. The music was turned off and not heard again for fifteen years.

The club enhanced its standing as a premier site for championship golf by hosting a U. S. Women's Open in 1961. The legendary Mickey Wright won this one going away, dominating the Lower Course with her power. During the practice rounds, spectators had watched in awe as she hit one solid 5-iron after another to the pin at twelve Lower, a shot of 180 yards, all carry. Wright's prowess and the overall strength of this Open field showed that women's golf, too, had entered the modern era and helped to win new respect for the women's game.

At Baltusrol, there had always been a strong tradition of women's golf, and during the 1960's one of the club's most talented and tenacious competitors, Helen Hockenjos, rounded out her career. She had won her first club championship in 1948, and she won her last – and her thirteenth – in 1968. This was the capstone of a career that included six New Jersey State Championships as well as victories over the leading women players of the day. Helen was one of several Baltusrol women who carried the club's banner in regional tournaments: Collette Ramsey won four club championships and New Jersey and Metropolitan events, and Harriet Hart – who took up the game when she was 24 – became one of the oldest rookies in professional sports when she qualified for the LPGA tour, having won the New Jersey title in 1969 and 1970, the Metropolitan championship in 1970, and the Baltusrol club championship in 1973.

In addition, Baltusrol women continued a long-standing pattern of serving as officers in the Women's New Jersey Golf Association and the Women's Metropolitan Golf Association. The Baltusrol Women's Golf Committee has conducted one of the most active programs of women's golf in the country, and the number of women golfers at the club has grown steadily.

Baltusrol was in the news again in 1963, when the club was the site of another fire. This one was a forest fire and it took place in broad daylight when a spark somehow ignited in the woods above the practice

*Jack Nicklaus, 1967 Open Champion.*

range. Fanned by high winds, the spark turned into a spectacular blaze that ravaged the woods all along the first three holes of the Upper course and threatened both the garage and the clubhouse. The large crowds who came to see the fire had to be controlled by the Springfield Police, and the fire itself was brought under control by the Springfield Fire Department—a considerably more advanced outfit than the brigade that had fought the 1909 clubhouse fire!

American golf in the 1960's and '70's was dominated by one player, Jack Nicklaus, and Baltusrol was the scene of two of his most dramatic and significant major championships.

The Opens in 1967 and 1980 were both won by Nicklaus, of course, and they came at crucial points in his astonishing career.

In 1967, Nicklaus was still the upstart and Arnold Palmer was the king as far as golf fans were concerned. It didn't matter that Nicklaus had already won a batch of major titles, or that he had beaten Palmer in a head-to-head contest in the 1962 Open at Oakmont. Golf fans still wanted to see Palmer win, and they particularly wanted to see him beat Nicklaus. As the 1967 Open got underway, the galleries were filled with fans carrying signs that let Nicklaus know just how they felt about him, and they were vocal in their preference for Palmer.

Palmer and Nicklaus were paired with each other the last two rounds. The turning point came at the long seventh, where Nicklaus rolled in a sizeable birdie putt. Palmer had just hit a screaming 2-iron to eight feet; he was visibly shaken and missed his putt, losing a stroke where he had expected to gain one. But no one was going to make up ground on Nicklaus on this particular day, who even won over the crowds with golf of a rare high order. His final round score was 65, his record-setting Open total 275. This would be the last of the great Nicklaus - Palmer showdowns, and it established exactly which golfer was at the top of the heap.

In 1980, when the Open next came to Baltusrol, the Nicklaus era seemed to have run its course. Jack was 40 years old and he hadn't won a tournament for more than a year. But he answered all questions about his game during the first round as he roared around the course with a record-setting 63. This amazing round could just as easily have been a 62, for he missed a 3-foot birdie putt on the eighteenth. His closest pursuer throughout the tournament was Isao Aoki, of Japan, who putted like a magician. The two men happened to be paired all four days of the tournament, and they poured all their pride and experience into their memorable duel. When it was all over, Aoki would break Nicklaus' old record by shooting 274, and Nicklaus would set a new one with 272, winning the championship by two strokes.

The scoreboard carried a huge message that has become the famous summa-

tion of the 1980 Open: JACK IS BACK.

These two historic and emotional Opens had shown just what kind of drama golf at the highest levels could provide, and they confirmed Baltusrol's role as one of the great showcases in the sport. Huge galleries had attended both events, with more than 100,000 spectators on hand for the tournament rounds in 1980. That Open was also a huge financial success both for the club and for the USGA, with significant revenues coming from the sale of corporate tents.

Baltusrol's proximity to New York City had once again proven, just as it had in 1901, to be a major advantage when it came to putting on a successful tournament. It meant that both spectators and sponsors were close at hand. The existence of the dual courses – Tillinghast would probably roll over in his grave! – insured plenty of room for corporate tents, media areas, and parking. All in all, the existence of a facility like Baltusrol, a green kingdom within sight of the New York skyline, was seeming more and more like a marvel.

After the Nicklaus victory,

Baltusrol still had work to do—and wasted no time in getting to it. Bob Finney, chairman of the 1967 Open,

*Aoki and Nicklaus at awards ceremony.*

*The scoreboard announces JACK IS BACK.*

was elected President that same year, and within a year's time he had both courses stripped to install a

new irrigation system, improve the drainage, and reseed with bentgrass (replacing the native fescue and bluegrass). Finney, whose memory reached back to halcyon days he had enjoyed as a boy on the Old Course, was so imbued with the spirit and tradition of the club that he was known as "Mr. Baltusrol."

The club presidents who followed Finney found that they had to address themselves to two related problems: declining revenues and declining membership. The number of members had hovered at around 500 for many years, but it took a significant dip in 1974 when the energy crisis brought about a severe economic downturn. In March 1974 the membership fell to 468, one of the lowest levels in club history. Given the large amounts required to maintain the club facilities – the irrigation system alone had a $400,000 price tag – every member was important.

John F. Roberts was President at the time, having replaced Matthew Glennon (1970-1973). Roberts was also the president of F.W. Woolworth, and he took a merchandiser's approach to the cost-revenue squeeze.

*Vice President Richard Nixon, presents the Eisenhower Trophy to Johnny Farrell and Bill Burke. Nixon joined Baltusrol in 1965.*

*Bob Finney, "Mr. Baltusrol."*

*Carl Jehlen.*

*The Golf Shop circa 1954.*

*Mark De Noble.*

His strategy was not to economize but rather to boldly expand revenue-producing operations. One of Robert's proposals, the development of paddle tennis courts, was ultimately voted down by the board. Baltusrol was to remain exclusively a golf club.

Another project was the enlargement of the Golf Shop. Original estimates for the work began at $90,000 – approximately the same amount that had been spent to build the clubhouse back in 1909 – but the final cost was $200,000, and the members had one of the most spacious, inviting, and attractive pro shops to be found at any private club. In 1977 Bob Ross took up the reins in the pro shop, after experience as a touring pro and head professional at five other clubs.

The presidents who followed Roberts were B. P. Russell (1976-1979) and Robert J. Boutillier (1979-1982), and they continued to seek ways to expand. One idea was the "Hill Property Development Project," which involved the construction of condominiums on land owned by the club at the top of the mountain. These would be offered for sale to Baltusrol members. Discussion of this idea advanced to the point where the club actually sought an IRS ruling on how the project would affect the club's tax exemption, but at that time the project was abandoned.

The management of the club underwent a change of regime in 1981 when Carl Jehlen, "Mr. Inside," retired. The citation read at the large reception held in his honor noted not only his professionalism but his unfailing cordiality: "Carl was ready to receive the members and their guests as host of Baltusrol—every day." Throughout its long history, Baltusrol was fortunate in having staff members who not only gave the club long and able service, but who also had the strength of personality to make their presence felt in a large institution. Mr. Inside had been one of them. His successor, Mark De Noble – who has held the position of club manager for 14 years now – was cut from the same cloth.

Paul J. Hanna became Baltusrol's twentieth President in 1982. He presided over the most extensive, and expensive, renovations to the clubhouse that included the complete overhaul of the plumbing, electrical, and heating systems. When all the bills were in, this overhaul was by far the most costly endeavor in the club's history, costing a total of $1.6 million.

*The Golf Shop in 1995.*

33

# Bob Ross
# *The Consummate Pro*

*A*n exceptionally well rounded and versatile golf professional player, teacher, and statesman, Robert A. Ross, Baltusrol's pro at the time of this writing, has met the club's ever-expanding needs admirably.

A native of Vermont, Bob graduated from Admiral Billard Academy in New London, Connecticut, and Pasadena City College in California, and he attended PGA business schools and merchandise seminars. He was head golf professional at five other clubs before coming to Baltusrol in 1977, including the prestigious Philadelphia Cricket Club and Sawgrass Country Club in Ponte Vedra, Florida.

Bob Ross was part of the Professional Golf Association tour from 1959 to 1976, and he participated in three National PGA Championships and three U.S. Opens as well as winning both the Pennsylvania Open and Philadelphia PGA Championships in 1967. Ross was voted National Country Club Professional of 1980 by Country Club Golfer Magazine and the New Jersey Section of the PGA.

A former president of the Philadelphia Section of the PGA and a one-time member of the National PGA Rules Committee, Bob has also worked with many organizations concerned with the business of golf.

A remarkably attractive and personable gentleman, as well as a popular golf teacher, Bob has attracted able assistant professionals, and as a skilled merchandiser, he has run one of the largest and most beautiful pro shops in all of New Jersey.

In 1985, a quarter century after Mickey Wright's sterling performance, the women returned to Baltusrol for the 40th Open Championship, played over the Upper Course. The media attention focused almost entirely on the young Nancy Lopez, who had just burst upon the scene as the hottest player on the LPGA. She was expected to win her first Open at Baltusrol, and she was the outright leader at the halfway point. On the third day, though, she fell a shot behind a relative unknown, Kathy Baker, who

*Kathy Baker, 1985 U.S. Women's Open champion.*

had posted a fine 68. In the fourth round, Lopez fell quickly out of contention and Baker shot a 2-under par 70, one of only four sub-par rounds of the day. Her winning total of 280 was an achievement as the Upper Course, playing to a par of 72, had proven a most exacting test.

The chairman of that Open, Robert A. Potter, became the next club President and held the office from 1985-1987. Like other presidents during the club's tenth decade, he concerned himself with

essential improvements, but they were the kind of improvements that don't really show—unless you're looking for them. They were like improvements that Rolls-Royce makes to its automobiles, the kind that insure permanence and durability, not the kind that are intended to make a flashy show. To speak plainly, Baltusrol didn't really need any major changes; at some point in its history – club members could argue exactly when – it had simply become a landmark, one of the permanent features in the landscape of golf.

One indication of the club's status came in the form of an accolade from *Golf Magazine*, which selected the clubhouse as the second best in the world. A dubious honor, perhaps, only to be second best—but Baltusrol was second only to the Royal and Ancient Clubhouse at St. Andrews. The club and the golf courses belonged, in a sense, to history and to golf lore.

The prestige of Baltusrol was certainly a major factor in attracting new members during the 1980's, and the membership rolls expanded steadily (at the present writing, the club has more than 1,200 members including 500 proprietary members and a long waiting list). The cost of proprietary certificates increased, too, and with other revenues the club has enjoyed a period of steady solvency. Club Presidents Kenneth Nichols (1987-89), David Baldwin (1989-91), Alan Reed (1991-

*The Front Lobby.*

93), and F. Duffield Meyercord (1993 - present), have all had the benefit of leading a strong, thriving institution. Most recently, under Duff Meyercord's presidency, the Club has embarked on a new irrigation system and a major renovation of the Clubhouse.

One sign of the club's tremendous popularity, both as a tournament and outing site, was the establishment of the policy in 1991 that one golf course will always be available for member play. Shades of 1916, when

*The landing overlooking the Lobby.*

*The Dining Room.*

*The Grill Room.*

*The Terrace.*

*The East Lounge.*

demand for tee-times led to the building of the dual courses!

At the same time, the club was quietly preparing itself for its second century. In 1990 an ad hoc committee was appointed to make arrangements for the Centennial Celebration, and in 1991 the club engaged Rees Jones to prepare master plans for both the Lower and Upper courses. Even here tradition prevailed, since Rees is the son of Robert Trent Jones; and, like his father, he has made a reputation as a golf course architect who knows how to preserve and enhance the character of the classic Open courses.

In preparation for the 1993 Open, many of his recommendations were implemented—new tees at No. 3 and No. 9, several extended tees, new bunkers at No. 7, No. 8, and No. 14. These changes added some length to the course, posing difficulties for the long-hitting pros without really altering the course as played by members. The grass in the rough was also changed from bent to a mixture of rye and bluegrass, though this would turn out to be the one vulnerable point when the Open was played. A dry spring made the rough grow in sparsely, and there was some worry that the best players in the world would break all kinds of scoring records.

A multitude of other preparations, all orchestrated by Open Chairman Richard Miller, had been undertaken for the tournament. The scale of the operation was larger than ever, with some 700 club members volunteering for assignments. The U. S. Open was now unquestionably in the ranks of big-time sporting events, and not even the best-laid plans could avoid the traffic snarls

*Chairpersons of the 1993 U.S. Open.*

that occurred on the first day as record numbers of fans flocked to the course. Another sign of the Open's cachet was the huge merchandise tent that was erected just inside Baltusrol's gates; throughout Open week a long line of customers waited outside the tent for their turn to buy souvenirs.

As it turned out, even in perfect scoring conditions, the players had their hands full—and still they lavished praise on the Lower. Record crowds turned out to see golf stars from several generations, starting with Arnold Palmer and descending in age through Jack Nicklaus – who was mobbed every time he stepped off the course – to Tom Watson, Nick Price, Ernie Els, and 16-year-old sensation Ted Oh. Almost overlooked for the first two days was Lee Janzen, who moved quietly in the lead on the second day and stayed there. His totals after his second, third, and fourth rounds were identical to those of Nicklaus 13 years earlier, and

they were good enough to hold off his most determined pursuer, Payne Stewart.

The 1993 U. S. Open made it quite clear just what Baltusrol has come to mean in American golf. While golf writers dug into the club's history to find their stories, the television cameras captured scenes that evoked Baltusrol's rich heritage. Every step of the way, there were reminders of previous Opens and earlier champions. Out on the course, as Janzen was in the process of winning his tense duel with Stewart, several shots went straight into golf lore. One was Janzen's 5-iron on the tenth hole of the final round, a shot that had doom written all over it as it sped toward a towering oak—and when it came out on the other side and bounded onto the green, it seemed that word written on it was not doom, after all, but destiny. Another was his chip-in at the sixteenth, when by all odds he looked as if he had to bogey. Another shot was not played by Janzen, and not even in

the final round—it was John Daly's mammoth 1-iron on the seventeenth, at 630 yards the longest par 5 on an Open course, with a green that had never been reached in two shots. Well, Daly reached it, and everyone who follows golf has read about it, and will read about it again the next time an Open comes to Baltusrol.

Louis Keller would surely have enjoyed the 1993 Open, and he would have approved of the way that Baltusrol had adhered to his vision. Over a century, first and foremost, Baltusrol has been a golf club. Other activities came and went, but golf was always the centerpiece. And not just good golf, but superior golf—golf that would set a national standard and test the abilities and fiber of the greatest golfers in the world. Every time that it seemed that the game was about to catch up with Baltusrol, the club took action to guarantee that it would retain its preeminence. It went without saying that all the facilities,

inside and out, would be expected to measure up to the same exacting standards. The majestic clubhouse, with its commanding views of both courses, added to the exceptional beauty of Baltusrol's setting—a setting that became only more remarkable as the years passed and the suburbs grew up all around the club. Altogether, Baltusrol succeeded in creating one of golf's greatest stages, and there can't be many golfers who set foot on the place without taking a deep breath trying to take it all in.

Baltusrol started with a ghost, the man who lent his name to the mountain, and now the place is populated with the shades of all the golfers who have left their trace on these storied golf courses. The player who makes his way around Baltusrol, no matter how he plays, is always in the exalted and honorable company of the great players who have gone before. From Harry Vardon to Bob Jones to Jack Nicklaus to Nancy Lopez— the list goes on and on and on.

The name Baltusrol now evokes the exploits of a host of golfers, and the elusive, enduring, gracious spirit of the game itself.

*1993 Open Champion, Lee Janzen.*

# The Evolution of the Golf Courses

# Introduction

For a full century, golf has been played on Baltusrol's fabled fairways. Beginning with nine rudimentary holes, the golf course was soon transformed into a respected 18-hole championship layout, and then doubled once more to become the two world-renowned golf courses that exist today, the Upper and Lower.

During this rapid and sometimes painful evolution, Baltusrol managed to keep itself in the forefront of American golf. Many other clubs that figured prominently in the early chapter of our golf history have faded from sight, unable – or unwilling – to make the changes necessary to keep pace with developments in the game.

Not Baltusrol. It has hosted a national championship in every decade of the twentieth century except one, a record no other club can match. The United States Open has been played seven times at Baltusrol, on three different courses—another unique record.

If Baltusrol's success now seems inevitable, we should remember that it was achieved only through bold and constant innovation. The first 18-hole course, the Old Course, was originally designed as a one-of-a-kind combination layout, a short course and long course rolled into one. In time the short course would be abandoned and the long course would evolve into what became known as the Old Course. It featured huge cross bunkers, the first island green, and pit bunkers faced with railroad

ties. In the boldest innovation of all, this Old Course was scrapped to make way for the Dual Courses!

So many changes could have led to disaster, but at every critical juncture Baltusrol was guided by

*Louis Keller.*

men of conviction and foresight. The founder of the Club, Louis Keller, set the standard when he made it clear that he would be satisfied with nothing less than a superior golf course. It was Keller who commissioned the layout of the original nine holes, Keller who then dynamited these holes to make way for the combination course, and Keller who initiated the development of the Upper and Lower. Keller wasn't alone. He had

*George Low.*

the able assistance of George Low, Baltusrol's esteemed professional and greenkeeper, who played a major role in shaping the Old Course. He was also supported by Baltusrol's green committee, especially Chairman C. F. Watson, who oversaw the construction of the Dual Courses.

And then there was Albert W. Tillinghast, the self-styled "Creator of Baltusrol," the talented and charismatic architect and builder of the Upper and Lower. It was said of Tillinghast that he was the first golf course architect to be given an unlimited budget—which he then exceeded! Tillinghast was one of the first to articulate the princi-

*A. W. Tillinghast.*

ples of modern golf course design, and he applied those principles at Baltusrol.

He was followed by a series of able men who left their mark on the Dual Courses. First came Major Avery Jones, who planted many of the trees that now line the fairways, then there were architects Robert Trent Jones and his son Rees, who readied the Lower for major tournaments; and through every change the golf

courses were kept in superb playing condition by green superintendents like Robert Casey and Joseph Flaherty. It goes without saying that such a record of unbroken success can be achieved only when a golf club is committed to excellence, and when

*Robert Trent Jones.*

vigilant green committees, led by dedicated chairmen, have the support of an enlightened membership

Some of the impetus for change came from within the club, and some came from without—specifically, from the United States Golf Association. Each time that Baltusrol was selected to host a national tournament, the golf courses were improved, strengthened, and modernized. Some of the most remarkable people in American golf – men like Bobby Jones, Francis Ouimet, Joe Dey and P.J. Boatwright – looked over Baltusrol with a critical eye, making suggestions that led to significant alterations.

Yet the golf courses retained their essential character throughout these changes; they are inalterably Baltusrol's Upper and Lower, and so they will remain. What follows is the story of these courses and the people who fashioned them into one of golf's great landmarks.

# The Old Course

When Baltusrol was founded in 1895, Americans were just discovering their passion for golf. At that time there were fewer than eighty courses in the country and the United States Golf Association was not yet a year old. Nearly all of those early courses were primitive affairs, laid out and built by men who had no experience whatsoever. The first professional "Architects" were Scotsmen hired for an afternoon to drive 18 stakes on a golf course site. The greens were often indistinguishable from the fairways, and the most fashionable hazards were steep earthen berms, cop bunkers, fences, and other man-made obstacles.

Baltusrol had all those features, but the rapid, dramatic changes to the golf course provide a perfect illustration of the trial-and-error that led to modern principles of course design, construction, and conditioning.

Louis Keller took it upon himself to employ an Englishman, George Hunter, to design Baltusrol's original nine-hole course in 1895. One of Baltusrol's charter members, Hunter designed a course that measured 2,372 yards. Early advertisements proudly announced that the course had "40 foot greens." Only two holes were more than 300 yards in length, but the ninth hole was a monster that stretched out some 517 yards. According to club lore, Hunter had sited his eighth green far from the club house and needed a long hole to make the return.

Of these holes, the fifth followed the same routing as three Upper. Nothing else remains of this golf course today.

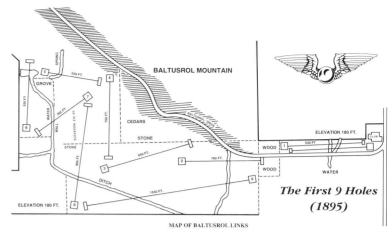

MAP OF BALTUSROL LINKS

*The First 9 Holes (1895)*

## The Short and Long Courses (1898)

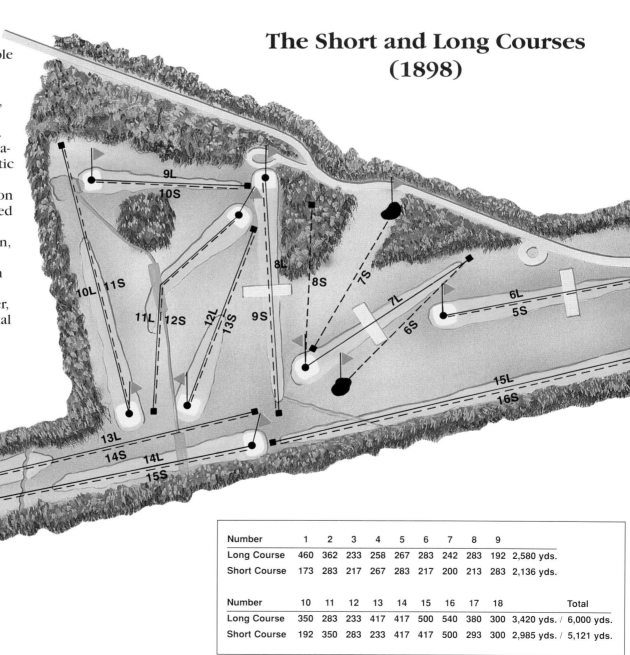

| Number | 1 | 2 | 3 | 4 | 5 | 6 | 7 | 8 | 9 | |
|---|---|---|---|---|---|---|---|---|---|---|
| Long Course | 460 | 362 | 233 | 258 | 267 | 283 | 242 | 283 | 192 | 2,580 yds. |
| Short Course | 173 | 283 | 217 | 267 | 283 | 217 | 200 | 213 | 283 | 2,136 yds. |

| Number | 10 | 11 | 12 | 13 | 14 | 15 | 16 | 17 | 18 | Total |
|---|---|---|---|---|---|---|---|---|---|---|
| Long Course | 350 | 283 | 233 | 417 | 417 | 500 | 540 | 380 | 300 | 3,420 yds. / 6,000 yds. |
| Short Course | 192 | 350 | 283 | 233 | 417 | 417 | 500 | 293 | 300 | 2,985 yds. / 5,121 yds. |

### The Short and Long Courses

Under Louis Keller's leadership, Baltusrol quickly became one of the prominent clubs in the Metropolitan area. Baltusrol's nine-hole course was the site of regular interclub, invitational and open tournaments; and the membership grew quickly from thirty to nearly 400. To meet the needs of its members, and to keep its place as a leading tournament site, Baltusrol had to expand.

The Chicago Golf Club had opened the first 18-hole course in 1895, and other leading clubs like St. Andrews, Shinnecock Hills and Morris County had soon followed suit. So in June of 1897, the Board of Governors approved raising

$500 in debt through a subscription to the members, with the proceeds to be devoted to the opening of an 18-hole course. And on Labor Day, Baltusrol's first 18 holes were opened for play. This course was less than a year old when Keller decided that it needed improvement. In early 1898, he presented to the Board plans for a unique combination course designed by a Surveyor, A. H. Woodruff.

The goal was to provide a short course for women and beginners and a long course for experienced players. The long course measured

6,000 yards and the short course 5,128 yards. There were twenty-two greens, fourteen of which were shared by both courses.

The work on the combination course was quickly done, and this hybrid 18 opened for play in the summer of 1898. The green committee made the two courses as similar as possible. The short course would shift off the long course at regular intervals to avoid the longest of holes and enable slow players to keep out of the way of the faster ones. For example, the first hole of the short course was routed the same

as the first of the Lower, except there was a short green 173 yards from the tee. If two pairs of players met at the first tee, the players on the longest course had the right of way. They would clear the first bunker of 130 yards, and on their second stroke leave the first short hole clear for the short-course players to approach.

### Makings of the Old Course

The desire to host national championships would lead to significant improvements to the golf course. Baltusrol had successfully hosted a number of interclub invitational and open tournaments, and Keller and the Board began to lobby the USGA for its first national championship—the 1900 U.S. Women's Amateur. In anticipation of securing this event, a six-inch water main from the Short Hills Water Company was connected to the links for watering the greens. New bunkers were built and changes were made to the fourth, sixth and seventh holes. The fourth was stretched to 501 yards by blending the former fourth and fifth holes. The sixth became the fifth, and a new sixth hole of 350 yards was created with Baltusrol Way becoming a hazard for a short drive. The seventh was lengthened with a new tee to a distance of 505 yards. This revised long course was shaping into what is known today as the "Old Course."

Despite these improvements, the 1900 Women's Amateur went to Shinnecock. But Baltusrol did not have to wait much longer, for it was awarded the Women's Amateur for the following year.

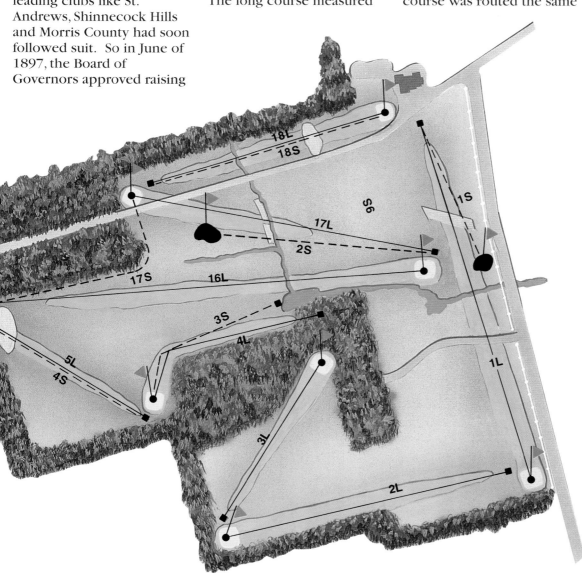

# The Old Course
## (1900)

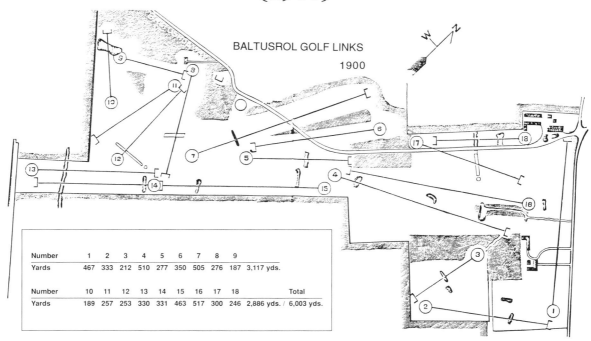

BALTUSROL GOLF LINKS

1900

| Number | 1 | 2 | 3 | 4 | 5 | 6 | 7 | 8 | 9 | |
|--------|-----|-----|-----|-----|-----|-----|-----|-----|-----|------------|
| Yards | 467 | 333 | 212 | 510 | 277 | 350 | 505 | 276 | 187 | 3,117 yds. |

| Number | 10 | 11 | 12 | 13 | 14 | 15 | 16 | 17 | 18 | Total |
|--------|-----|-----|-----|-----|-----|-----|-----|-----|-----|-----------------------|
| Yards | 189 | 257 | 253 | 330 | 331 | 463 | 517 | 300 | 246 | 2,886 yds. / 6,003 yds. |

The 1901 Women's Amateur was played on a combination of the long course and the short course, for the short seventh and eighth holes were used in this event. The green of the short seventh and tee to the short eighth can still be seen today in the woods short of the second green of the Upper.

After 1901, the short course was abandoned. One of the reasons for its demise was the latest technological advance—the new lively rubber ball. The Women's Amateur marked the passing of the gutta percha, or "gutty." The new rubber ball flew farther and lasted longer than the gutty. In the Amateur, the majority of contestants had used the new ball.

### The Island Green
Prior to the 1904 Amateur Championship, a new hole was put into commission that was to become known as the "Island Green." The hole was a short par 4 that played downhill to a green surrounded by a moat. In the practice rounds shortly

*The Island Green (No. 10) seen from the twelfth tee.*

before the tournament, considerable discussion arose as to the merits of the hole. Some contended that it was absolutely impossible to hold the green while others claimed that it was one of the very best holes on the course. The final decision on using the hole for the tournament would rest with a committee of Baltusrol members: Messrs. Leighton Calkins, Wm. Fellowes Morgan and Lionel H. Graham. They accordingly went out and subjected it to a practical test. None of these gentleman possessed championship qualities. Their tee-shots were 40 or 50 yards behind where good players would go. Consequently, their second shots had to be played with a mid-iron (2-iron) instead of a mashie (5-iron), and they found it impossible to hold the green. Accordingly, they voted against its being played in the championship.

In its place, the old green was used, which was slightly to the left of the pot bunker on the left side of the fairway.

> *I remember at one time watching Walter Hagen in one of the big tournaments drive the ball from the (tenth) tee into the water. In those days we used balls that floated on water and were called "floaters". Walter took off his shoes and stockings and played the ball out of the water and got his birdie three. I will never forget this as long as I am able to think about golf.*
>
> Fritz Leuders
> Baltusrol Member

**The tenth was one of the most photographed holes in the country.**

In the years following the 1904 Amateur, the Island Green came to enjoy both local and national notoriety. It was Baltusrol's "signature" hole. There were two tees for the hole; the first was directly behind the pond and the medal tee was 30 yards up the hillside. These tees can still be seen behind the third green of the Upper. To the best of our knowledge, Baltusrol's Island Green was the first of its kind. Today, of course, island greens are common-place, especially on resort courses.

### Consequences of the 1904 Amateur

The 1904 Amateur Championship was extremely important in shaping Baltusrol. In a mere nine years, Baltusrol had transformed its original unin-spired nine holes into a course worthy of hosting the most prestigious tourna-ment in the nation. Granted, Baltusrol had played host to the Women's Amateur and the Men's Open, but in these times, the Men's Amateur was the "Championship." What happened after this tournament was more significant than what happened during the week of play—criticism led to a better course.

The defects of the course were bluntly listed by Leighton Calkins, the inventor of the handicap system and noted golf writer of the time:

"During the Champion-ship in that year (1904) there were no side traps, and no traps in close proximity to the greens. There were thirteen cop bunkers (cop bunkers had an artificial appearance with straight lines and a crest with steep sides) stretched across the fairway in dull monotonous array; but, except at those particular points a bad shot was rarely punished because the "rough" had a hair cut, and in most cases the woods could be given a wide berth. The fairgreen generally was in poor turf, thin, and infested with worm casts. As one player remarked, the rough was smooth and the smooth was rough."

Throughout the next decade, the Green Committee directed continual improvements in an effort to upgrade the Old Course. New tees and greens were constructed. Over 75 new bunkers were built in strategic locations. The old fashioned cop bunkers were removed. Miles of fairway were sanded, top dressed and fertilized. By 1910, the changes had paid off, and Baltusrol was regularly recognized as one of the finest courses in the country.

As noted by Leighton Calkins, "Half a dozen years ago Baltusrol, despite its good length and some hard holes, was hardly a championship course. Today it ranks with Fox Hills, Appawamis and Nassau, and is more difficult than any of them."

### The Colossal Cross Bunker

Baltusrol did not rest on its laurels. In the years prior to World War I, a massive rebunkering program replaced the old fashioned cross bunkers with modern bunkers built at diagonals to the line of play. Simple as it seems, this principle was radical and modern, for it opened new routes from tee to green and laid the groundwork for strategic design.

Other major improvements were also put into play almost every year. On the first hole, now the first of the Lower, a tremendous modern cross bunker was

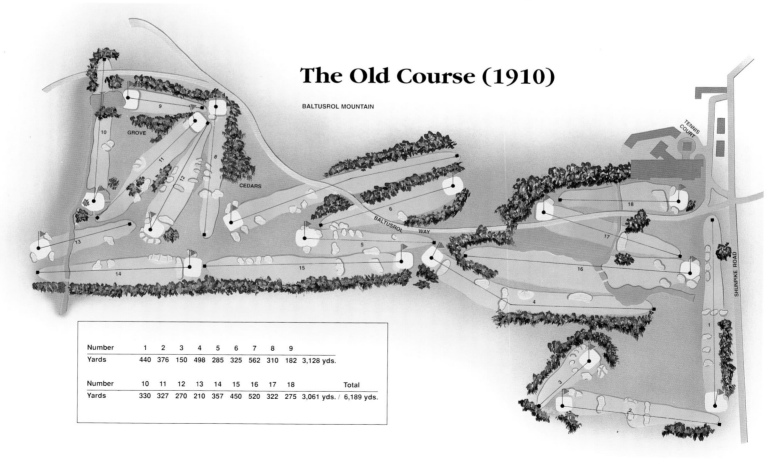

## The Old Course (1910)

BALTUSROL MOUNTAIN

GROVE

CEDARS

BALTUSROL WAY

TENNIS COURT

SHUNPIKE ROAD

| Number | 1 | 2 | 3 | 4 | 5 | 6 | 7 | 8 | 9 | |
|--------|-----|-----|-----|-----|-----|-----|-----|-----|-----|------------|
| Yards | 440 | 376 | 150 | 498 | 285 | 325 | 562 | 310 | 182 | 3,128 yds. |

| Number | 10 | 11 | 12 | 13 | 14 | 15 | 16 | 17 | 18 | Total |
|--------|-----|-----|-----|-----|-----|-----|-----|-----|-----|----------------------|
| Yards | 330 | 327 | 270 | 210 | 357 | 450 | 520 | 322 | 275 | 3,061 yds. / 6,189 yds. |

constructed across the fairway to replace the existing cross bunker 30 yards beyond it.

The construction of this bunker was exceedingly difficult since it was dug in a clay soil, which often necessitated the raising of a cop, or crest to make it effective; and in raising a cop the danger is that the bunker will become too artificial in appearance.

The Green Committee avoided this problem by sloping the back of the bunker gradually into the surface of the ground, and providing an irregular curve to the line of the bunker and its surface limits.

### The Infamous Pot Bunker

The pit which guarded the eighteenth hole, and had been a factor in the finish of many close matches, proved to be a mine of gravel that supplied much of the needed material to make concrete for the new clubhouse in 1909 .

During the excavation, it was expanded into a turfed punch bowl that sloped into a sand bunker with a palisade of massive timbers on the far side holding up the green.

Unfortunate players who caught this bunker had to play a shot over the timbers. It was a wonder that no one was ever seriously injured by a ricocheting ball.

The architectural use of timber supports was not revolutionary, as this hazard strongly resembled bunkering at North Berwick in Scotland.

*The original cross bunkers on the first hole.*

*Diagonal cross bunkers replaced the original ones on the first hole.*

*The deep pot bunker on the eighteenth hole.*

45

### The 1915 Open

The Old Course was improved further and stiffened for the 1915 Open. The Board of Governors wanted no adverse criticism of its links as a championship test. The course was lengthened, several new bunkers were built in strategic locations near greens and drive zones, and an obsolete cross bunker on the twelfth was removed.

After the Open in December of 1915, the Green Committee made the following report to the Board of Governors:

"Since the last Annual Meeting of the Club your committee has made a number of changes in the course. Whether these changes are improvements or not, we leave to the members to judge. In the beginning, in order to avert adverse criticism and also to give the members a chance to express views, we placed a notice on the bulletin board stating that the Committee would be glad to receive any written suggestions in regard to improving the seventh, eighth and eleventh holes. We received just one written suggestion and we did not avert all criticism.

In June we held the Open Tournament of the USGA, which was described by the officers of that Association as one of the most successful ever held.

A large share of the credit for the improvements and condition of the course, is due to George Low, who has been indefatigable and has given much time and thought to it."

Despite the changes and generally perfect course conditions, the Old Course received some criticism after the 1915 Open, direct-ed primarily at the shortness of certain par 4 holes. The Board of Governors responded. They voted in December of 1915 to substitute new holes for the tenth (Island), eleventh and twelfth. The new tenth and eleventh had roughly the same routing as the current fourth and fifteenth of the Upper. The new twelfth followed a diagonal routing to sixteen Upper, returning to the old twelfth green. Incidentally, the old twelfth tee can still be seen in front of the rain shelter on four Upper. The Green Committee's report of December 1915 explained the proposed changes as follows:

"The Baltusrol links have been criticized adversely for the following four reasons:

Similarity in length of the eighth, tenth, eleventh and twelfth holes.

The fact that a brassey (2 wood) cannot be used after the seventh hole until the fifteenth.

The congestion caused by the proximity of the eleventh and eighth greens.

The objection to climbing the hill a second time.

Your Green Committee believes that all these objections can be corrected by substituting for the tenth , eleventh and twelfth holes the following new layout:

New No. 10—410 yards. along the foothills practically a continuation of the present No. 9, with a tee near No. 9 green, and playing lengthwise over the pond.

New No. 11—135 yards at right angles down to small foothill.

New No. 12 - 500 yards back to the present No. 12 green, the fair green skirting the red barn.

These changes with the lengthening of the No. 2—20 yards; No. 3—32 yards; No. 4—20 yards; and No. 7— 20 yards would add 188 yards to the course, making it 6,400 yards long.

This change would involve the taking of additional land owned by your Secretary."

These new holes were begun in 1916 and completed in early 1918. It is believed that George Low was responsible for the design and construction. The new tenth, which followed the routing of four Upper, was criticized so vociferously for the steep grades on the green and fairway that the hole was substantially reworked that winter. The green was regraded and the approach was widened. During these alterations, the former Island Hole (tenth) and the Hill Hole (eleventh) were utilized.

*The USGA tent at the first tee of the 1915 US Open. Seated left to right: Howard Perrin, Parker Page, Francis Ouimet, M. Louis Crosby, Louis Bayard, Jr., Howard Whitney, Percy R. Payne, II( on ground), and Frank L. Woodward, President of the Association.*

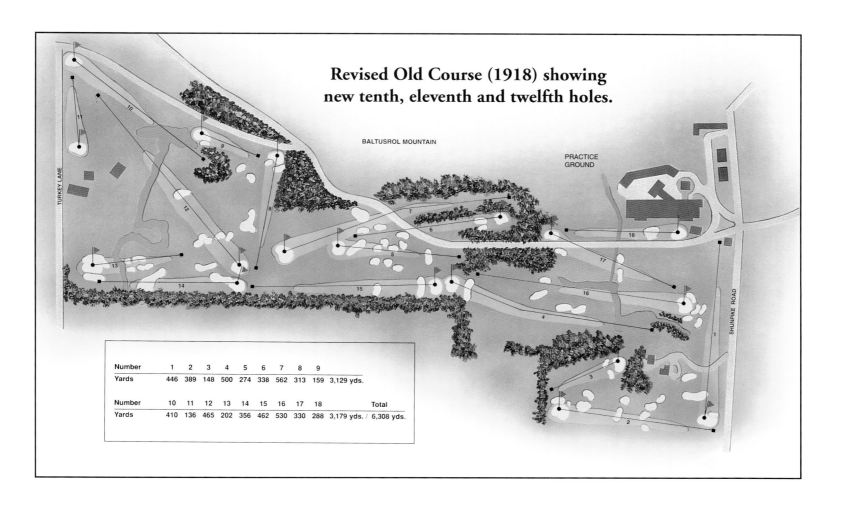

# Revised Old Course (1918) showing new tenth, eleventh and twelfth holes.

BALTUSROL MOUNTAIN

PRACTICE GROUND

TURKEY LANE

SHUNPIKE ROAD

| Number | 1 | 2 | 3 | 4 | 5 | 6 | 7 | 8 | 9 | |
|--------|-----|-----|-----|-----|-----|-----|-----|-----|-----|-----------|
| Yards | 446 | 389 | 148 | 500 | 274 | 338 | 562 | 313 | 159 | 3,129 yds. |

| Number | 10 | 11 | 12 | 13 | 14 | 15 | 16 | 17 | 18 | Total |
|--------|-----|-----|-----|-----|-----|-----|-----|-----|-----|------------------------|
| Yards | 410 | 136 | 465 | 202 | 356 | 462 | 530 | 330 | 288 | 3,179 yds. / 6,308 yds. |

*The new tenth fairway can be seen beyond the old ninth green and the pond.*

47

# The Old Course: Hole by Hole

**Described by Robert Finney and Fritz Leuders, Baltusrol members.**

> *What an experience it was to play that first round at Baltusrol! I do not think there ever was a finer, lovelier golf course. The old course was only 6,189 yards long but it did not play easy. It was not as hard as either of our present courses. There were not too many traps or bunkers. It was one of the most interesting and thrilling golf courses I have ever played. Each hole had a name descriptive of the hole.*
>
> Robert Finney,
> Baltusrol Member

## No.1 *Shunpike*
### Par 5  440 Yards

This was roughly the same as one Lower. However, the tee was at the left of the present men's tee. The green was in the same place as now but many bunkers have been added.

## No.2 *Orchard*
### 376 Yards  Par 4

This was also essentially the same hole as two Lower, except that again many bunkers have been added. The present tee and the green are in the same area now as they were on the Old Course.

## No. 3 *Alps*
### 150 Yards  Par 3

This was an easy par 3. The tee was in the same place as the three Lower front tee—the only difference being that the old tee was elevated. The green was at the top of the hill of the present third Lower fairway. The downhill part of the present third fairway was dense woods which were in back of the old green.

### No. 4 *Pond*
490 Yards  Par 5

After playing the third hole, you walked through woods (now part of three Lower fairway) to the fourth tee located somewhere to the left of the present pond on four Lower. The pond was much smaller in the old days as the current pond was man made and came into existence with the Lower Course. The fourth Green of the old course is now the green for five Lower. The old fourth was a little longer than our present fifth and was a slight dog leg to the right. The fairway somewhat paralleled the present eighteen Lower fairway. This was an easy par 5 reachable in two. The short hitter, though, had to cross two series of traps, one for the second shot and one for the third.

### No. 5 *Outlook*
285 Yards  Par 4

The tee for this hole was about where the back tee of the present eighteen Lower tee is located. The green was halfway in the middle of seventeen Upper fairway on the left-hand side. This was an easy par 4 and with present-day equipment, could be driven by good players.

### No. 6 *Sleepy Hollow*
325 Yards  Par 4

The tee for this hole was on seventeen Upper fairway. The level part of the tee still can be seen. The green was on a side-hill and located on one Upper fairway about 100 yards short of the green. While the hole was an easy par 4 the green was tricky, very sloping, and difficult to putt.

## No. 7 *Long Hole*
### 562 Yards Par 5

This was the longest hole on the old course and was a fine par 5. The tee was not elevated and can still be seen along the woods behind the present tee for two Upper. The tee shot landed roughly on the left side of the Fairway on two Upper. The fairway of the old seventh then cut across the seventeen Upper fairway to a green situated about where the ladies tee for the seventeen Lower is now located.

## No. 8 *Mountain*
### 310 Yards Par 4

An interesting but short par 4 hole. The tee for this hole was to the right of fifteen Lower and a little towards the mountain. The green was behind the upper tee on three Upper. The tee shot was towards a steep hill and the second shot up to a flat green. This green was very high up and had bunkers all around the front. When walking up to the third tee from the second green, you can see the old green to the right, although it is very much overgrown. Dense woods was on the right hand side of the fairway going up the hill.

## No.9 *Half Way*
### 182 Yards Par 3

This was roughly the same hole as the present three Upper. However, it was a bit longer—the tee being to the right, behind and above the present upper tee.

## No. 10 *Island Hole*
330 Yard Par 4

This was one of the most famous and photographed holes in the United States, and much was written about it. The tee was up in the woods in back of the pond behind the third Upper green. The pond is now dry but the outline is still visible. The hole played downhill over the pond to a green that is now the sixteen Lower green. The green was then completely surrounded by a moat of water.

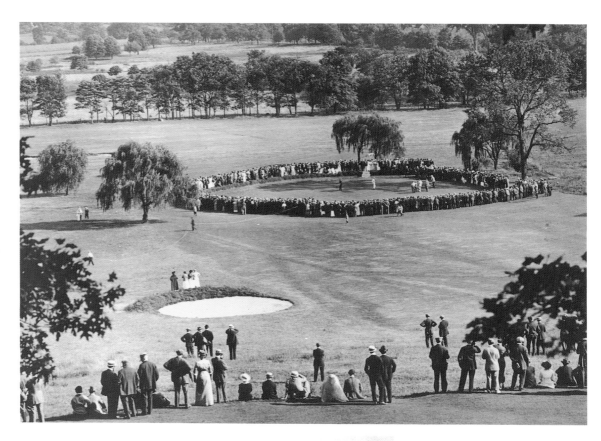

## No. 11 *Hill Hole*
327 Yards Par 4

The tee for this hole was situated just to the right of the present sixteen Lower green. You drove uphill toward the mountain. The green was situated just below the present third Upper tee. This was a beautiful hole but not particularly difficult until you got older and had to climb the hill.

## No. 12 *Fairview*
270 Yards Par 4

The tee for this hole was also just below the third Upper tee, and the drive was to a green in the area of the present rain shelter alongside the men's tee of seventeen Lower. This also was an easy hole.

## No. 13 *Lone Maple*
210 Yards  Par 3

The tee for this hole was also in the area of seventeen Lower men's tee. The green was the present fifteen Lower green. This was the most difficult par 3 on the Old Course.

## No.14 *Homeward Bound*
357 Yards  Par 4

The tee for this hole can still be seen, located to the left of fifteen Lower green along the row of trees beside fourteen Lower tee. The old hole was really the reverse of fifteen Lower. The old green was part of the present fifteen Lower front tee. There were dense woods and out-of-bounds all along the right side. Sandy's Garden was just short of the old green. It was rough terrain and had heather from which it was very hard to recover. Some of the outlines of the old traps can be seen around fifteen Lower tee.

## No. 15 *Long Tom*
450 Yards Par 5

The tee for this hole is now the back tee for fifteen Lower. The green was to the right of seventeen Lower green. The flat area can still be seen. There were two sets of traps on this hole, which the short-hitter would have to cross on his drive and third shots. However, the green could be reached in two by today's big hitters. Dense woods and out of bounds were on the right side of the fairway.

## No. 16 *Burn Hole*
### 520 Yards Par 5

The tee for this hole was the eighteen Lower front men's tee. The green was the present three Lower green. There was a bunker that could catch your drive. Also there were small bunkers near the front and three in the back of the green. This was a rather long par 5 in those days, but would not be particularly difficult today. A burn formed a hazard on the right which would later be converted into the pond on four Lower.

## No. 17 *Shady*
### 322 Yards Par 4

The tee for this hole was between the practice green and three Lower green. The green was at the beginning of the fairway on eighteen Upper (left hand side). There were no traps but you had to cross a road on your second shot. In those days there was no lifting out of the road, as you played them "as they lie." The second shot could be caught in the road, which was Baltusrol Way. It was even more difficult to get out of the road than a bunker. In those days wagons generally went through the course and left deep ruts in the dirt road. There was dense woods behind the green. The flat area of the green can still be seen.

## No. 18 *Tappie*
### 275 Yards Par 4

The eighteenth was essentially the same as our eighteenth Upper, although some 170 yards shorter and much easier. The tee for this hole can still be seen above the depression that marked the old seventh green. There was a great big bunker in front of the green that had railroad ties on the side toward the green. If you caught the trap, you couldn't shoot toward the pin without hitting directly at the railroad ties. It is amazing that no one was ever killed playing out of this bunker.

Scenes from the Old Course

# Seeds for the Dual Courses

In 1916, the seeds for the Upper and Lower Courses were sown. The popularity of golf was spreading, and Baltusrol was feeling the growing pains. The membership of the Club exceeded 700 and the congestion on the golf course had become unbearable at times, particularly on Saturdays and Sundays.

Many golf clubs of the time were also feeling the strain on their facilities because of the enormous popularity of golf. But the usual decision was to build merely a second course, often one that was decidedly inferior to the first, on land that was left over. The approach that Baltusrol would follow was certainly more courageous and has paid huge dividends over the years.

### Keller's Vision
Recognizing the need for a second course, Louis Keller submitted a letter to the Board suggesting a new course and lease extension. Keller offered Baltusrol the

---

To the Governors of the Baltusrol Golf Club,

Gentlemen:

In 1909 before embarking in the construction of the new clubhouse, the Governors requested me to grant a 25 year extension of the existing lease of the links. Although this lease still has 17 years to run several Governors have expressed to me a feeling that an ownership of the links would make for greater prosperity in the club. I think that I have convinced these gentlemen that practically a perpetual lease would accomplish their object in a manner more economical for the Club than an actual purchase of the property. Such a lease would naturally have to be based upon an accurate survey and as the suggestion of providing an additional course has met with so much favor among the members at large, it would seem that the two propositions should be considered simultaneously, and to that end a committee, say of five Governors, should be appointed to report back to the Board upon the feasibility of both propositions.

You are probably aware that I have some 500 additional acres back of the present course from which you are at liberty to pick out whatever portion you need for the additional 18 holes. Such a course, in my opinion, would be superior to the present one and so far different in character that many of your members would want to cover both courses during the day. I am bringing the matter up at present because I am told that both propositions may be mentioned at the next Annual Meeting and it would be a graceful thing for the officers to be able to answer such inquires by stating that the Board of Governors have already started the necessary machinery to ascertain the feasibility of both propositions.

For the past year members have been discussing this duplicate course and it is high time that its feasibility or infeasibility should be determined on so that if the location back of the Clubhouse be abandoned, the owner may make other use of the property and the Club may look in other directions for the necessary duplication of its links.

Doubtless within the next few years all the leading golf clubs in the country will find a duplicate course necessary and Baltusrol should certainly be in the van, for it certainly is more in need of it than any other.

Louis Keller, October 1916

---

pick of a site for a new course from 500 acres he owned behind the clubhouse on top of and beyond Baltusrol Mountain. In response, the Board passed a resolution to begin negotiations with Keller, formed a Committee on the New Golf Course, and set to work. Committee members C.F. Watson, Parker Page and William G. McKnight reported back to the Board in early 1917 with two solutions to relieve the congestion on the golf course:

"Two plans have been suggested to meet the situation, the first being a reduction in membership, but after consideration, we do not feel that such a plan is feasible or could be carried out successfully. It is the *playing* membership that must be reduced in order to relieve congestion and although a large increase in the dues would result in a considerable number of resignations we do not believe that playing members would resign. The only

---

*Playing in a four-ball match, Mr. Robert C. Watson, the Secretary of the USGA, incidentally remarked to George (Geordie) Low, the Baltusrol pro, while we were waiting our turn on one of the tees and had an opportunity of witnessing the play generally "Do you know, I think Baltusrol has more duffers to the square inch than any other two clubs put together. Now just look at those men!"—pointing to four who had just hit off their tee shots to the twelfth hole, and had made an awful mess of the job. "Why," retorted Geordie, "those are not Baltusrol men, they come from Englewood". "Well," said Mr. Watson, pointing to another four-ball match approaching the eleventh green and acquitting themselves very badly in the undertaking, "where do they come from?" "Midlothian" said Geordie, determined to be loyal to his club.*

*The American Golfer*

---

*Clockwise: Steps at seventh tee, Seventh green, From the mountain behind eight, Fourteenth tee and "Sandy's Garden," Moat around the Island green, Pond and Clubhouse from fourth fairway, Fourth fairway, Bunker at eighteenth green.*

alternative which suggests itself to your Committee is the establishment of another eighteen hole golf course and we recommend that your Committee be authorized to continue its efforts in this direction."

property until a new arrangement was made with Louis Keller.

In October of 1917, Mr. Keller offered to sell to Baltusrol the land for both the existing and new course. The purchase of the existing course of approximately 140 acres, was made at a price of $1,000 per acre, and Louis Keller accepted a purchase money mortgage.

For the additional land, Louis Keller had obtained rights and options to several tracts adjoining the present course, totaling

3) The Holmes tract, which was covered with underbrush, lying south of the Bodinsky tract and of approximately 33 and 1/2 acres.

4) The Dengler tract of approximately fourteen acres adjoining the Bodinsky tract to the east. This was a part of the Dengler farm of approximately 39 acres.

Louis Keller's offer and the plan to finance the purchase was ratified by the membership in a special meeting. In raising the additional revenues for the new course, the Board of Governors resolved that there would be no increase in the number of members without express instructions from the members of the Club.

Seth Raynor and the Committee, this land was deemed unsuitable and the property adjacent to the Old Course was recommended for the new course.

It is worth noting that Baltusrol had for the first time sought the advice of established golf course architects. Previously, changes to the course had been carried out under the supervision of George Low, whose duties as a pro included course maintenance and construction.

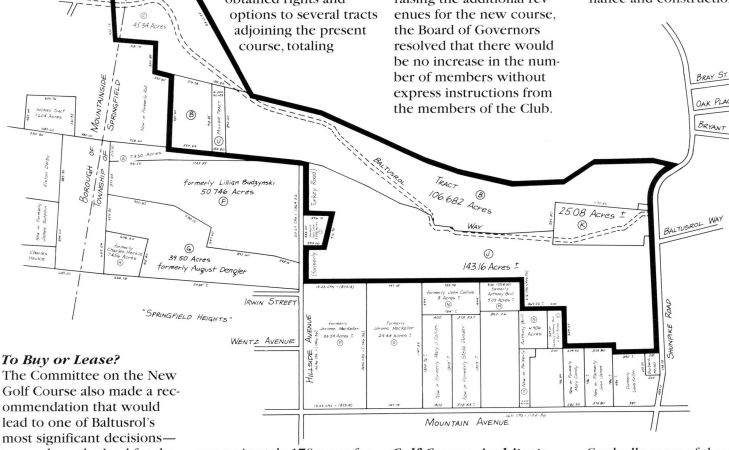

### To Buy or Lease?
The Committee on the New Golf Course also made a recommendation that would lead to one of Baltusrol's most significant decisions—to purchase the land for the new course and the existing course.

The Old Course was owned by Louis Keller. In 1908, he leased the property to the Club for a term of twenty-five years. The Committee believed that no considerable expenditure should be made on the clubhouse, new construction on the present golf course, or acquisition of additional

approximately 170 acres for approximately $52,000, which he offered to the Club at his actual cost. The additional properties were:

1) The McKellar tract of approximately 65 acres adjoining the old fourteenth fairway.

2) The Bodinsky tract of approximately 60 acres to the south of the new tenth and eleventh greens, on the Old Course.

### Golf Course Architects That Might Have Been
The Committee also had toured the land behind the clubhouse that Keller had originally offered, but they had doubts about its suitability for a golf course. They therefore recommended hiring Donald Ross to inspect the property, but for reasons unknown they hired Seth Raynor instead. In June of 1917, upon examination by

Gradually some of these pros had demonstrated a flair for designing golf holes and became the pioneers of a fledgling profession. Donald Ross was one such person, having made a name for himself as the architect of the famed resort courses at Pinehurst.

Seth Raynor had followed a different route, learning the architect's trade as the engineer for C.B. Macdonald,

architect, always impeccably dressed and groomed, poring over the plans for a golf course. He was very much a hands-on architect who liked to make his designs "in the dirt," relying on the inspiration of the moment to fashion the details of each hole as it emerged from the landscape. In the accounts passed along by old-timers, Tillinghast's working method was to seat himself in the shade of a tree, bottle in hand, and call out directions to his workmen as they shaped the course with their mule-pulled scoops. As golf historian Herb Graffis wrote, "The laborer and mule would occasionally get a sniff of Tillie's richly-flavored exhaust and knew they were working for a man of great power and artistry."

In 1918, when Baltusrol hired him to construct two new courses, Tillinghast was just hitting his stride. His services as an architect had been in demand, but his golf courses were spread across the continent in Florida, Texas, and California. In New Jersey, he had built courses at Shackamaxon and Somerset Hills, but he had never won a commission of the magnitude and prestige of Baltusrol. Strictly speaking, no American golf architect before or since has ever

received such a commission, and Tillinghast stood to gain more from Baltusrol than Baltusrol stood to gain from Tillinghast.

As it turned out, both Baltusrol and Tillinghast were winners, and Tillinghast's work at Baltusrol placed him securely in the first rank of American golf architects. Throughout the 1920's he was a whirlwind of activity, building or remodeling golf courses all over the country. Some of his more notable courses included Winged Foot, Ridgewood, Quaker Ridge and the Bethpage Black. His career lasted until the Great Depression brought golf course construction to a standstill, but Tillinghast managed to stay in the game as a course inspector for the PGA. When that job ended, Tillinghast had a fling as an antique dealer in Beverly Hills, where he seems to have sold off many of the possessions he and his wife had collected over the years. In 1940, after a heart attack, he went to live in Toledo, Ohio, with his eldest daughter. He died there in 1942.

For several decades he was forgotten by the golf world, though his courses continued to give pleasure and to serve as tournament sites. In recent years the extent of his legacy to

American golf has come to be better understood and appreciated, for it is abundantly clear that Tillinghast had a genius for building golf courses that endure. In retrospect it seems that he deserved all along the title he gave himself—the "Creator of Baltusrol."

*The Fourth at Baltusrol*
*Short Hills, New Jersey*

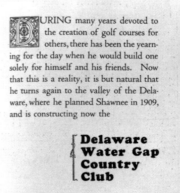

### The Second Design Consideration

The next fact of paramount importance was the character of the property. Its western border was formed by the steep, wooded slopes of Baltusrol Mountain, down which the land tumbled to a relatively flat, open expanse. On the eastern side, the property included a tract, roughly in the shape of a square projecting out from the rectangle, that had previously been farmland. It was gently rolling land with trees in isolated groves and along the fence lines.

How could this site be used to its greatest advantage? Now that the Upper and Lower course have been in play for more than 70 years, the answer seems inevitable. In 1919, however, when Tillinghast set down his original plan for the routing, the concept was far from self-evident. As Tillinghast wrote, "In planning 18 holes there were thousands of combinations, each offering a mute appeal for recognition." At Baltusrol,

rather than designing a second course, as was his original charge, Tillinghast designed two. In doing so, he recommended that the Old Course be discarded, and he would salvage what he could.

This was a bold recommendation. For Tillinghast could have decided to keep the Old Course and let the new course range up and down the slope and in and out of the woods, combining the features of the land-

scape – as the Old Course had – thus giving each layout the greatest possible variety. His decision, however, was to tuck the Upper Course into the slopes of the mountain and to spread the Lower Course out on the flatter land. This arrangement determined once and for all the character of the golf courses. They were to be "Dual

Courses," and they might very well be equals, but they would be as different from each other as a brassie from a birdie. And they would be "equally sought after as a matter of preference."

### Presenting the Plans

Tillinghast's plans for the Upper and Lower were presented to the Board in December of 1918. The Green Committee recommended acceptance of the plans in January of 1919. The plans were approved as

*Louis Keller, seated center, and the Board had to make many difficult decisions.*

60

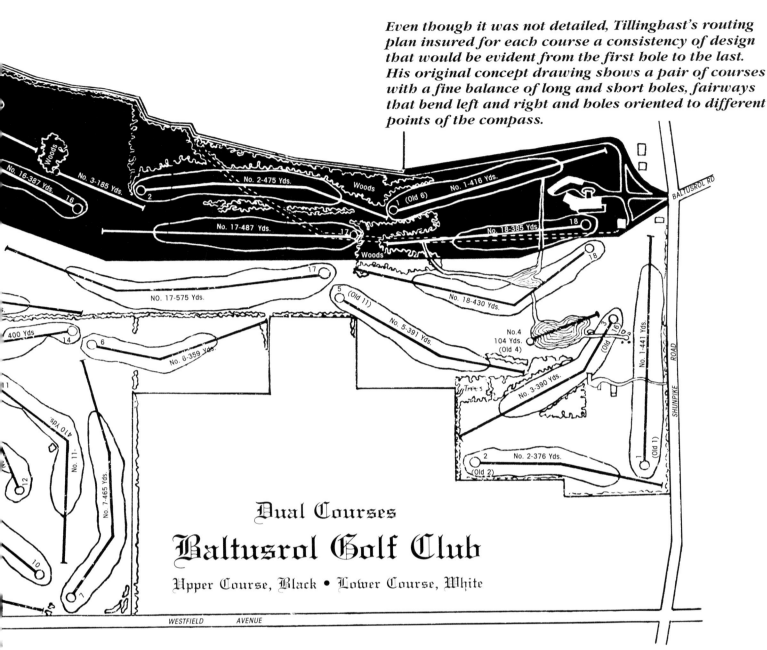

*Even though it was not detailed, Tillinghast's routing plan insured for each course a consistency of design that would be evident from the first hole to the last. His original concept drawing shows a pair of courses with a fine balance of long and short holes, fairways that bend left and right and holes oriented to different points of the compass.*

## Dual Courses

# Baltusrol Golf Club

### Upper Course, Black • Lower Course, White

submitted with one improvement—Louis Keller informed the Governors by letter that he could obtain the Collins property skirting the old fifteenth hole for a length of 785 feet. This acquisition provided needed elbow room. As described by Keller "by simply advancing the present Fourth Green, which is going to be the Fifth Green, sufficiently, so as to make it a short walk around the corner to a tee for the new Sixth, which would be located on the Collins Plot."

The audacity of the Board's decision to accept Tillinghast's plans can hardly be overstated, for no club with a comparable history had ever undertaken a challenge like it. Baltusrol was one of the most celebrated clubs in the country, and the Old Course was a landmark. It had earned its spurs as a worthy test of championship golf - hosting five USGA National Championships - and Baltusrol was now prepared to plow it under! Having reached the top rank in golf,

and after twenty-five years of improvements and investments in the Old Course, Baltusrol was taking the risk of starting all over again.

As *Golf Illustrated* declared, "they are planning at Baltusrol on a vaster scale than has ever been attempted in American golf for the opening of the Dual Courses." These two courses were to be equal in every respect—equal in length, difficulty, shot values, and attractiveness. Both were expected to give pleasure in member play,

and at the same time to meet a standard that would enable them to serve as tournament sites.

With each hole playing at different angles, Tillinghast provided thirty-six different challenges. This provided variety to the members who often made golf an all day affair. Members and their guests, typically traveled by train or motor coach from New York City, played eighteen in the morning, had lunch, and played eighteen in the afternoon.

61

# Opening the Forest

*But often we find a large copse or a thick forest which must be penetrated. Those who grieve because of this necessity do not realize fully that opening up the fairway will not be a program of indiscriminate destruction but rather a painstaking effort to cut through in such a manner as to bring to view the best trees which long have been hidden away among unlovely companions. Woods are like communities and trees are like men. In each there are a lot of common nuisances and parasites that are best out of the picture altogether. In every forest you will find some rare old trees, oaks and elms, sycamores and hickories that have been hidden away from sight for many years with a tangle of nondescripts all about them. These we save, of course, as much as possible, but there are times when some truly grand trees have to go and it is not without a pang at their passing.*

A.W. Tillinghast

Tillinghast was a hands-on builder who came to work at Baltusrol in a style befitting a Wall Street tycoon. He arrived in a chauffeur-driven limousine, and typically supervised his construction crew dressed in a suit, necktie and hat.

Today's architect would probably prefer less formal attire, for the first tasks that needed doing were basic and dirty. Once the preliminary stakes had been set, showing both the Upper and Lower courses beginning and ending at the clubhouse, the great work started. Clear the trees. Move the dirt. Grow the grass.

By November 1918, Tillinghast had the old hedge rows brushed up and the forest cleared to permit the laying out of the new courses. Incidentally, some 100 cords of wood were gathered for consumption in the clubhouse.

Tillinghast made every effort to save fine specimen trees and groups of trees. Not only did he have sentiments about trees, but he incorporated them in his designs to create doglegs and elbows, serving a definite purpose in playing the game.

As if it wasn't challenging enough to design and construct two course simultaneously, Tillinghast was instructed to keep 18 holes in play during the construction period and utilize as much of the existing links as possible. In doing so, he used all the fairways and greens of the Old Course. Some green sites were used although the holes were routed completely different; the rest of the greens had their turf lifted and moved to new green sites.

### Eliminating Hills

Tillinghast eliminated the hilly Old Course holes that had played alternately up and down Baltusrol Mountain at right angles to the general east-west deployment of the new courses.

Tillinghast's working of the Upper along Baltusrol Mountain was masterfully done. Along the second through the sixth holes he provided wider fairways where the ground slopes from the right to the left side and he graded parts of the fairway to offer a check against the ball moving fast from the natural side slope on the right. The slopes of hills were cut away, twisted and turned and graded to a most satisfying fairway, approach or green. To guard against wash – surface water guttering new earth and washing away turf, topsoil and young grass – ditching was constructed above the fairways to carry the water away without causing damage.

It should be noted that the only fairway not graded was the second of the Upper. Tillinghast originally contemplated locating the tee to this hole short and to the left of the current first green. The angle of the tee shot would have minimized the slope of the Mountain. We do not know whether this tee was ever built.

However, we do know that the first hole was originally a par 4 to the old sixth green. Shortly after opening in 1922, the first hole was stretched to a par 5 with the construction of the existing first green.

### A "Mighty" Turf Grass Experiment

The tree and stump removal continued through the winter and was completed in June of 1919. Then came a bold new experiment.

The new fairways were sown with soy beans and cow peas that were treated with a secret fluid guaranteed to hasten the nodules that attract bacteria, a process called inoculation. The objective was to stimulate the soil, accelerating the normal two to three years required for woodland soil to gain the nutrients required to support turf. Within weeks these virgin fairways were covered with a carpet of green—but, alas, it would take years to establish first class turf.

### Trees and the Course Beautiful

In constructing the Upper and Lower, Tillinghast would plead guilty to the removal of many old trees, but he never would have "given instructions for the destruction of a fine one without genuine regret." He had a soft heart for trees. He used trees to add comfort to teeing grounds, twist and turn fairways, frame holes and provide attractive vistas.

His cardinal principle on trees though was "that every possible beauty be featured so long as it does not interfere with the sound play of the game." It was fine to "play around trees but certainly the only route to a hole must never be over or through them."

*Uphill holes like the eighth were eliminated. Note the second green Upper under construction on the right.*

*Last of the old chestnuts near the ninth tee Lower.*

*Certainly, no worthy builder of modern courses will conceive a hole directly up-hill if there is any way to avoid it. In working from one level to another it is a good rule to look for the longest way up and the quickest way down, and by the longest way up, I mean the least arduous with the old-time cow-path as an example.*

*...Avoid directing shots in any direction other than into the side that breaks. For example, if the fairway shows a rather pronounced slope from the right side, the teeing ground must be placed well to the left, and vice versa. The reason for this is quite obvious to any man that plays much golf. Playing into the slope straightens a ball out and it will not go racing away with the throw of the ground as it would if played directly along the slope, or worse still, with it.*

*...And when it comes to building greens and their approaches into side slopes, it is well to work over a great area in order to have sufficient space to give long slopes to your contours, that the work, artificial as it has to be, may appear natural and pleasing, and not, like a railroad embankment, an offense to the eye.*

• • • • • • •

*It may be interesting to green committees to learn that the new fairways of the Baltusrol courses have been sown with cow peas and soybeans, while the new putting greens are covered with buckwheat. Later the crops will be turned under preparatory to fall grass seeding.*

A.W. Tillinghast

**The half dead maple near the old twelfth green.**

He had specific ideas about what trees were appropriate on the various parts of a golf course. For instance, he liked to see "an occasional green or teeing ground among birches." And he encouraged wherever possible "evergreens as the most desirable neighbors for the putting greens." Although trees around greens can be messy when dropping their leaves in the fall, he wrote that "after all it means only a concentration of labor for a period and the charm of such greens surely is worth it." His emotional attachment to sylvan beauty appeared frequently in his writings.

Although he liked trees around putting greens, he despised them directly by the green "for their branches deflected many erring shots to fortunate finishes, falling leaves clutter the greens and the roots sap the soil of vitality that the turf needs."

He also warned that greens built in the woods must provide avenues for air circulation or the "turf is likely to suffer from brown patch and smothering ailments."

### Sweet Revenge

Tillinghast's opinion on the improper placement of a tree on the course may have been influenced by a tragic twist of fate early in his career as an amateur player. When he began his work at Baltusrol, one of his first deeds was to dispatch an ax crew to chop down a certain maple tree growing close to the twelfth green of the Old Course. He did this with no genuine regret. As Tillinghast told the story, in the purple prose he always preferred, that maple conjured up the memory of one of his "life's darkest moments"—when he lost a key hole in the 1904 U.S. Amateur.

Even when his claims seem extravagant, melodramatic or sentimental, it is clear that he had experienced the intense emotions of competition. When he turned to golf course architecture, he designed superb courses that provided a stage not simply for championship golf but for all its agonies and ecstasies—with trees as a sort of soothing chorus.

### Construction Delays

The original plan was to spend about $100,000 and complete the courses in two years—it would actually take six years and around $180,000 to complete.

The delays and cost overruns could be attributed to two factors. The first was the scarcity and high price of labor during World War I, and the second was A.W. Tillinghast. Green Committee Chairman C. F. Watson made this report:

"When the course was first started, men were receiving some $2 per day, and all through last year they received $4, and then $3.50 and now $3, and that the elaborate bunkers, as laid out by Mr. Tillinghast, had cost the Club more than the cost of building the greens.

The bunkering of the new course has turned out to be much more elaborate than was originally expected, but the comments made upon the new bunkers seem to have justified the cost, which has been really double the cost of building the greens. Already, 2,000 tons of sand have been purchased and spread in these bunkers and more is coming."

Watson directed the construction effort on behalf of the Green Committee. For his tireless efforts in overseeing the construction of the new courses, he was awarded an Honorary Life membership.

### The Official Opening

The Upper and Lower officially opened on June 16, 1922, two years late. Despite the prolonged period needed to complete the golf courses, play was never interrupted. Tillinghast did a remarkable job juggling his

*On sixteen Lower, Tillinghast replaced the moat of the famous Island Green with a girdle of sand.*

work schedule, since all of the land occupied by the Old Course was eventually utilized for the two new courses.

Although the passing of the Old Course brought some dismay, the spirit of the Old Course still lives in the Upper and Lower. For the first and second of the Lower and the third, fourth, fifteenth and eighteenth of the Upper have the same green sites and follow similar routings as the first, second, ninth, tenth, eleventh and eighteenth of the Old Course. Also, the third, fifth, fifteenth and sixteenth greens of the Lower are Old Course green sites, but with completely different hole routings.

Essentially then the first tee of the Lower and the eighteenth green of the Upper are where Baltusrol's first five National Championships began and ended. And the ghosts of Willie Anderson commenc-

BALTUSROL GOLF CLUB

*Celebration Dinner*

to commemorate the opening
of the dual golf courses

Saturday Evening, June 17, 1922

BALTUSROL, NEW JERSEY

toric playoff and Jerry Travers being carried off the eighteenth green can be visualaized on today's courses.

### Completing the Courses

Following the opening of the Upper and Lower, there was general disappointment with the condition of the new courses. Consequently, an additional $50,000 was appropriated in October of 1922 for Tillinghast to complete the two courses. And over the next two years additional improvements were made.

The first tee was moved from behind of the Upper Clubhouse to an area in front of where it is today. Later a new green was built about 100 yards back from the original, making it a par 5. A major tree planting was completed in March of 1924. This planting included the screening of Westfield Road, now Mountain Avenue, which runs along eight Lower. Many of the improvements were overseen by Major Jones, who was hired as the green keeper in October of 1923.

By 1924, the Upper and Lower were finally complete. Although Tillinghast had intended to make them playable for the average golfer, some members complained loudly about their length and difficulty, particularly the Upper. At the Annual Meeting of the Club, in November of 1924, in response to a member's concern over the difficulty of the courses, Mr. McKnight, Chairman of the Green Committee fended off criticism at length by saying that "the Green Committee was simply following out the plans laid down by Mr. Tillinghast, Course Architect, which had been approved months ago by the Board."

# The "Course Beautiful" and Strategic Design

*Baltusrol's two finishing holes, the finale of Tillinghast's "Course Beautiful."*

A natural appearance was of paramount importance for "the course beautiful." This was one of Tillinghast's favorite notions, and in his regular column for Golf Illustrated, he often hymned the virtues of "the course beautiful," by which he explicitly meant a golf course in harmony with its natural setting. It is not really the task of the golf course designer to build beautiful golf holes—but Tillinghast made it his task. His visual sense was strong, bold, and uncompromising.

Tillinghast's ability to visualize a golf hole was one of his greatest assets as an architect, as was his gift for finding on each site the natural "models" for greens, mounds, and bunkers. His courses were always built with their surroundings in mind, and his aim was to make each feature, from the teeing ground right though the green, dovetail with all the others. "Without all of them," he wrote in 1916, "there is something lacking which spoils the whole. It is not Nature's ensemble." He would not countenance "distortions" or "sorry imitations." On almost every hole on both courses at Baltusrol, it is immediately clear how Tillinghast applied his principles, using the land as a great laboratory in which his theories could be proven.

Tillinghast also advocated the importance of golf course conditioning. He recognized that the green committee and the green superintendent were critical in keeping the course beautiful. In his opinion, the green committee should be kept small with little turnover to maintain consistency in policy and programs from year to year. He also encouraged members to take great pride in the golf course and encourage their green superintendent in every effort to keep the course in first-class condition, and to give him "a kindly word or a little noise now and then, commenting on his good work."

### Twisting Fairways
There were certain features on golf courses that Tillinghast simply could not abide. His twin pet peeves were the straight line and the right angle, both of which he detested—and neither of which occurs very often in nature. He was forever railing against parallel fairways, those "great and ancient evils," and fairways straight as "bowling alleys." He likened fairways cut with ruler-straight precision to the bowl haircuts sported by boys from the backwoods. In contrast, his fairways twist and turn around encroaching areas of hazard or rough.

More pronounced angles are formed with elbows and doglegs. He defined a dogleg as having some pronounced obstruction forming a corner in a fairway, that could not be carried. The only route to the green was around the obstacle. By contrast, if the obstruction could be carried by a courageous shot, rewarding the brave golfer with a distinct advantage, we have an elbow.

On the Lower Course, he took as his models the gentle undulations of the meadow land, and on the Upper Course the golf holes are at peace with the mountain. There are a few – but only a very few – fairways cut in a straight line, but everywhere that Tillinghast could find a natural feature, even the slightest jutting undulation, he used it to create elbows and a twisting line. Where there was no natural feature handy, he constructed bunkers and mounds to give the fairway the shape he was after, as he did with the bunkering that pinches into either side of the fairway on five Lower.

### Numerous Angles of Attack
As for teeing grounds, Tillinghast was justly proud of the fourth tee on the Lower, with its irregular shape "somewhat after the fashion of an immense horseshoe." That tee permitted numerous angles of attack to the fortified green across the water, and served Tillinghast whenever he needed an example of a

*It costs no more to follow Nature than to ignore her. If you must introduce artificial creations into a golf design, take efforts to make them appear natural.*

*Summing it up briefly, the course beautiful adds much to the pleasure of golf without detracting in the least from its qualities as a test. Even those players who are not analytical will have strong inclinations to certain courses over others. Aside from the fact that they probably fancy the places where they have scored best, the chances are that subconsciously they have admired the scenery a bit.*

*The saying that "A thing of beauty is a joy forever" undoubtedly is just as much applicable to the golf course as to the most extravagantly laid out lawn or garden.*

. . . . . . .

*As to the featuring of open play around woods, here usually is provided opportunities for dogleg holes—a type which has done much to improve the plan of modern courses. The chance to feature prominently specimen trees is greater than in cutting directly through the heart of timber and it is highly desirable that an especially striking tree or group, should mark the turn of the play.*

A.W. Tillinghast

*The fourth tee's irregular shape as seen in the 1926 Amateur.*

*Fifteen Lower depicts the natural Tillinghast teeing ground.*

*A towering elm seen from the fifth tee Lower.*

"perfectly natural teeing ground."

The typical tee boxes of the time, "almost invariably small and mathematically formal." struck Tillinghast as "pawky little terraced, box-like pulpits, which seemed to shriek of wheelbarrows and spades." The ideal teeing ground for Tillinghast "is nothing more than a great level area, which will permit the placing of tee-markers in many, places." The slopes around the tee blend gently and harmoniously so they "cease to be slopes." On the Upper and Lower his tees are natural in appearance and not easily worn out if the markers are shifted each day. In situations where the natural slope made a terrace necessary for the tee, the slopes of the terrace were gently made to allow cutting with the regular fairway mower. The tees on eighteen lower and seven Upper are prime examples of gently sloped terraced tees .

### Comfort and Hope

On other holes, especially on the Upper Course, Tillinghast situated his tees in order to feature "lordly, towering Oak, Elm, Tulip and Beech trees" for—despite his ruthlessness when a tree stood in the wrong place— he had a weakness for trees and a faith in their power to comfort the golfer who has just played a bad hole. "Teeing grounds," Tillinghast declared, "may just as well be beautifully located as not for here is born every new hope in a round of golf."

*Years ago teeing grounds almost invariably were small and mathematically formal but early in my career I ruthlessly tore away from these and wherever possible graded large teeing ground areas which permitted of a constant change of the tee plates to suit weather conditions and to lend variety by playing from different angles. The short fourth, the water hole at Baltusrol, with its irregularly shaped teeing ground, somewhat after the fashion of an immense horseshoe, is a sample of this.*

· · · · · · ·

*Often when there are two or three teeing grounds provided for one hole, they are laid out in a dead straight line. This not only looks artificial, but the arrangement robs the hole of variety. Playing to the fairway from different angles not only is pleasing, but often the wind dictates a different angle almost as much as length.*

· · · · · · ·

*No matter how distressing has been the hole just finished fresh determination surges as foot falls on the next teeing ground. Why not let men get determined in comfort? An honest old tree can be very sympathetic and comforting if the golfer will take the time to look into its serenely complacent face and feel that way about it. It may be another weakness, but I do like to find such settings for teeing grounds. Possibly it is an inviting group, maybe a lordly, towering centenarian which still lifts an exalted and glorious head. I have known it to be an old apple tree, long since beyond the bearing of fruit, but offering a sturdy trunk about which a circular bench may be built whereon one may relax awhile.*

A.W. Tillinghast

## Natural Greens

By the same token, he prided himself on the ability to discover natural greens, that would blend harmoniously with their surroundings. He had harsh words for the green committees who wanted to build greens when perfectly natural greens lay right under their noses, waiting to be discovered. The antiquated greens of the day were not only without character; they were frequently blind to the approach and located in basins which collected surface water rather than draining it off easily. By far the worst fault was a flat putting surface, which offered no encouragement for firm shots played correctly up to the pin.

In building greens, Tillinghast employed horse scoops to create contouring. This enabled him to sculpt "pleasing undulations which are effective, easily kept in condition and above else harmonious with natural surroundings."

*Sixth Green Lower during the 1926 Amateur.*

On the Lower Course it is readily apparent that many of the greens were "found," for they lie flush with the fairway and present a continuation of its slope and contour. Like the greens on the classic British courses, they look as if they had been there forever, having been transformed into putting surfaces merely by cutting the grass a bit shorter.

*I think that the proper contouring of a course is more readily appreciated by golfers generally than any other department of construction work and the presence of an old-fashioned featureless green would be just as much out of place on an up-to-date course as cobble-stone paving along Fifth Avenue.*

A.W. Tillinghast

*Sixth green Lower in 1994, with its subtle undulation, lies flush with the fairway.*

68

On the Upper Course, Tillinghast did not so much find natural greens as natural sites for the greens. Because of the slope of the land, several of the greens had to be elevated, and he took advantage of the ridges and knolls radiating out from the mountain to raise the greens. The greens not only took their pitch but their shape from their surroundings, and they come in a complete variety of forms—oblong, oval, punch bowl. The same is true for the greens of the Lower Course, where the greens vary from circular to squarish and include many other shapes in between. Tillinghast is often said to have favored pear-shaped greens such as the eighth green on the Lower. However, he did not make many of them at Baltusrol, where his imagination ran free and the greens come in all shapes and sizes.

### Greens with Bite and Roll

Tillinghast built Baltusrol's greens "to conform with the dictates of the various strokes of golf play." They are "open to approaches after a carefully placed drive." They are raised in the back and on the sides to offer "bite" to shots correctly played to the pin, and to insure good surface °drainage.

The 190-yard third hole on the Upper is an example. Its green is an elongated punch bowl that falls away from a high-faced bunker at the right entrance. Only a perfectly executed shot with plenty of cut spin can be expected to hold the green within a reasonable distance of the flagstick. The ball, which comes in from the right, receives no help from

*Natural green on thirteen Upper circa 1935.*

*Pear shape green on eight Lower.*

*Elongated punch bowl green of three Upper.*

the green and "its roll is hastened to the side pits on the left."

*Consequently a green, built to receive such a shot (cut shot) should offer every assistance to the ball truly hit with this "work" imparted to it, and a slightly raised right side, or right rear, offers the greatest encouragement to the player....*

*And if the green is to help the correctly played shot, it is but proper that it lend no aid to the ball that comes up with the wrong spin; in fact, such a shot should fall upon a surface which will emphasize its fault...*

*Of course the situation is reversed in the case of a green, constructed to receive a long shot, and such a ball very properly may "show its legs" a bit after it strikes. The flaring up of the left side of such a green will help to straighten out the slightly pulled ball, that is not running too fast. Here, the right side of the green should possess cunning throws to treat the sliced shot with scant ceremony but conduct it directly to retribution.*

*Bobby Jones playing out of the front greenside bunker on seventeen Lower in the 1926 Amateur.*

### Bunkers and the Proper Placement of Sand

As for the bunkers—well, bunkers in profusion and variety are the signature of any Tillinghast course, but there is no such animal as a "Tillinghast bunker." The man was infatuated with bunkers and constitutionally incapable of building two that were alike. The large flat-bottomed bunker, regular in shape, set down in a predictable location—that is not a Tillinghast bunker. For Tillinghast a great bunker was an artistic creation, perfectly designed for its own unique setting.

At Baltusrol each and every hole received individual attention and treatment, and the pattern of bunkering was tailored to the precise requirements of the hole. These requirements were sometimes aesthetic, for on many holes – like fifteen Lower – the bunkers are scooped and scalloped into the slope beneath the green, too far away to be a hazard except for the most badly mishit shot. As for the cross bunkers, or cop bunkers, the huge bunkers which crossed the fairway at right angles and were all the rage at the turn of the century, Tillinghast found them "grotesque." At Baltusrol he wasted no time in removing the massive cross bunkers which had been among the chief features of the Old Course.

*Any hazard that is worthy of the name will not offer a large, flat floor, and this is particularly true through the fairway, where it is small punishment for the erring player. Great hazard areas had better be a combination of undulating tough or grassy stretches and sand. Let it exact a true penalty but not one that is unnecessarily severe.*

*A.W. Tillinghast*

*Par 3 sixteen Lower in 1994.*

Hazards built in echelon and greens opening up diagonally to a straight line from the teeing grounds, make the true line play something other than indifferent hitting straight ahead, sauce for goose and gander alike. In brief, the oblique lines make it possible for every class of player to extend shots only to the limitations of power, thus making it easier for the duffer to enjoy golf more, but at the same time calling for greater effort for the scoring of par and "birdies" than in the times when carries were obligatory and greens were faced at right angles and accepting, without great favor, shots from either side of the fairway.

A.W. Tillinghast

*Par 5 seventeen Lower in 1978.*

*Par 5 eighteen Lower in 1978.*

*Par 4 fourteen Lower in 1926.*

*Thirteen Lower in 1978.*

### The Oblique

When it came to shot values, Tillinghast once again based his theories on a distaste for the straight line and right angle. His preference was for the "oblique" line, or diagonal angle. He may have been the first to articulate this simple principle, which permits holes to be played in numerous ways, introducing elective play and finesse.

The Baltusrol courses offer examples of the "oblique" on almost every hole, but thirteen Lower, with its ditch running diagonally across the fairway, is a perfect risk-reward hole. The golfer has to decide on the tee how much of a carry he wants to risk. The shortest route to the flag is down the right side, but that route requires the longest carry. This hole, incidentally, made

a profound impression on Bobby Jones when he played in the 1926 Amateur, losing the final match after he tried, and failed, to carry the ditch on the right. He used Rae's Creek to create a similar hazard at the thirteenth at Augusta National, perhaps the most celebrated risk-reward hole in all of golf. Jack Nicklaus also considers thirteen Lower one of his favorites.

### Friend of the Duffer

In designing courses and Baltusrol, Tillinghast always considered the wide range of latitude in playing abilities. He was particularly concerned for the duffer. To him the ideal course "presents pleasurable golf to everyone, and it is exacting to the expert alone."

On play directed through or along the woods,

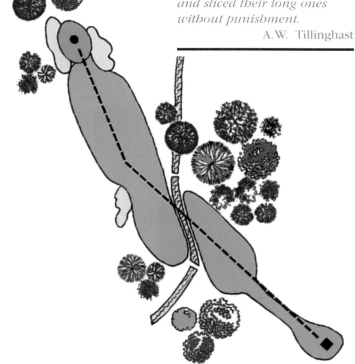

Tillinghast strongly recommended that "the underbrush should be cleared thoroughly for a considerable distance off the fairway."

Again he was looking out for the duffer for he wrote "it is quite enough to penalize a wayward shot by making the player get out without vexation and over-heavy punishment of a lost ball."

### Guile that Lies Therein

One last strategic consideration at Baltusrol is Tillinghast's guile. Though strongly opposed to blind shots on par 3's, or on any par 4 and par 5 where the golfer has played his drive or second shot, respectively, to the correct position, he was perfectly willing to employ other forms of deception. Blind drives he did not oppose, nor did he object to greens that were "half-blind to long shots," permitting the golfer to see the flag but not the bottom of the flag stick. On several holes—eighteen Upper, for instance—unless the drive is hit far enough, the front of the green is concealed by a rise in the terrain, creating doubt not only about the placement of the approach but the distance of the approach.

Tillinghast also removed trees and placed bunkers to create illusions about the correct distance to the hole, and he built bunkers so that their slopes collected balls that looked as if they ought to stay out.

On the greens of the Upper Course, he seems to have taken a diabolical pleasure in tilting the putting surfaces so that a putt that reads as if it breaks in one direction instead breaks sharply in the other.

Altogether, these cunning-

ly placed illusions add an element of intrigue to the golf at Baltusrol, and place a high premium on course knowledge. Two of the closest students of the Lower Course, Robert Trent Jones and Jack Nicklaus, have both noted the deceit that lurks on the Lower. "The guile," wrote Jones, "can be most deceptive and an insidious stroke-waster." And as noted by Nicklaus "it can nibble at you with bogeys that you do not really understand how you got"

Those remarks would surely have made Tillinghast smile wickedly under his waxed mustache.

*Three Lower—A wayward drive in the trees on the right or left is easy to find and play.*

*Four Upper— A putting green with deceptive breaks that belie the natural slope.*

*Eighteen Upper— A long drive will be rewarded with a clear view of the green.*

*One of the new courses at Baltusrol furnished a splendid example of the greatly changed aspect of a shot through the removal of several prominent trees close by the green. The hole in question is the tenth on the new Upper Course. The green is situated upon the top of a knoll and the line of play is slightly across the slope. When the several trees were removed, particularly one old wild-cherry, the distance immediately appeared longer than the iron-length, which it is.*

. . . . . . .

*Recently I was asked to express an opinion concerning a green which was half-blind to a mashie pitch from the teeing-ground. The stand that I take on this question is most decided. Such a green should allow the player to see his pitch strike on the green and to observe its every hop or twist. This applies to any green which should be reached by a lofted iron either from teeing-ground or fairway. There are some truly excellent holes whose greens are half-blind to long shots, and an absolutely blind drive at times is no objection so long the objective is not a green. Often there are blind shots to greens when the preceding shots have not been hit far enough or placed with sufficient accuracy to open up the flag to full sight. Certainly this goes a long way to the making of a good hole. But a blind approach from teeing-ground to green or from fairway after the drive has been played to the queen's taste? Never!*

A.W. Tillinghast

***Ten Upper circa 1935.***

***Ten Upper in 1994.***

***Five Upper in 1994.***

### The Home Hole
The unorthodox finish of the Lower Course, with its back-to back par 5's, is a glorious Tillinghast finale, a doubling of the principle that the Home hole should reward the courageous. Both greens certainly loom up in a mighty way, and intimidating hazards—on the seventeenth the double expanse of bunkers, on the eighteenth the stream and the bunkered face of the hill on which the green perches—cut directly across the line of play. In the opinion of Bobby Jones, eighteen Lower is one of the strongest finishes in American golf.

Yet these two holes, with the forced carry on seventeen and the partially blind approach on eighteen, deviate slightly from Tillinghast's theories of correct design—and that is precisely the point. Theory went out the window when Tillinghast had an opportunity to create a unique pair of golf holes. Theory also took a back seat to psychological considerations, for Tillinghast clearly understood that golf was a drama and that the last act had to be conclusive.

### Eighteen Inspirations
Tillinghast had tremendous gifts as a designer of golf courses—rich imagination, strong intelligence, a marvelous eye for beauty. But the quality that kept all the others in balance was his feeling for what can only be called the spirit of the game, with its ebb and flow of deep delights and disappointments every bit as deep, its splendid allure and exacting demands, its constant hopefulness and dreadful finality. Each and every golf course is imbued by its designer with a personality

that transcends its playing qualities, and in the end it is this personality that determines the fate of a golf course.

Like other Tillinghast courses, the Dual Courses at Baltusrol express at every turn Tillinghast's endless fascination for the game. His own standard was that a golf course should present nothing less than eighteen "inspirations"—a standard that few golf course architects could have stated, for the very good reason that few could have conceived it. An inspiration! To make such a declaration, the designer would first need to have been inspired—not amused, or challenged, or interested, or intimidated, but inspired.

From his writings, it is clear that Tillinghast always kept in mind the demands of an "average golfer" who was in fact very much like Tillinghast himself, and this golfer was always open to inspiration, and always seeking it. He was deeply stirred by his success or failure, but "no matter how distressing has been the hole just finished fresh determination surges as foot falls on the next teeing ground. Why not let men get determined in comfort? An honest old tree can be very sympathetic and comforting." In passages like that Tillinghast is no doubt guilty of gushing emotionalism, but is there anywhere a golfer who doesn't know what he's talking about? A golfer whose own emotions have been kept in perfect control and exact proportion?

Tillinghast was a man deeply stirred by the game of golf, and it shows in his golf courses. He expected the "average golfer" to approach the game with the same passion, to respond to

*Seventeen Lower in 1994.*

*Eighteen Lower in 1994.*

*Panorama of the eighteenth greens around 1926.*

the beauty of the setting, to appreciate strategic values, and to undertake every round as if he were the hero – or victim – in a rousing drama. His golf courses are artfully constructed stages where a golfer can endure all the vicissitudes of a

round without once being tempted to quit the game.

Just as a child knows that a certain man is handsome or a certain woman is beautiful, a golfer knows in his bones whether or not a golf course has captured the magic of the game.

At Baltusrol, Tillinghast succeeded in capturing that magic twice.

*Undoubtedly the last, the Home hole, should be one of the most exacting of any. No matter what its character may be, the hole must demand precise judgment and accurate execution. Under no circumstance may it be of the length that allows one man to half hit a shot and get home with an opponent, who has hit his. I like to see the Home hole looming up from the teeing ground in a mighty, impressive way. When a match arrives there on even terms, let that hole reward the courageous. There is more yellow spilled all over the teeing grounds of good Home holes than at any other spot on the course.*

· · · · · · ·

*A round of golf should present 18 inspirations - not necessarily thrills, because spectacular holes may be sadly overdone. Every hole may be constructed to provide charm without being obtrusive about it. When I speak of a hole being inspiring, it is not intended to imply that the visitor is to be subject to attacks of hysteria on every teeing ground. It must be remembered that the great majority of golfers are aiming to reduce their previous best performance by five strokes if possible, and if any one of them arrives at the home teeing ground with this possibility in reach, he is not caring too much whether he is driving off from a nearby ancient oak of majestic size, or from a dead sassafras. If his round ends happily, this is one beautiful course. Such is human nature.*

A.W. Tillinghast

# The Continuing Evolution

During the construction of the Dual Courses, the membership had declined significantly. Disruption during construction was cited as a primary cause. Consequently, in 1925, a Ways and Means Committee was formed to study and report on ways to increase membership. Their report cited the difficulty of the new courses and made the following request of the Green Committee:

"Consider the advisability of building front tees on a number of the holes on both the Lower and Upper courses with a view to making the courses more attractive as regards distance to the average player. Back tees in such cases would be reserved for championship events, tournaments, etc., where low handicap men are competing and the championship quality of

the courses should not be affected. We believe that the installing of front tees and the resulting shortening of the distances of a number of holes on each course would be pleasing to the general membership, and would not invite adverse comment from the low handicap men. The course would still present a good test of golf during general play when the front tees were in use."

However, rather than a shortening, a lengthening of both courses occurred. Over the next five years, both courses were lengthened from around 6,400 yards to 6,700 yards. The added length may have been a response to the next major innovation in golf equipment—the steel shaft.

At the 1926 Annual Meeting, Mr. Monroe for the Green Committee reported that both courses were in

excellent shape, although he hoped to make some improvements in the fairways. In reply to a question, he stated that "no material changes in the Upper course were contemplated".

Thank providence that the Green Committee and the Board did not yield to any vocal criticism, for today the Upper is virtually the same as laid out by Tillinghast, with just a few major improvements. During the middle and late twenties some of the holes on the Upper were modified, but always in line with Tillinghast's basic design. For example, the ninth tee was short and to the right of the current eighth green instead of to the left, where it is today. And the ninth fairway ran close to the right property line. The fairway was rerouted due to the encroachment of the existing housing development.

There were other changes to the Upper that represent improvements or completions of Tillinghast's original design. For instance, the green of eight Upper was originally 30 yards in front of its present location. With the rerouting of this hole, the green was moved back, to the knob on which it presently lies. The current eighth hole more closely resembles Tillinghast's original design.

Also, consistent with Tillinghast's "Course Beautiful," the pond on thirteen Upper was constructed in the late 1920's—fishing was the ulterior motive. This pond was regularly stocked with trout, and fly fishing only was permitted.

### The Amateur and the Open
The 1926 U.S. Amateur Championship was the coming out for the Lower

*Panoramic view taken in 1924 from the Terrace*

Course which played to 6,750 yards. The tournament was a smashing success. The Lower was instantly embraced as one of our Nation's best. A.W. Tillinghast was on hand for the event, basking in the praise for his creation from USGA officials, the players and the press.

The Upper's debut was the 1936 Open. The course was modified and improved in preparation for the event and played to 6,866 yards. The most radical change was made to the fourteenth hole. Prior to the event, the USGA and Baltusrol were debating whether to hold the Open on the Lower or the Upper. Two of our greatest amateur players, Bobby Jones and Francis Ouimet, inspected both courses. They recommended the Upper, but insisted that the fourteenth was a weak hole that had to be improved. Accordingly, the green was moved to the left of its original location. What is now a dry ditch was then a small dammed pond

in front of the original green. The green required relocation primarily due to drainage problems. The men's tee was extended to its present location, having originally played from the current women's tee. Today the fourteenth is considered one of the Upper's most beautiful and memorable holes.

There was also some debate on eighteen Upper. The stir was over a large swale in front of the green—the last remnant of the old pot bunker on the Old Course. Instead of eighteen Upper, the USGA suggested using eighteen Lower. After some debate the Board insisted on using the Upper in its entirety and the swale was filled.

### Major R. Avery Jones
The improvements to the Upper were overseen by Major R. Avery Jones and the Green Committee. In May of 1925 Major Jones was promoted to General Manager. But, he continued to oversee course mainte-

nance. Jones always gave priority to the golf courses, for he recognized the importance of the courses to the success of Baltusrol. And he saw to it that the courses would "not be starved for the newer toys" by the "pulling at the treasury for funds" by other Club committees. His leadership maintained the continuity of this policy throughout the regular change of officers on the Board of Governors.

Since the 1936 Open, there have been practically no modifications of note to the Upper. There were,

however, pro tees on the seventh and eleventh that fell from use and were later removed. The back tee on seven Upper can still be seen in the woods behind the existing tees. The eleventh played to over 600 yards from the old pro tee. (The recently completed Master Plan developed by Rees Jones calls for the restoration of these tees.)

In the Lower's case, we know of no major structural or routing changes since its opening in 1922. The only significant changes have been those undertaken to

*It is safe to say that not more than 5 per cent of the members of any club take the trouble to study the treasurer's report; but 95 per cent are deeply interested in the standard of golf course maintenance. If that standard is poor, the members are unhappy and there is no pleasure for the board, the golfers, nor the staff.*

Major R. Avery Jones

modernize the course for championship play.

### The Flexible Design
Tillinghast had the foresight to design the Upper and Lower with flexibility in mind. This flexibility would allow the modernization of the Lower and Upper to keep up with technological advances in equipment. For instance, many of the original teeing grounds were built with room for lengthening. In Tillinghast's own words:

"In these days of long flying balls we are forced to insure the future values of the various holes against even more lively balls than those of the present. A few years since, a course which measured up to six thousand yards was regarded as a thoroughly satisfactory, championship test. Now we are creeping up to sixty-five and sixty-six hundred yard totals from the back teeing grounds, with the average daily play several hundred yards less. Holes of four hundred and twenty-five yards once were regarded as long two-shotters. Today we are adding fifty yards to this length because of the constant introduction of longer flying balls.

We must endeavor to make modern courses as elastic as possible, and when we are forced to lengthen out it is far more economical to build new teeing grounds and hazards than to construct new putting greens."

### Tillinghast's Friend
In June of 1948, desiring another Open Championship, the Board of Governors formed a committee to consider improving and modernizing the golf courses. The commit-

tee wanted an outstanding architect to oversee the work and selected Robert Trent Jones. In addition to Jones, Francis Ouimet had agreed to act in an advisory capacity. In late 1948, the Committee reported that Mr. Jones suggested changes to make the Lower course fairer for the average golfer and more difficult for

**Robert Trent Jones.**

the low handicap golfer at a cost up to $25,000.

The Lower was lengthened and modernized at the hands of Robert Trent Jones, but it is still, unmistakably, a Tillinghast creation. Jones, a personal friend of the original designer, went to considerable effort to maintain the "Tillinghast touch," explaining, "In remodeling any golf course of quality, the object is to complement the work of the original. Any major changes should be in keeping with its style. What I did at Baltusrol, I believe, was faithful to the Tillinghast concept."

Many of the changes effected by Jones involved lengthening the course by approximately 400 yards to make it commensurate with the high-powered game that

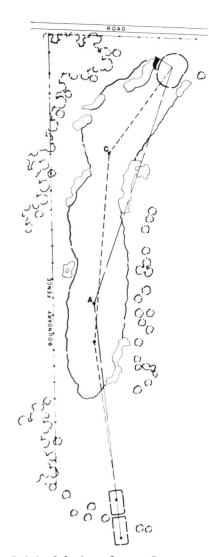

**Original design of seven Lower.**

*The equipment and the ball have been improved. The maintenance of courses has been brought to fine perfection. Rough is no longer the factor it used to be, because mechanized equipment has made it possible to maintain rough in better condition. However, during all this change the architecture of many courses has remained exactly the same. Naturally, the advantage has been to the player, who has outmoded the values previously set up to penalize him, perplex him, make him maneuver, and above all, to make him play his shots accurately.*

*For nine years, now, we have made tests at the Open Championships. These tests have been made for a definite purpose: to find out how accurate today's players are, and what should be considered a poor shot or a good shot.*

*Throughout these tests we have come to two definite conclusions: first, that modern players are hitting the ball farther, and second, that they are hitting the center of the fairway more often. Therefore, it is my contention that values should be tightened to meet the high standards which the great improvements in clubs and balls have made possible. In doing this, traps must be moved out to where they will have the same meaning they had in the Jones era, and fairways must be narrowed to develop a comparable latitude for error as when they were played by wooden-shafted clubs.*

*In tightening these values we have one sole objective—to test the play of modern golfers, so that the best man wins, and the golfer who has made the least shots and played the most brilliant golf is declared the champion. The tightening of any values must be done fairly. There should be no tricks, nor any trickiness on any part of the course.*

Robert Trent Jones

had evolved since Baltusrol last hosted the Open. In stretching the course to more than 7,000 yards, he added a number of fairway bunkers to emphasize the need for tee-shot accuracy. He also consolidated or enlarged sprawls of strategic sand near the greens, and he eliminated bunkers that were no longer of consequence. As predicted by Tillinghast thirty years earlier, improved course conditions, coupled with longer and more consistent golf balls and precision manufactured and balanced steel shaft clubs, had turned the Lower into a relatively short course.

Jones' most conspicuous changes were made to the

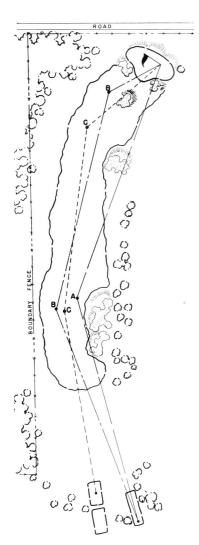

*Revised design of seven Lower.*

beautiful fourth hole and the dogleg seventh. In both cases he enlarged the greens to receive longer shots. The fourth was lengthened by nearly 70 yards with two tees of 160 yards and 194 yards. The elbow of the seventh was sharpened with an alternate tee on the right. This hole was also reduced from a short par 5 to a maximum par 4 of 470 yards for Open competition.

In designing the fourth hole, Tillinghast had used a pond that requires an absolute over-the-water carry to the green. Jones enhanced and strengthened the hole with a longer carry, a terraced green, and a narrow extension of the putting surface backed by

bunkers. Both before and after Jones' modernization, four Lower has consistently been ranked as one of the best par 3's in the world.

The "famous fourth" was also the scene of an ultimate squelch by Robert Trent Jones. After remodeling the hole, he was criticized for making it too difficult.

"Let's go play the hole and see if there is anything that needs to be done," Jones suggested as he led the critic along with C. P. Burgess, General Chairman of the 1954 Open Championship, and pro Johnny Farrell to the fourth tee, where each struck a shot.

After each of the first three had put his ball on the green, Jones played his and sank it for a hole-in-one.

"Gentlemen, I think the hole is eminently fair," the architect is reported to have said.

The fourth also has been the scene of several notable catastrophes. Arnold Palmer dumped his ball into the water during the 1967 Open. Augie Kammer, the Baltusrol great, took a 9 on the hole in a qualifying round of the 1926 U.S. Amateur. And another member, Henry Topping, vented his particular frustrations by throwing his entire bag of clubs into the pond.

### 1967 and 1980 Opens
When Baltusrol was awarded the 1967 Open, the decision on which course to play had still to be made. Upon touring both the Lower and the Upper, Joseph C. Dey, Jr., Executive Director of the USGA, commented that the Upper was a nice course for the members, but the true test for the pros was the Lower. His opinion carried weight, and the decision was made to

*Four Lower from the back tees.*

play the Open on the Lower. The Lower played to 7,015 yards, essentially as it did in the 1954 Open, although, on Dey's recommendation, two relatively minor structural changes were made. The right hand tee on the seventh was extended forward to shorten the hole to under 470 yards so it would play as an easier par 4 for the Open competition. On the sixteenth, a new tee was built behind the present front tee, extending this hole to approximately 214 yards.

Dey made one other recommendation that would dramatically change the Lower's look. This was the renovation of the bunkers. Over the years the edges of the bunkers had become

quite ragged. To redefine the bunkers, over two acres of Merion blue grass sod was laid and 700 tons of sand were added. The purpose of the blue grass was to provide a uniform and fair lie. Pop up sprinkler heads were installed to keep the banks in verdant turf. Unfortunately, the blue grass was laid all the way to the floor of the bunker, eliminating the natural working of sand into the slope of a bunker that Tillinghast had so prized, and which brought the hazard into the player's view. Tillinghast was convinced that "a splash of white sand here and there does go a long way to dress up a golf course ... use it with discrimination

*Bunkers undergoing renovation prior to the 1967 Open.*

and above all,— put it where it may be seen."

For the 1980 Open, P.J. Boatwright, the respected USGA Tournament Director, recommended no structural changes, but he did want the rough grown in on numerous fairways. The impact was most pronounced on the seventeenth and eighteenth fairways—the rough was grown in on the left, removing from play the Tillinghast opening to the green on both holes. This eliminated the choice of the left side as a landing area for the second shot and made the third shot to these holes a blind pitch.

### The 1993 Open
In 1992, Rees Jones, son of Robert Trent Jones, was called in to make modifications for the 1993 U.S. Open. Rees had established his own reputation as Open Doctor through his restoration of The Country Club in Brookline, Massachusetts for the 1988 U.S. Open and his remodeling of Hazeltine National Golf Club in Chaska, Minnesota for the 1991 U.S. Open.

The most noticeable change was increased length—the Lower was now 7,152 yards from the tips. Rees engineered a new pro tee on the third, a new alternate tee on the ninth, the enlargement of the twelfth

*Rees Jones.*

*The approach to seventeen Lower prior to 1980 provided a landing area on the left side.*

*Prior to 1980, the fairways on eighteen Lower and Upper were connected .*

tee, and the lengthening of the fifth, thirteenth, and fourteenth tees. New fairway bunkers were built on seven and eight, and the greenside bunker on fourteen was tucked around the left front of the green.

Despite the modernization, the Lower retains the flow and flavor of Tillinghast's design. The routing has remained unchanged, even in its most idiosyncratic feature—the audacious finish of back-to-back par 5's. This double whammy at the end of the round was regarded by Bobby Jones as "one of the great finishes in golf." And thanks to the sensitive renovations by Robert Trent and Rees Jones, the shot values have remained essentially the same.

If the ultimate critics are the great players, than the Lower has remained one of the world's supreme tests. The consensus after the 1993 Open was unanimous—the golfers loved the course. One after another, they sang its praises as a strong fair golf course that put the driver back in their hands. They had nothing but respect for this venerable course which, they observed, was the first Open course in years that didn't

need to be tricked up.

### The Future
While Tillinghast was well aware that all golf courses were living organisms, and that they had to grow and change, he urged caution, consistency, and faithful adherence to a single concept of design. As a course consultant for the PGA, he

*Lower Baltusrol is different from the golf course that Tillinghast opened in the 1920's, but it doesn't feel that way. Length has been added, bunkers repositioned, and greens slightly enlarged to accept the shots characteristic of modern play. Many of the Tillinghast features that come into play only for the average golfer have remained unchanged, while additional bunkering has been added for the better players and the improved equipment. A general characterization of the most recent improvements would be that we merely updated the golf course. In the early 1950's, my father updated the course, too, with many of the changes having been occasioned by the improved equipment of the day as well as the improved quality of play."*

Rees Jones

had witnessed many courses that had been changed "without any thought of a preconceived scheme of hazards. Consequently, the poor course resembles a crazy quilt." Tillinghast attributed this to no continuity on the Green Committee. He noted that "each new chairman blindly rushes to a complete change on everything. And so it goes, every year or two there is a new regime and they each pull against the other, but in the meanwhile the course goes to the bow-wows."

Over almost fifty years under the tutelage of the Jones' the Lower had been continually improved to keep up with the modern game. The Upper, however, had been left relatively unchanged since the 1936 Open. The club now felt that it was time for the Upper to catch up with its sister course, and, consequently, after the 1993 Open, Rees Jones was retained to prepare a long range master plan for the Upper.

The objective was to provide a harmonious program to improve the Upper over a five year period. The con-

cept behind Jones' master plan was twofold—bring the course forward for the modern game and return it as closely as possible to the philosophy that Tillinghast articulated.

Rees made approximately 80 recommendations. Most of them were relatively minor, such as restoring mowing patterns on greens and approaches, and trimming trees. The major changes involved modernizing the course much as Rees' father had done years earlier on the Lower. Implementation of the mas-

ter plan began in 1994. To date, several tees have been lengthened or enlarged including the eighth, eleventh, twelfth, thirteenth, fourteenth and fifteenth.

Recognizing that Baltusrol cannot rest on its laurels, Rees was also retained to develop a master plan for the Lower, which will be completed in 1995. Little structural change is anticipated given the last 50 years of improvements.

Under the watchful eye of Jones, the Upper and Lower will continue to remain true to the ideals of their creator.

*We are going back to past records to find as much of Tillinghast's original concepts for the courses as possible. We are reinstituting pin positions on greens and the open fairway approaches into greens that he spent so much of his energy perfecting. We are also extending tees back and shifting fairways to bring original hazards back into play. In Baltusrol, Tillinghast left the world a pair of golf courses that have multiple shot options, requiring a premeditated strategy. The Upper Course is tighter and requires more finesse, the Lower is a bold, demanding course. Our work has been an effort to reinstate the definition, the fairness and the challenge that Tillinghast courses are famous for. Joe Flaherty and his predecessor, Ed Casey, have been extremely faithful about preserving the style and character of the courses very much the same as they were when Tillinghast completed them. I'd like to imagine that Tillie would be proud if he stood on the terrace today overlooking his creation.*

Rees Jones

***Payne Stewart barely misses a birdie to tie Lee Janzen in the final round of the 1993 U.S. Open.***

# The Lower's Ultimate Critics—The Players in the 1993 Open

*This is a great golf course. It's one of the fairest set ups for an Open in years*—Ray Floyd.

*I love this golf course. It's my fourth U.S. Open, and this one I feel the most comfortable*—John Daly.

*You can run the ball up here, and that's a nice option we haven't had at other courses. This is a shot makers' course*—Paul Azinger.

*It's a good, hard golf course out here*—Craig Stadler.

*This is one of the fairest Open courses as far as rewarding the good shots and penalizing the bad ones*—Scott Simpson.

*I'm going to drive the ball all week*—Mark McCumber.

*It's a true test of golf. They haven't tried to trick it up*—Greg Norman.

*These are the best greens I've ever played*—Rocco Mediate.

*This course is going to stand on its own. It doesn't need any special treatment*—Corey Pavin.

*This is extremely fair, the way they have the course*—Scott Hoch.

*This is the best Open course we've played in a long time*—Blaine McCallister.

*It takes all your game to play this golf course*—Tom Watson.

*Par is a good score on any hole out here. You may be on in two on eighteen, but par is a still a good score*—Payne Stewart.

*First tee Lower—1926 Amateur.*

*First fairway Lower—1926 Amateur.*

*Four Lower—1926.*

*Fifth green Lower—1926.*

*Sixth green Lower—1926.*

*Twelve Lower—1926.*

*Thirteenth green Lower—1926.*

*Eighth green Lower—1926 Amateur.*

# Tillinghast's Creation

*Twelve Upper—1936.*

*Thirteenth green Upper—1936 Open.*

*Nine Upper—1936.*

*Fifteen Upper—1936.*

*Eighteenth green Upper—1936 Open.*

*Seventeenth green Lower—1926.*

Baltusrol

Lower and Upper
Courses
1995

# The Lower Course

The essential character of Baltusrol (Lower) is unlike that of any golf course we play on the tour, and only occasionally does it look like any other course in the north-eastern United States. In fact, if someone put a blindfold on me and led me out to four or five holes on Baltusrol I would think I was at a Scottish links, or perhaps at Royal Birkdale. This is especially true on many holes between the seventh and sixteenth, where there are stretches of flat, almost treeless land and the greens are surrounded by mounds and bunkers that have a rugged natural quality.

Jack Nicklaus

## No. 1
## Par 5
## 478 Yards

This is a fine opener as either a par 4 for championship play or a par 5 for everyday play. Shunpike Road flanks the left side and is out of bounds, and fairway bunkers and a brook on the right pinch the landing area, adding to the tension every golfer feels starting out. A straight and extremely long tee shot will be rewarded with a view of the green. Otherwise a slight rise in the fairway will hide the bottom of the pin for the long approach or lay-up. The green is rather small and tightly bunkered.

In 1967, Deane Beman made U.S. Open history on this hole by making a total of 12 strokes over four rounds—he went eagle, birdie, birdie, par. This equates to eight under par for member play as a par 5.

# No. 2
## Par 4
## 381 yards

A straight and accurate drive is required to a tight landing area that is bounded by cross bunkers 240 yards off the tee, pine trees and out-of-bounds on the left, and a deep bunker on the right. A drive that is too long will find itself in the cross bunkers. A well positioned tee shot will leave a short-iron approach to a large and tightly bunkered green that slopes from right to left. An approach that ends above the hole will risk a three-putt.

# No. 3
## Par 4
## 466 yards

*I like this hole because it sets up such an interesting approach. The left side of the green slopes sharply to the left. A shot from the right side of the fairway— undoubtedly with one of the mid irons—will tend to bounce left and may run right off the green. Ideally, then, the approach should be hit from the left side of the fairway so that it will land into the slope of the green. But the left side is far more dangerous off the tee. The hole doglegs slightly from right to left and a drive that misses the fairway to the left will be, as we say, in jail.*

Jack Nicklaus

# No. 4
## Par 3
## 194 yards

*I like this hole very much. One of its most important features is the fact that the front of the green is faced with stone—like a sea wall. Most water holes have the greens that slope gently down to the water fronting them. This brings too strong an element of luck into play, a kind of it-depends-on-the-bounce situation. Not this hole. You know where the hazard ends and the green starts. You are either sunk in the water or nicely on the green. The green is wide and has two levels, a feature that sets up an interesting variety of tee shots, depending on where the flagstick is positioned and which tee is used.*

Jack Nicklaus

This famous hole was the scene of one of golf's most memorable vindications. After stiffening the hole for the 1954 Open, Robert Trent Jones was roundly criticized for making it too severe. In response, he took a group of his critics to the tee and knocked a 4-iron into the hole for an ace. He then remarked, "Gentleman, as you can see, the hole is eminently fair." Here he points out where he made his hole-in-one to Club Pro Johnny Farrell.

# No. 5
## Par 4
## 413 yards

A challenging and handsome par 4, it plays harder than its yardage might indicate. The fairway is pinched by fairway bunkers, and the uphill second is difficult because the elevated green is sloped from right to left and back to front. The green is one of the most difficult to putt on the course.

# No. 6
## Par 4
## 470 yards

*There are some truly excellent holes whose greens are half-blind to long shots, and an absolutely blind drive at times is no objection so long as the objective is not a green.*
A.W. Tillinghast

A partially blind tee shot calls for length and accuracy. The fairway is a hogback sloping sharply down on both sides and is hard to hold with a drive. A good drive will still leave a long iron to a large green hemmed by traps on either side.

# No. 7
## Par 5
## 505 yards

Normally a par 5 for member play, this hole plays as one of the hardest par 4's in U.S. Open competition.

*This hole doglegs to the right, with an out-of-bounds fence on one side and trees on the other. A long drive must be hit here, of course, but hooking the ball could be very dangerous. The trees on the right are very much in play from the tee, and too much hook will carry the ball clear across the fairway and into the rough on the left. The approach shot will be partially blind because of a large mounded bunker about 50 yards short the green and must be worked toward the pin from the front portion of the green. This shot should be faded in if the pin is on the right and hooked or drawn if the pin is on the left.*
Jack Nicklaus

## No. 8
### Par 4
### 374 yards

*I like the eighth which has a tight area for the drive and an interesting little pitch shot over a bunker.*
Jack Nicklaus

## No. 9
### Par 3
### 205 yards

*The ninth is one of the most British looking holes on the course, featuring a green with a very narrow opening between two traps, a crescent-shaped bunker circling around the rear and demanding a variety of shots that alter radically as the pin position is changed.*
Jack Nicklaus

# No.10
## Par 4
## 454 yards

The back nine starts off with this demanding par 4. The fairway, partially hidden from the tee, narrows to a bottleneck around the 280 yard mark. A trap on the left and trees on the right put a premium on accuracy off the tee. In the final round of the 1993 Open, Lee Janzen was facing bogey or worse when the towering oaks on the right blocked his shot to the green. He tried to carry the trees but hit a five iron low into the thickest part of the oak's crown. Somehow, his ball sailed unscathed through the trees and onto the green. After the shot Janzen believed he had destiny on his side.

*No hole can be condemned as blind if it is so because the feeble hitting of the player makes it so. Some of the best holes are great because visibility of the green is only gained because a fine shot opens it to sight.*

A.W. Tillinghast

# No.11
## Par 4
## 428 yards

This severe dog-leg played as one of the hardest holes in the 1993 Open. A precise and long draw down the left side around two large sassafras trees will be rewarded with a short iron and a view of the large and undulating green. A straight or pushed drive to the right side of the fairway will leave a shot to the green, but a rise in the fairway will hide the foot of the pin, creating a bit of deception.

# No. 12
## Par 3
## 193 yards

A huge frontal trap and a high mound on the right guard a large sunken green. Distance is hard to judge on this hole as the foot of the pin is hidden.

# No. 13
## Par 4
## 401 yards

A diagonal creek makes this is a very good dogleg. Bobby Jones lost the 1926 Amateur here when he tried for too big a carry and caught the creek. This hole left such an impression on Jones that it was his model for the design of the thirteenth at Augusta National.

*Naturally, I have a favorite hole, ... it is the thirteenth. When you stand on the tee you see a bunker on the left side of the fairway. It is about 240 yards out, where the fairway turns slightly to the right and up towards the green. A creek cuts diagonally across the fairway angling towards the hole and forces the tee shot to carry from 170 to 225 yards. Well down the right side of the fairway is a large and threatening clump of trees. The problem is obvious. You must keep the ball away from the trees on the right. You must also keep it away from the bunker on the left. The player who likes to hook his tee shots is faced with an almost impossible situation. To stay in the fairway and avoid the trap on the left, a hook has to be aimed almost directly at the trees. The way to play the hole is to drive toward the left-hand bunker with a left-to-right fade that will carry the ball away from trouble.*

Jack Nicklaus

# No. 14
## Par 4
## 415 yards

The most direct route is over the elbow formed by a fairway bunker on the left. A drive over the bunker will be rewarded with a short iron and clear view of the green, although, there is danger lurking in the tree line that stretches the length of the left side. A safe drive to the right of the bunker will leave a partially blind mid-iron to the green.

*A dog leg hole provides some pronounced obstruction, which forms a corner in a twisted fairway from either side. If it be impossible to carry over this obstruction, but at the same time necessary to get beyond it in order to open up the next shot, we have a Dog-leg. If a similar obstruction may be carried by a courageous shot, which is rewarded by a distinct advantage, we have an Elbow.*

A.W. Tillinghast

# No. 15
## Par4
## 430 yards

This attractive hole has bunkers left and right awaiting the errant tee shots. Two huge diagonal traps guard the approach to a beautifully green sighted on top of a rise, while three smaller traps flank the right hand side. The fast undulating green with a definite frontal forward pitch is one of the most difficult on the course.

# No. 16
## Par 3
## 216 yards

Played from an elevated tee, this hole requires a long iron from the back tee and a middle iron from the forward tee. Traps completely encircle the large undulating green which has numerous subtle rolls, both seen and unseen.

# No. 17
## Par 5
## 630 yards

This is often referred to as one of the great par 5 holes in America. An accurate drive in the fairway is required to enable the second shot to carry the cross bunkers at about 400 yards. Provided the rough is avoided and two solid shots have been played, the uphill approach to the well-bunkered green will require a short iron.

In 1993, Open history was made when long-hitting John Daly became the first man ever to reach this green in two shots. His second was a 1-iron from 295 yards away. Prior to the feat, John Daly told his caddy, "If I reach 17, at least I'll make history."

## No. 18
### Par 5
### 542 yards

*It could make for a lot of excitement, if you come to 18 needing an eagle. It is the only hole on the course where you've got that chance.*
Payne Stewart

*The fairway is downhill from the tee, but nothing less than a very long drive will permit reaching the green in two. A safe second shot played short leaves a little pitch to a tabled green, no easy stroke if the Open is at stake and you need a birdie.*

Jack Nicklaus

Bobby Jones considered this one of the finest finishing holes anywhere. It has been the scene of many heroic Open finishes, such as Furgol's zigzagging in 1954, Jack Nicklaus' perfect 1-iron in 1967 and Payne Stewart's attempt to reach the green in two in 1993. Water, heavy rough and thick trees lie along the fairway, but if a player needs birdie or eagle, two perfect shots will make the green.

# The Upper Course

The Upper course cannot be described by likening it to any other well known championship course. It possesses a character all its own. It is laid out across the eastern foothills of what is locally known as "Baltusrol Mountain." The greens are closely trapped but through the fairways the contours of the ground, lakes, streams and the natural woodland render numerous artificial hazards unnecessary.

Play is definitely influenced by the natural elements of the setting—the higher, more rugged terrain of Baltusrol Mountain. Obviously, Tillinghast utilized this influence to create a course of implicit strategic design, which forces players to determine where and how they have to play every shot – especially a putt – to compensate for the unrelenting influence of the mountain. This is conspicuously evident on the first six holes, which run along the base of the mountain before the course moves onto terrain that does not have such a strong pitch and roll.

The course plays somewhat longer than the actual measurement, for most of the tee shots are played to rising ground. The length is well distributed—interesting drive-and-pitch holes have not been sacrificed to secure length.

The wooded hillside which extends along the entire western boundary of the property furnishes a beautiful natural setting for the course. It gives the impression that the course itself is hilly but in the fairways there are no steep slopes and in an entire round usually not more than one shot has to be played from a side hill lie.

There are no out-of-bounds fences and although the skyline of New York City is clearly visible from the third and fourth holes there are no public roads or buildings nearby to spoil the natural beauty.

The greens occupy natural sites. In the entire construction there have been minimal changes in the natural features. The greens are ample, although they are generally less expansive than those of the Lower, and also are situated so as to have a "right" or "wrong" side from which to putt.

## No. 1
### Par 5
### 473 Yards

This splendid opening hole is reachable in two, but its bunkers are trouble. The green slopes from back to front and right to left. The ideal approach should be left or below the hole or else a three putt is highly likely.

# No. 2
## Par 4
## 422 Yards

The woods guard the fairway on the right and the fairway slopes steeply from right to left. Care is required in placing the tee shot to avoid catching the slope and rolling into the left rough. The second shot will likely have to be played from a side hill stance. The ideal putt is from the left because it will be uphill on the biggest green on the Upper course (8,300 square feet).

# No. 3
## Par 3
## 191 Yards

This hole calls for a high shot with a cut, especially if the hole is located in the hollow in the right front. With the cup in the middle of the green or back left, caution is paramount as a bold approach can run off the left side of the green. Putting can be a nightmare, as four putts are quite common.

This may be the oldest hole at Baltusrol, making it 100 years old. It follows the same routing as the fifth of Hunter's first nine holes and the ninth of the Old Course. In the 1903 U.S. Open, this is where defending champion Laurence Aucterlonie incurred a controversial penalty in the first round that cost him a tie with Willie Anderson for the Open lead and the 18-hole Open record of 73. It is also where Willie Anderson, the eventual champion, lost a chance to break the 72-hole Open record, and almost lost the Open, after making an eight in the final round.

# No. 4
## Par 4
## 384 Yards

*Keep in mind that one word 'Blend.' I cannot emphasize it too strongly— blend your slopes so gently and harmoniously that they cease to be slopes.*
A.W. Tillinghast

A carefully controlled tee shot is necessary. The player can place his tee shot on high ground to the right or play to the left to secure a wider opening to the green. The green is a ledge at the base of the mountain, and is protected on the left by a grassy slope and sand bunkers. The approach must come in high with plenty of spin to stay on the surface.

# No. 5
## Par 4
## 390 Yards

Broken ground and the forest form a natural hazard all along the edge of the fairway to the right. The green is closely trapped, but provided the tee shot is well placed the second shot is not difficult. A slight crown in the green makes it mandatory to stay below the hole with the approach shot.

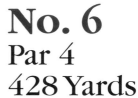

# No. 6
## Par 4
## 428 Yards

The first 270 yards of this hole are cut through woods and the tee shot must be straight. Bunkers cross the fairway 40 yards from the green. The back-to-front slope makes this green one of the most receptive, but the influence of the mountain can produce some diabolical putts.

# No. 7
## Par 3
## 214 Yards

*I am not contending that on certain occasions, when fields of crack golfers are contesting that the long one shotter may not be stretched just a bit. With these occasional events in mind it is perfectly sensible to provide a back teeing-ground but for the steady diet of the family, bring them closer to the table.*

     A.W. Tillinghast

Tillinghast originally designed this hole with a back tee at 230 yards. The terrace behind the current pro tee may be a remnant of that tee. This hole still is a true one-shotter to a pedestal green. Six bunkers embrace the putting surface. And a lateral ridge can't be ignored in trying to hole a putt.

# No. 8
## Par 5
## 541 Yards

Woods border the fairway the entire length of the hole on the right. The tee shot is trapped on both sides at 260 yards. The second has a wide fairway. The green is built on a natural plateau 20 feet above the fairway and is well protected by steep-faced bunkers.

# No. 9
## Par 4
## 338 Yards

From an elevated tee a lake calls for a carry of about 185 yards. The water is no hazard except for a painfully short hitter. This is a drive-and-pitch hole to the narrowest and smallest green (4,300 square feet) on the course, so the second shot must be precise.

# No. 10
## Par 3
## 151 Yards

This slightly uphill hole requires a bit more club than the yardage would indicate. The green is on top of a knoll surrounded by sand and has more than its share of surface variations.

In constructing this hole, Tillinghast removed several trees close to the green to add a little deception. He wrote later that "when the several trees were removed, particularly one wild-cherry, the distance immediately appeared longer than the iron-length, which it is."

# No. 11
## Par 5
## 551/604
## Yards

This hole originally played to 602 yards from a championship tee behind the existing men's tee. This tee fell from use in the 1950's. As part of Rees Jones' master plan, the tee was reinstated.

The ideal way to play this hole is down the right side to avoid a 100-yard stretch of bunkers on the left. There is a slight dip before the green, which is flanked by sand sprawls. The green has a lateral terrace sloping toward the left front, but it is not unduly difficult to read.

# No. 12
## Par 4
## 359 Yards

This hole funnels between trees to a pedestal green with a steep bunker sprawled across its entire face. There also are bunkers on the left and right. The elevated green is one of the hardest to hold and calls for a carefully played pitch.

# No. 13
## Par 4
## 386 Yards

*I still think that the sand-pits should nestle close-up, with sand showing up into the slopes, and in such a manner as to open the green to a second shot, that has been accurately placed on the proper side of the fairway.*

A.W. Tillinghast

There is water on both sides of the fairway. A pond on the right will catch only a short slice, but a creek on the left is not evident and borders the fairway from 180 to 280 yards. The green is set on a right-to-left diagonal. The ideal approach from the right sets up a putt that will follow the line of the green.

# No. 14
## Par 4
## 395 Yards

A trap crosses the left side of the fairway 195 yards from the tee  The player must carry it or play into the face of the hill to the right, from where one cannot see the green.  The long green slopes back-to-front and is protected by sand on either side.  For obvious reasons, any putt below the hole is desired.

   This hole was modified in preparation for the 1936 Open on the recommendation of Bobby Jones—length was added with the construction of the existing men's tee and the green was moved from a site that was to the right of the existing green.

# No. 15
## Par 3
## 140 Yards

This is the shortest hole on course and the last of the one-shotters.  It requires a pitch shot from a high tee to a green on top of a small hill.  Although an ample target, it should not be missed as the green falls sharply away on each side—to the right is a deep gully and traps are in the front, left and rear.

   Despite the large target, both Tony Manero and Harry Cooper missed the green and bogeyed this hole in the final round of the 1936 Open.  Cooper's ball actually hit a spectator and bounced into a trap.

# No.16
## Par 4
## 435 Yards

Fairway bunkers guard the left while the right is open but a large pin oak may stymie a second. The closely trapped green is the biggest worry on this hole. Any putt from above the hole is frightening. Keeping an approach shot right of the flagstick is a must.

This hole was the climax of the 1936 Open and the 1985 Open. In 1936, Tony Manero sunk a 12 foot birdie putt to give him a two shot lead with two to play. While in 1985 Kathy Baker, who was in a duel with Judy Clark, also made birdie to give her a commanding lead.

# No.17
## Par 5
## 557 Yards

This long hole can be seen all the way. The tee shot is slightly uphill with traps and rough on the right. From the left to the center of the fairway at 450 yards punishing bunkers catch a poorly hit second. Flanking bunkers frame a green that is tilted forward and naturally favors a putt from below the hole.

# No.18
## Par 4
## 459 Yards

This is the longest and most difficult par 4 on the course. The tee shot is played from high ground to rising ground. All along the right of the approach to this hole is a steep bank into which traps are cut. The large and deep green is not trapped, but the second shot must be long and accurate. Even though the green is one of the most reasonable to putt, birdies are rare.

A shorter version of this hole formed the eighteenth of the Old Course and was the final scene for

Baltusrol's first five national championships, including Jerry Travers historic 1915 Open victory. The last remnant of the "infamous pot bunker," a pronounced dip in front of the green, was filled in preparation for the 1936 Open.

1901

1903

1904

1911

1915

1926

1936

1946

1954

1961

1967

1980

1985

1993

reatness is measured in many ways. Certainly a golf club such as Baltusrol has at its core a strong social camaraderie and an abiding sense of tradition. Yet, a number of clubs in the United States have these elements. What separates Baltusrol? Simple. A one hundred year history of hosting our great country's national championships.

Since Baltusrol's inception in 1895, the desire to serve as host to the game's pre-

mier championships has been evident. Only six years after its founding, Baltusrol hosted its first national championship—the 1901 Women's Amateur. And over Baltusrol's first one hundred years a total of fourteen United States Golf Association (USGA) national championships have been played on its courses. Naturally, much attention has been centered on Baltusrol's role as host to a record seven U.S. Open Championships.

The U.S. Open has become *the* championship of American golf. And, as any golf fan knows, the prerequisite for aspiring hosts

# THE NATIONAL
*Championships*

is to fulfill the most exacting conditions. Baltusrol has not only met these tests, but served as a model for others. Consider that Baltusrol's seven Opens have been on different courses—the original Old Course in 1903, a revised Old Course in 1915, the Upper in 1936 and the Lower in 1954, 1967, 1980 and 1993. Beyond the Men's Open, Baltusrol has hosted seven other USGA Championships—three U.S. Amateur's, two Women's Opens and two Women's Amateurs.

Virtually every celebrated champion in the history of

American golf has strolled the grounds at Baltusrol. That roster includes the likes of Willie Anderson, Walter Travis, Harry Vardon, Francis Ouimet, Jerry Travers, Walter Hagen, Chick Evans, Bobby Jones, Gene Sarazen, Ben Hogan, Arnold Palmer, Mickey Wright, Nancy Lopez, Tom Watson, Nick Faldo, and most notably Jack Nicklaus.

As one of the oldest clubs in the United States, it is fair to say that Baltusrol played a major role in shaping American golf. Certainly in playing this role, Baltusrol has had the everlasting commitment of its membership.

Prior to the 1993 Open, David Egar, the USGA Senior Director of Rules and Competitions, explained the enduring alure of Baltusrol as follows:

"There is something about Baltusrol—something that has made the USGA return here a record seventh time, something that has brought us to Springfield, New Jersey, for a National Championship at least once in every decade of the twentieth century.

What is it?

Success. The history of the U.S. Open at Baltusrol is a chronicle of dramatic championships, each of them staged with care and efficiency. Fundamentally, Baltusrol is a golf club—not a country club. All of its members know and love the game, and within their club is a century-old culture that has taught them how to deal with both the traditions and the travails of the National Open. They know how to make an Open work."

What follows is a chronicle of Baltusrol's national championships.

*The U.S. Open Men's Championship trophy. Above: The "Gutty" (gutta-percha) ball and The "Haskel" (rubber) ball.*

# 1901

# U.S. Women's Amateur

*Driving from the first tee in the shadow of the Clubhouse.*

*Hecker Vanquishes Herron*

*Baltusrol Successfully Stages its First National Championship*

 In 1901, the national spotlight shined on Baltusrol's links for the first time with the seventh annual Women's Amateur Championship held October 8-12, just a few weeks after the assassination of President William McKinley.

 In the final round, Genevieve Hecker of Essex County CC in West Orange bested Lucy Hayes Herron of the Cincinnati CC, adding the title of National Champion to her two Metropolitan Champion titles. *The New York Times* ran a banner headline, "Crowd on Baltusrol Links," as nearly 1,000 spectators took in all the action. In reviewing the match, The New York Times remarked that "Miss Hecker was both straighter and longer on the long game and steadier in the short putts."

**The Haskell-Gutty Debate**
Miss Hecker earned the title from among a record 84 entries. The qualifying scores ranged from 97 to 104, including seven women from Boston who "created consternation by their steadiness of play." The New York papers expressed concern that the tournament would be swept by the Bostonians. A fast pace was set in the qualifying round, with four players tying for low scoring honors at 97. This was a significant record, since in past championships very few women were able to break 100.

 The reason for the low scores was that most players used the lively new rubber ball, the Haskell, in preference to the old gutta-percha ball or "gutty." Miss Hecker had experimented with a rubber ball on the first day, but her putting was so erratic that she decided to finish out with an ordinary gutty. She scored a 101 in the qualifying round.

 The longer-flying rubber-filled ball, in general use throughout the championship, unquestionably aided in the lower scoring. The ball was again in evidence in the long-driving competition, which was won by Miss Margaret Curtis with a poke of 193 yards, two feet, and five inches. At Shinnecock Hills the prior year, the winning drive by Miss

Louise Maxfield was 189 yards and five inches on a downhill slope. At Baltusrol, the ground was level, and the improvement was attributed to the new ball.

### Marion Oliver's Rubber Ball

Great attention was focused on the first round match between Miss Bessie Anthony of Chicago and Baltusrol's own Miss Marion Oliver. The match pitted East vs. West, and the fact that Miss Anthony was using the gutty

*Miss Margaret Curtis wins the long drive contest.*

ball and Miss Oliver the new rubber ball afforded an excellent opportunity for comparison. Miss Oliver had the advantage from nearly every tee and generally reached the green on even terms with her opponent, only to be outputted, which seemed to prove that the gutty had a truer roll on the putting surface. The match was won by Miss Anthony five up and four to play. The defeat of more than one player was attributed to the rubber ball, and some of those who started with it gave it up before the week was through.

*Miss Marion Oliver driving from the eighth tee. Miss Herron is seated on the sand box.*

### The Key Match

Without a doubt the most sensational match of the tournament was between Miss Hecker and Miss Bishop on the third day. Miss Hecker started out with the lively rubber ball, but her work around the green was so unsteady that after a few holes she returned to the gutty. Miss Hecker was three down to Miss Bishop after the front nine, and could not make up any ground on the back nine. When it came a case of dormie three, the friends of the Essex County lady gave up all hope. But Miss Hecker turned to her caddie and advisor, the Scotsman John Harrison, and said, "Do you think I have a chance to pull out this match?" Just what the Scot said is not known, but it was enough to rally Miss Hecker to capture the next two holes. And when the match was halved at the home green, everyone was sure that Miss Hecker would win the match. This she did.

*Mrs. Manice and Miss Hecker at the seventeenth tee.*

*Gallery watching the driving from the sixth tee.*

*Miss Hecker and Mrs. Manice on the eighth green.*

### The Final Match

Miss Hecker met Miss Herron in the championship match. The key hole of the match was the fourteenth. Miss Herron was three down, but a comeback seemed plausible when Miss Hecker drove out-of-bounds. After hitting her second shot from the tee (at the time out-of-bounds was penalized with distance only), Miss Herron failed to take advantage by making two abominably short shots for an eight, handing the hole to Miss Hecker who scored six. With the match, dormie four at the fifteenth hole, Miss Herron stumbled to another eight, losing the match 5 and 3.

### Championship Notes

Among the more prominent players in the field was Margaret Curtis from Boston. After being beaten in the finals the year before, Miss Curtis came to Baltusrol as one of the leading players. If not for the steady play of Miss Herron, who defeated Miss Curtis in the semi-finals, Miss Curtis

*Runner-up Lucy Hayes Herron.*

would have reached her second straight final. She would win the Amateur Championship title at Baltusrol later in her career in 1911.

More championships awaited Miss Hecker who successfully defended her title the following year at The Country Club in Brookline, Massachusetts, and later added a third Metropolitan title in 1906. Miss Hecker also is known as the first woman to write a book on golf, entitled, simply enough, *Golf for Women*, which she described in a subtitle as being aimed at "the feminine inquiring mind and from a woman's point of view."

In wrapping up its coverage of the event, *The New York Times* commented, "The tournament was splendidly managed by the Baltusrol Golf Club, and the large crowds during the week have been entertained with comfort to all." This marked the beginning of Baltusrol's tradition.

# 1903 U.S. Open

*Stewart Gardner putting on the eighth green.*

## Anderson Captures His Second Open

*Baltusrol Hosts Its First*

At the turn of the century, the U. S. Open played second fiddle to the Amateur. The Amateur was a prestigious and gentlemanly affair. The trouble with the Open was just that—it was open to all comers. The professionals, a clan of hardy Scots with a handful of Englishmen thrown in, had dominated the Open since its inception in 1895. To the amateurs of the day, wealthy club members who wanted to fashion golf in their own image, the professionals looked like a "gang of ringers."

### An American Scot

Willie Anderson fit the pattern of the dour, bibulous Scottish professional. The son of the green keeper at North Berwick, he emigrated at age 14 and quickly established himself as a gifted player. In 1897, Willie was all of seventeen. He would have won his first Open at the Chicago GC if Joe Lloyd hadn't made an amazing three on the final hole, a brute of 465 yards, to beat him by a stroke. The next year, Anderson finished third at Myopia Hunt Club. In 1899, he was fourth at the Baltimore CC. In 1900, at Chicago GC, the year Harry Vardon won, he finished eleventh (Vardon's easy victory underscored the superiority of the top

British players over the American professionals). In 1901, at Myopia, Willie finally broke through, winning a playoff with Alex Smith, one of his good friends and drinking companions, after they had tied with scores of 331.

Willie Anderson had also been the pro at Baltusrol for about a year. He was hired by Louis Keller in 1898

mainly because he had been born in Scotland, and no self-respecting club then considered itself a real golf club unless it had a Scottish pro. What Keller may or may not have known was that Anderson had never hit a serious golf shot in Scotland. He had picked up the game in America.

### A Record Pace

In 1903, Willie Anderson came down to Baltusrol from the Appawamis Club in Rye, NY, to try for his second Open championship. In the opening round, he shot an Open record 73, and the rest of the field was chasing him. Anderson fired a 76 in the second round to finish the day with a total of 149 (the championship was played in two days, 36 holes per day), thus establishing new competitive records for both the 18 and 36 holes, and beating all previous records on the first day of any open championship, wherever played.

*Willie Anderson and Mr. Carnegie on the eighth green.*

### Aucterlonie's Mistake

The ninth hole was the scene of a major rule interpretation for the defending champion, Laurence Aucterlonie. (This hole essentially followed the same routing as the third of the Upper.) The hopes of the West depended on Aucterlonie who represented the Glenview Club in Illinois. But he was bothered a great deal by the gallery and more than once they had to be restrained for pressing too close and for loud talking. In the first round, Aucterlonie was the early leader with a 31 through eight holes, and should have finished the outward nine in 34, but his high cleek shot on the ninth imbedded in a soft place on the green. Aucterlonie thought he could lift and replace the ball, a privilege not granted by a recently instituted rule change. The scorer supported his opinion, but as he touched the ball his partner, "Nipper" Campbell, called out, "Dinna lift, mon; ye may be disqualified!" Aucterlonie at once withdrew his hand. The scorer then told him to play the imbedded ball and also another ball from the same place, and they would put it before the rules committee later. Aucterlonie got a four with the imbedded ball and a three with the extra one. Under the rules of the time, the committee could make only one ruling, which was that he should have played the imbedded ball without complaint. He was therefore penalized a stroke for having touched it. He finished the round with a 75, two shots behind Anderson. Without the penalty, Aucterlonie would have shared the first round lead with Anderson and the new 18 hole Open record of 73. In any event, Aucterlonie faded on the second day and finished the Open in seventh place.

### The Snowman

In the third round, Anderson shot a 76 and had a six shot lead heading into the last round. Setting out in the afternoon with 225, there were high hopes that Anderson would do 75 or better and tie or beat Harry Vardon's 300 at Prestwick or his own 299 in the Western Open at Euclid. He was on his way to a new record and an easy victory when he reached the par 3 ninth hole. Anderson heeled a brassey spoon into a clump of trees. Instead of playing safe, he tried to hit the ball onto the green through a narrow opening in the trees. The ball pitched high, hit a branch and bounded back

*Mr. Douglas and Willie Smith on the fourteenth green.*

*Alex Smith and Walter Travis at the first tee.*

to where he stood, lodging in some stones down the hillside. His next poke with a niblick did not dislodge the ball; it took him five shots to reach the green, and he finished the hole with an abysmal eight. Unshaken, Anderson pressed on, making par on the next two holes, but after a bogey on the twelfth, he learned that he had to finish in 38 to tie David Brown, who was in at 307. Thereafter Anderson played with extreme care, finishing in 38 and an 82 for the round. He had saved his bacon and made the 18-hole playoff.

### The Controversy

The night before the playoff heavy rains drenched the course, making it barely playable. Nevertheless, under the direction of the rules committee, USGA President G. Herbert Windeler ordered both contestants to began play at nearly 11 o'clock with heavy rain falling. David Brown, a contentious fellow who had won the 1886 British Open on his home course at Royal Mussel-burgh, played under protest. As reported by the New York Times, Brown declared that "It's na gowf, the water's sure to stop the roll o' the ball." Anderson won the front nine by two shots 40 to 42, but Brown fought back on the thirteenth and fourteenth holes picking up one shot on each and squaring the match. Anderson gained a shot on the fifteenth and sixteenth holes even after scoring a six and five, respectively. The two players halved the seventeenth and eighteenth holes with fours, and Anderson became the first two-time Open champion,

*Walter Travis and Alex Smith on the seventh green.*

*Runner-up David Brown.*

winning the cup, the medal and $200.

### An Unbeatable Record

Anderson's victory set in motion consecutive Open wins in 1904 and 1905, making him the only man to win three successive Opens. This record has stood for almost 90 years and may never be broken. Also, his record of four Open victories puts him in the company of Bobby Jones, Ben Hogan and Jack Nicklaus. In addition to his four Open titles, he also won the Western Open, a major event of the day, four times.

*The gallery watching the returns.*

Although he was esteemed, respected, and well liked by his fellow professionals, Anderson never enjoyed the respect or recognition he felt he was due. One of his friends reported hearing Anderson mutter, "They don't know me. They don't know me." He died in 1910, at the age of 32. It has always been thought that his early death was brought on by drink.

### Open Notes

As reported in *Golf*, a magazine of the time, "the course, putting greens included, was quite fit for a National Championship." The length of the course was 6,003 yards. As far as could be judged, the entire field of 91 players used the new rubber ball or Haskell, thus ending for good the debate on the superiority of the new ball over the gutty.

*Baltusrol Caddie*

113

# U.S. Amateur

In September 1904, Baltusrol held its third national championship—the U.S. Amateur. There were 54 holes at medal play to qualify for match play. Of the 144 entries, 128 players completed the first 18 hole medal play, with 64 qualifying to compete in the final 36 holes of medal play. The low medal honors went to H. Chandler Egan, who shot 80, 80, 82 for a three round total of 242. Egan was a handsome blonde lad of 20 from Chicago and a student at Harvard. He would go on to win the Amateur, defeating Fred Herreshoff, 8 and 6 in the final 36 hole match.

### A Record Field
The field was the largest assembled to date and included several notable players. Among them was A.W. Tillinghast, who would eventually become eternally linked to Baltusrol. Egan defeated Tillinghast 3 and 1 in the first round. There also was Jerome D. Travers of Upper Montclair Country Club, who would go on to win four National Amateur titles. Travers was eliminated in the first round by Dr. D.P. Fredricks from Oil City. And there was the great Walter Travis, an Australian born American from Garden City, a previous three-time winner of the U.S. Amateur (1900, 1901 and 1903) and

**H. Chandler Egan
Champion**

**F. Herreshoff
Runner-up**

*USGA Officials (Left to right) Daniel Chauncey, Alex Britton,
G. Herbert Windeler, S. Y. Heebner, W. Fellowes Morgan.*

runner-up in the 1902 U.S. Open. He was eliminated in the second round by G.A. Ormiston from Oakmont. Three other notable Oakmont players were in the field—the club's founder Henry C. Fownes shot 103; William C. Fownes shot 96; and C.B. Fownes shot 92 to win one of the two playoff spots for the 64 hole qualifying.

Baltusrol also was well represented with 11 players in the field. None of the Baltusrol players qualified for match play and only two made it past the first 18 holes. They were J. H. P. Wharton, and E.A. O'Connor, who each shot 90 in the opening round. Another Baltusrol player, Frank O. Reinhardt, the Inter-Collegiate Champion for that year, was expected to make the final 64, but he shot a 92 and was eliminated in a playoff for the last two spots. Another noted Baltusrol amateur, James A. Tyng, also shot 92 and lost in the playoff.

### East vs. West
In the final match, Herreshoff, the New Yorker, squared off against the Chicagoan Egan. The newspapers of the day played the story as a regional battle, Herreshoff against Egan, "The Westerner."

On September 10, 1904, The Daily Tribune commented, "A heavy dew had put the course in fine condition for the contest and (although) Egan had the advantage of about four years in age, Herreshoff, while almost seventeen, seemed the brawnier of the two."

Herreshoff got off to a fast start, winning two of the first three holes. However, Egan won eleven of the next fifteen holes, gaining an overwhelming nine-up morning advantage. In the afternoon round, the Daily Tribune said Herreshoff "appeared in better spirits and made an admirable rally." The nine-up advantage remained through 27 holes, and though the match was dormie, the New Yorker played the game for all he was worth. At the tenth green Herreshoff overcame a stymie, using his mashie to loft his ball over Egan's and into the hole for a three. With two perfect shots he won the eleventh, but the match was ended when Egan made a brilliant three at the twelfth.

### Egan's Legacy
H. Chandler Egan, whose first name was Henry, was one of the most impressive, popular, and enigmatic players in the early years of American golf. After graduating from Harvard in 1905, he successfully defended his title at the Chicago G. C., where he was also the runner-up in 1909. In 1911, for reasons known only to himself, he moved to Oregon to become a fruit farmer in a place that was 300 miles from the nearest golf course. Years later, he tried his hand at golf course design, laying out several notable courses in the Pacific Northwest, including the original at Eugene C. C. in Oregon and Indian

*Herreshoff approaching the eighth green.*

*Travis playing out of the twelfth bunker.*

*Ormiston driving to the fifteenth hole.*

*McBurney approaching seventeenth green.*

Canyon Golf Course in Spokane.

In 1929, twenty years after he had last played in the Amateur Championship, Egan decided to make a comeback in the Amateur held at Pebble Beach. He was then 45 but still able to defeat three nationally ranked younger players before bowing out in the semi-finals. Egan is also remembered for creating the magnificent eighteenth hole at Pebble Beach as part of a redesign prior to the 1929 Amateur.

Ironically, for a man who could take his golf or leave it, he caught pneumonia on a golf course seven years later and died within a week.

### Championship Notes
The Baltusrol course played to a length of 6,159 yards, and was generally considered to be a fine championship test. However, many players did voice criticism of the course. The common objection seemed to be that dry weather had made the soil too hard for proper golf and the rough was not the kind generally associated with the name. No doubt the cloud of dust that followed an iron shot gave some support to this contention. In some respects Baltusrol was easier than other first-class courses, principally because wild driving was not severely punished. Egan's success was proof of this, for he won the low medal with fine recoveries after a pulled or sliced ball.

*Travers and Captain Horne on the eighteenth green.*

*Semi-finalist D.P. Fredericks.*

*G. A. Ormiston.*

*Chandler Egan putting on the eighteenth green.*

*Douglas approaching the first green in the qualifying playoff.*

*Semi-finalist W.T. West.*

# 1911

# U.S. Women's Amateur

The seventeenth Women's Amateur Championship was played on the Old Course at Baltusrol from October 9–14. The field was exceptionally strong with players from the Pacific Coast, Canada, Chicago, St. Louis, Philadelphia, Boston and the metropolitan New York area. There were over 65 entries, including four from Baltusrol—Mrs. N. P. Rogers, Mrs. M.D. Patterson, Miss Maude K. Wetmore, and Mrs. W. Fellowes Morgan. Rogers, Patterson and Wetmore qualified for the match play round of 32, although each of them was defeated in the first round.

Mrs. Ronald H. Barlow, the Eastern Champion, won the qualifying medal with a fine score of 87. Miss Dorothy Campbell of Hamilton, Canada, the defending title holder, was next with 93. Miss Lillian Hyde had 95, while Miss Margaret Curtis required 96. Seven contestants had scores under 100, versus four in the prior Women's Amateur at Baltusrol in 1901.

### Power Hitter
Two of the longest hitting women players in the country found themselves pitted against each other in the final match—Miss Lillian B. Hyde and Miss Margaret Curtis. Miss Hyde clearly had the advantage in dis-

*Miss Lillian B. Hyde.*

*Mrs. Ronald Barlow.*

*A group around the eighteenth green.*

*Miss Eleanor Allen and Miss M.W. Phelps.*

*Miss Dorothy Campbell.*

tance; however, this was more than offset by indifferent putting which would be her downfall. Playing a steady, well-rounded game, Miss Curtis defeated Miss Hyde 5 and 3, and notched her second Amateur title. *The New York Daily Tribune* remarked, "It was another of the many illustrations of all around ability triumphing over brilliancy combined with mediocrity."

Throughout the match, Miss Curtis displayed a solid short game and made a number of crucial putts. By contrast, *The Daily Tribune* commented that "Miss Hyde's short game was sad. On something like seven greens the Bay Shore (New York) lady was guilty of taking at least three putts. Even with this deficiency in her short game, Miss Hyde thrilled the gallery with her prodigious length." Her drives consistently measured from 200 to 220 yards. This was impressive given the state of clubs and balls at that time.

Despite being outdriven, Miss Curtis managed a two-up lead after nine holes. Miss Hyde narrowed the deficit to two holes after the

twelfth hole but lost the next three and the match 5 and 3.

### The Curtis Legacy

Miss Curtis was one of the most formidable and influential figures in women's golf. She had she won the Amateur title in 1907 at Midlothian by besting the defending champion, her sister Harriot, in the final. This is the only time in which two sisters have met in the finals of a national championship. Miss Curtis would win again in 1912 at the Essex County Club, her home course near Boston.

All told, Miss Margaret, as she came to be known, played in 25 USGA Championships, her first coming in 1897, and her last in 1949, when she was 65.

Margaret and Harriot Curtis were also responsible for the creation of the Curtis Cup matches, which pit the finest women amateurs from the United States against those from Great Britain and Ireland.

### Championship Notes

One newspaper described the Baltusrol course as "not an easy one for women

golfers—the bunkering is both scientific and artistic. There are traps everywhere."

Interest in the day's play at Baltusrol did not cease with the final round of the championship. The Daily Tribune reported "with subsequent discussions at the luncheon table, attention was directed to the handicap mixed foursomes, which brought the 1911 Women's Championship to a close." Incidentally, this handicap tournament was won by Baltusrol's own Mrs. W. Fellowes Morgan with a net 83 (103 - 20).

# 1915

## U.S. Open

*The Amateur Travers Wins Open*

*Last Major on the Old Course*

*The new champion is carrried off on the gallery's shoulders.*

*Runner-up Tom McNamara.*

*Bob McDonald finished third.*

*Jim Barnes tied for fourth.*

*Louis Tellier tied for fourth.*

MAC DONALD SMITH, THE METROPOLITAN CHAMPION

TOM MAC NAMARA, WHO FINISHED SECOND

BIG JIM BARNES WHO PUT UP A GREAT FIGHT

"GIL" NICHOLLS A BIG FAVORITE.

"JERRY" TRAVERS THE WINNER

FRANCIS OUIMET WAS FIRST TO CONGRATULATE JERRY

BEN SAYERS OF SCOTLAND

MIKE BRADY OF BOSTON

LOUIS TELLIER AND HIS LONG DRIVER

FRED McLEOD AN EX-CHAMPION

ALEX SMITH WAS GLAD TO SEE "JERRY" WIN THE TITLE.

WALTER HAGEN, WHO LOST HIS CROWN

CHICK EVANS' SMILE AFTER HIS FIRST ROUND

J.A. DONALDSON WHO BROKE THE RECORD OF THE COURSE WITH A 70

H.B. Martin. BALTUSROL

After the great amateur Francis Ouimet won his stirring Open victory in 1913 against Ted Ray and Harry Vardon, another amateur victory seemed within the realm of possibility when the Open returned to Baltusrol in 1915.

### Travers' Record

The best amateur of the time was Jerome (Jerry) Travers of the Upper Montclair Country Club in Clifton, NJ. When Travers arrived at Baltusrol in 1915 he had won everything an amateur could be expected to win. He was a four time National Amateur champion, having won in 1907, 1908, 1912 and 1913. He won the New Jersey Amateur three times and the Metropolitan Amateur five times. He also had a penchant for Baltusrol's links, where he won the 1907 and 1913 New Jersey Amateur, finished second in the 1908 Metropolitan Amateur, and won the 1912 Metropolitan Amateur.

### A Last Minute Entry

Despite his impressive record Travers was not considered a favorite to win. He was known as a great match play player, but his medal play was subject to erratic spells. In fact, Travers almost did not compete in the Open. After the Open he wrote:

"I had no idea of playing until a few days beforehand. Business being dull and Baltusrol so very near home I decided to enter. What I hoped to do was to make a respectable showing, and if possible lead the amateurs, a position that would have fully satisfied me."

*Louis Tellier holing a putt on the eleventh while his playing partner, Walter Hagen, looks on.*

### A Chance to Win

To his own surprise, Travers played with exemplary steadiness, posting a total of 148 for the first day's play. Even though he was only two strokes behind the leaders, James M. Barnes of White Marsh Valley and Louis Tellier of neighboring Canoe Brook, Travers would later remark that "the idea had not yet entered my mind that an opportunity lay within my grasp." On the second day he shot a 73 in his opening round and led the field by a stroke with 18 holes left to play. For the first time Travers realized that he had a chance to win.

### The Historic Final

As a late starter in the fourth round, Travers had the advantage, or disadvantage, of knowing the score of the other leaders. Early in his round he heard that Barnes had played poorly going out and that Tellier had taken a nine at the seventh hole. He then thought, "If I could beat my partner Mike Brady, I would win."

At the tenth, or Island Hole, he was walking up to the tee when a friend told him that he had figured that if he came home in 39 he would win. Robert McDonald had come in with a total of 300 and no one else seemed likely to better this total.

Distrustful of his driver, Travers turned to his heavy driving iron on the tenth tee and promptly sliced out of bounds. His next effort was an equally wild hook, but a magnificent pitch from the rough to within a few feet of

the cup gave him an inspiring par. (In 1915, the penalty for out-of-bounds meant loss of distance only.) On the eleventh he pulled his drive and was able to sink another putt for a par. But on the easy to birdie twelfth, his approach went over the green and he missed a short putt for par.

Travers made par on the next two holes. Then on the 462 yard fifteenth, after he played his second shot, Travers was shocked to learn that Tom McNamara had come home in 36 and

*Walter Hagen, the 1914 Champion, teeing his ball at the twelfth.*

had posted a 298. He would now have to play the remaining four holes one under par to win. McNamara was a leading Boston pro who had been runner-up in two previous Opens, 1909 and 1912.

Knowing precisely what he had to do seemed to settle Travers. He was still some 35 yards from the pin, and he was able to knock his ball dead and make his birdie. Now he needed to get home in even par to win. Wisely, he left his wood in the bag, going to his driving iron on two of the last three holes. He made par on each, finishing the homeward nine in 37 for a four round total of 297, one stroke better than McNamara.

After holing out the final putt of a foot and a half, the gallery, which naturally was pulling for an amateur to win, carried the home town winner away on their shoulders.

### Open Notes

The honor of making the lowest 18 hole score during the championship and breaking George Low's course record of 71 went to Jimmy Donaldson, of Glen View, with a 70 in the final round. Donaldson, who finished the tournament at 308, went home with nothing but his record, however. Just before he left he made inquiries among his fellow professionals as to whether or not there was a prize for the best single round, and upon being assured that there was not he shouldered his bag of clubs with a sigh and left for Chicago.

This Open was heralded by the press and officials of the USGA as the best Open tournament ever, a sentiment that would be echoed again and again in future national championships to come at Baltusrol. Much of the credit was due to the dedication displayed by Baltusrol's officers, members and staff. John G. Anderson, a leading amateur player, wrote after the event that:

"It has been my privilege to attend almost all the Open Championships which have been held since 1905 and I may say frankly that at no other club has there been such fine control of the situation either in the club-house appointments, locker room service, or the care of the affairs on the links."

*The gallery follows Mr. Travers at the fifteenth hole.*

*The gallery surrounds the eighteenth green.*

*Jerry Travers holes the winning putt.*

# Jerry Travers playing the final holes on his way to the 1915 Open Crown

*Playing his tee shot to the short ninth hole.*

*Gallery on ten watch Travers recovery from the rough.*

*Holing his par putt on eleven.*

*Making the crucial birdie on fifteen.*

*Approaching the seventeenth green.*

*Approaching the eighteenth green over the deep bunker.*

*Gallery watches Travers winning putt.*

# 1926 U.S. Amateur

## Von Elm Dethrones Jones

## Lower Course Makes its Debut

The story of this championship was the heroic battle in the final round between Bobby Jones, a peerless champion, and George Von Elm, a contender who would not be denied.

Entering the tournament, Bobby Jones was the odds on favorite. He came to Baltusrol wearing three crowns—the British Open, the U.S. Open and the U.S. Amateur. In fact, Jones had won the last two Amateur Championships and was trying to secure a third straight and better the record of two straight shared with Jim Whigham (1896 and 1897), Walter Travis (1900 and 1901), H. Chandler Egan (1904 and 1905) and Jerome Travers (1907 and 1908 and again in 1912 and 1913).

### George Von Elm

There were only two or three players considered to have a shot at beating Jones. One of them was George Von Elm, a Californian who had won every amateur tournament of note west of the Mississippi. Von Elm had grown up in Utah and won that state's amateur title at 15. When he moved to Los Angeles, Von Elm elevated his game and took his place as one of the nation's leading amateurs, making a name for himself in the Walker Cup. However, against Bobby Jones, Von Elm had lost two previous encounters—the 1924 final at Merion by 9 and 8, and the semi-finals in 1925 at Oakmont by 7 and 6.

### Seeded from the Start

The 1926 Amateur seemed to be preordained. In a sense it had been pre-arranged, for this Amateur

*Von Elm and Jones before the contest.*

*Von Elm sinks what would be the winning putt on seventeen. Inset: USGA President Fownes. awards the new cup to Von Elm.*

marked the first time that the USGA seeded the qualifiers. The intent was to prevent the early elimination of the star players and match the best players in the later rounds. Jones was seeded first, Von Elm second.

### The Road to the Finals
Bobby Jones did not have a cakewalk to the finals. After earning the qualifying medal with a two round total of 143, he barely got by his namesake, Dick Jones, winning 1 up on the eighteenth. In his third match, he faced Chick Evans, the 1916 U.S. Open winner and two-time Amateur champion in 1916 and 1920. Never behind, Jones built up a 5-up margin and won 3 and 2. In the semi-finals, Jones faced Francis Ouimet, the 1913 U.S. Open and 1914 U.S. Amateur winner. The two titans battled closely in the morning round. Then Jones fired a 33 on the front nine in the afternoon and easily prevailed 5 and 4. In beating Ouimet, Jones headed into the final with all the momentum befitting a player of his status.

George Von Elm had a rocky start, shooting an 83 in the first round of the 36 hole qualifying and then squeaking by his first match, winning on the nineteenth hole against Ellsworth Augustus of Cleveland. He gained strength as he went, demolishing his opponents as he moved toward his showdown with Jones.

### The Final Battle
In the final, Jones was the overwhelming favorite of the gallery, but he was not facing a player short on experience or credentials. With 15,000 spectators in attendance, the match showcased two sharply different

*Von Elm concedes putt to Jones on eighteen during the morning round.*

*Von Elm teeing off on fifteen while Jones watches.*

talents. Although Jones was longer off the tee, Von Elm constantly hit closer approach shots—many times with long irons or woods.

The match was also a testimony to good sportsmanship. In the morning round on the seventeenth, Von Elm was a yard or more away, putting for a half, when the gallery began to stampede to the next tee without waiting for him to finish. Noting it, Bobby walked over and knocked George's ball away, conceding him the putt. The situation was reversed at the home hole. This time George returned the compliment, conceding a putt of similar length. Such generosity is rare, especially with the stakes so high.

After the morning 18, Von Elm stood one up. Bobby had a determined look as he came to the tee in the afternoon. He squared the match with a birdie on the first hole and stymied George on the third. But George holed a fifteen footer on the fourth and was never down again. Von Elm was one up at the turn even though Jones had played the front nine in 35, one under par versus Von Elm's 36, even par.

On the twenty-eighth hole (ten Lower) Jones outdrove Von Elm by 15 yards and it seemed likely that the match would go from 1 up to all square. Not quite. Uncharacteristically, Jones' second found a bunker, and Von Elm went 2 up.

The eleventh and twelfth holes were halved. Then on the tee of the risk-reward thirteenth, standing 2 down with 6 to go, Jones pressed for one of those long drives that might have turned the tide his way. Instead, he put it in the watery ditch. His lie was not that bad, but his second had a little fade and his ball kicked into a bunker.

This was the turning point of the match, as it cost Jones the hole putting him three down with five to go—difficult when facing the likes of Von Elm. The margin shrank to 2 when Von Elm missed a putt at the fourteenth, but Von Elm was determined. The battle ended on the seventeenth green when Bobby missed a putt by an inch that would have carried the match to the last hole. Straightening up Bobby shook George's hand saying, "I'm glad you won, George."

### Reflections
After his defeat, Bobby Jones remarked that Von Elm is "a fine sportsman, and one of the world's best golfers—he should go far in this game." And far he went. Von Elm

*The gallery watches the action on the famous fourth hole.*

*Jones downfall—in the ditch on thirteen.*

*Von Elm carried off the course on the gallery's shoulders.*

played in three Walker Cups, turned pro after the 1930 National Amateur and nearly won the 1931 U.S. Open at Inverness against professional Billy Burke. After four rounds Von Elm and Burke tied at 292. Incredibly, they finished the 36 hole playoff tied at 149. As weary as they were, they played another 36 holes and finally Burke prevailed by one stroke, 148 to 149.

For Bobby Jones the loss was a rare setback, for at this stage of his career Jones was almost unbeatable in major tournaments. In 1930 he won the Grand Slam – the Open and Amateur Championships of the United States and Great Britain – a feat which has not been matched, and in all likelihood never will.

*... I met George Von Elm for the third time in three amateur championships, and George was too much for me. I played as well as I could, and played very good golf; I was a single stroke over par for the 35 holes the match lasted; and I had the breaks on a couple of stymies. George did not have the luck. He simply outplayed me. It was coming to him. I had beaten him at Merion and at Oakmont, and Lord knows nobody is going to keep beating a golfer like George Von Elm. I wanted to make it three championships in a row, but it wasn't in the book. It was George's turn.*

Bobby Jones.

## Championship Notes

The 1926 Amateur marked the first time the new Havemeyer Trophy was awarded. The original trophy had been lost in the 1925 fire at Bobby Jones' home club, East Lake Country Club, in Atlanta. It was also the first time any Havemeyer trophy went home with a West Coast champion.

This Amateur was also the first national championship on the Lower Course. The course was barely four years old. For the championship, it measured some 6,750 yards and was considered by the contestants to be one of the most exacting championship tests they had ever played.

The galleries were the largest ever assembled for a golf championship. What better commentary on the growth of golf in America? From their inception in 1895, our National championships had grown from small gatherings, more like private parties, to the huge sporting spectacle that was witnessed at Baltusrol. The gallery was conservatively estimated to exceed 15,000 on the final day, far exceeding all previous Open and Amateur championships. Even the tremendous crowd that had gathered at Baltusrol to see Jerry Travers win the Open Championship was much smaller. This is quite remarkable since admission was free for the 1915 Open, while at this event spectators paid either $1.10 or $2.20 for tickets.

Once again, the Baltusrol membership showed what

*The galleries were the largest ever and they came well dressed.*

they could do in the way of staging a major championship. The results were a triumph of organization in a setting of rare natural beauty. As reported by P.C. Pulver, a leading golf writer of the time:

"The 1926 Amateur passed into history as one of the most successful championships ever played. The event wished upon Baltusrol was accepted by the latter in a spirit of good sportsmanship and it rose ably to the occasion, handling problems never before encountered and in the end, like the USGA, found itself thousands of dollars better off. And in conclusion it may be said that a championship in this country was never staged over a more testing course. Its architect, A.W. Tillinghast, was present throughout the tournament, and received the congratulations of many."

*Players had their badge numbers printed in the program and the caddies wore those numbers.*

*Thousands received reports of the tournament, but few knew from where the broadcast came.*

*Eustace Storey, well-known English player, shown in his rather unusual putting stance.*

*Bobbys' mother wishes her son good luck.*

*Jay Monroe, Tournament Chairman.*

# 1936 U.S. Open

*Surprise
Winner
Manero Sets
New Record*

*Upper Course
Makes its
Debut*

*Tony Manero.*

In 1936 the Upper Course was the scene of a most unpredictable Open in which two new Open records were set within 30 minutes. The "ghost champion" at Baltusrol in 1936 was Harry Cooper, the British-born but Texas-bred pro who had been dubbed "Lighthorse" because of the speed of his play. On the course he was tense and fidgety, a perfectionist of whom it could be said, "He never hit a shot he really liked." Plenty of other players would have been happy to have Cooper's game. In fact, his fellow pros had their own nickname for him, "Pipeline," because he was so unfailingly straight. In 1936, Cooper brought his best game to Baltusrol's Upper Course, hitting an amazing 49 of 54 greens in his first three rounds in route to a three-round Open record of 211.

### A Short-lived Record

For this Open the press was out in force, and the crowds were surging wildly across the course. There were no gallery ropes to restrain them. Until the final round, Cooper had handled the chaos and pressure with coolness. As he played the fourteenth hole, Cooper was told by another pro that all he had to do to win was finish standing up. Good news but Cooper bogeyed the hole. Then, at the par three fifteenth, the gallery blocked the route to the green, and Cooper – the man that liked to rush along – had to wait. He didn't wait long enough. He played away impatiently before the crowds were cleared; his ball hit a spectator and bounced into a bunker. Another bogey. Again at the eighteenth hole the crowd caused a delay, one of the most bizarre delays in the annals of golf —someone picked the pocket of Cooper's playing partner, Leslie Madison! There was milling, confusion, more waiting. When order was finally restored, Cooper, under-standably, three putted.

Cooper finished with a 73, for a total of 284, breaking the Open record by two strokes. However, his bogeys on fourteen, fifteen, and eighteen had spoiled what would have been a great round. It was hard for Cooper to fend off the congratulations showered on him as he walked to the locker room. Radio microphones were thrust in front of him, and reporters wanted to know how it felt to be champ. But he was not a happy man. "I haven't won this thing yet," Cooper answered cautiously.

### Manero's Charge

Suddenly the crowd of well-wishers began to evaporate when, almost impossible to believe, rumors filtered into the clubhouse about rela-

127

*Harry Cooper—King for twenty minutes.*

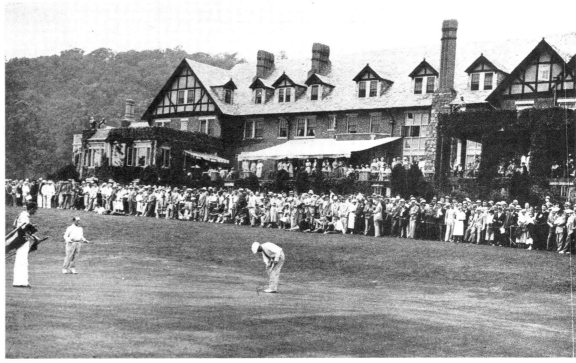

*Paul Runyan putting on the eighteenth green with "Wee Bobby" Cruickshank watching on the left.*

tively unknown Tony Manero, a dapper little ex-caddie from the Fairview Club in Elmsford, New York, and the current head pro of the Greensboro Club in North Carolina. It was at Baltusrol that most golf fans first heard of Tony Manero, even though he came to Baltusrol with several good wins under his belt, including championships at Glen Falls, Catalina, Pasadena and the Westchester Open.

Starting four strokes behind Cooper and playing with Gene Sarazen, Manero had gone out in 33. When word came over the grapevine that he had birdied the twelfth, the gallery poured back out to the course—just in time to see Manero roll in another birdie putt at the thirteenth. He was now five under par for the day.

Reporters who had begun to type their stories hailing Cooper as the successor to Sam Parks, Jr., the 1935 dark horse winner at Oakmont, reluctantly left their type-writers and plodded out to join the throngs now gathering around Manero at the fifteenth green. They saw a tense, nervous Manero trap his short iron and make a bogey four. Manero thought he had lost all chance for

the title then and there, but he was not bothered. He would later remark, "I didn't see much chance of catching up on Cooper anyway and I figured second prize money would be very welcome to Mrs. Manero." After the fifteenth, however, his focus was renewed by the encouragement he received from Gene Sarazen:

"I remember telling Gene Sarazen, who played with me, something about the tournament reminding me of the 1930 St. Paul Open, where I finished second to Cooper; and I must have been very chatty about it, because Gene told me to cut out the ancient history dope and play the hole I was on. Sarazen is the golf businessman, all right, and that advice of his, handed out in his plain-spoken way of 'do it or else' kept me right onto my knitting."

On the 439 yard sixteenth, reporters watched expectantly, knowing a new lead would have to be written within minutes when Manero dropped a 12-footer

*Henry Picard on the first tee.*

*Horton Smith and Johnny Goodman on the first green.*

for a birdie three to go five under for the day. He then finished with two pars to win by two, scoring 67 for the round, 282 for the tour-

nament, two strokes better than Cooper, setting the second new Open record of the day.

Manero had done what

was needed, and his composure never wavered though his homeward march was disrupted more than once by the gallery. At the final hole, after Manero played his approach, the crowd stampeded to form a circle around the green, with the result that Sarazen actually lofted his final shot over their heads!

### Support or Advice?
During the last hour of play, Sarazen coaxed, calmed, and encouraged Manero. The two men were good friends. Manero acknowledged "that it was a break for me that I was paired with Sarazen because I have more or less built my game on his body action and imitated his concentration."

Some reporters, however, thought that Sarazen had gone too far in helping Manero, that he had given not just encouragement but advice, and they brought a formal complaint to the USGA. After an hour-long closed-door meeting, the announcement came: Manero's victory would stand.

Many people have said that Cooper had lost the championship. However, no one could minimize the spectacular last round heroics of Manero, who made up four shots with the lowest final round in the Open to date. Manero never again came close to winning an Open, although he won 13 other tournaments against the best players of the day.

### Open Notes
This Open brought concerns over continuing improvements in golf equipment, particularly the ball. During the Open, the USGA and the leading golf ball manufacturers met, and the

USGA voiced its opinion that it would be inadvisable to build any greater distance into the golf ball. We can assume this fell on deaf ears, with more improvements in the golf ball to come in later years!

There were numerous indications that this Open marked the return of the pre-Depression gala days. The galleries were enormous and the half-million words of press copy filed was a new high. From a financial perspective, this Open ranked as either second or third in the USGA records at that time.

The Upper Course also received the praise of most pros and onlookers. In particular, it was noted that no attempt was made to trick up the course, which had not been the case at recent Open venues. The sand in the bunkers was not ridged. The greens were not close-mowed or rolled. The cups were in fair spots. And the rough was just long enough to cause trouble, but not punishment.

*Tommy Armour takes a break.*

*Manero strides up the eighteenth fairway while Sarazen (right) chants encouragement.*

*Manero besieged after sinking his final putt.*

*USGA President Jackson presents the Open cup to Manero. His wife is in the center.*

129

*Bishop
Defeats Quick
on 37th Hole*
❧
*First Amateur
after
World War II*

# 1946 U.S. Amateur

**B**altusrol's Lower course was the scene of the 1946 U.S. Amateur, the first since 1941. The tournament had been suspended for four years during World War II. In a classic final round, Stanley E. (Ted) Bishop, the New England and Massachusetts State Amateur champion, defeated Smiley L. Quick, the U.S. Public Links champion from California.

### Ted Bishop

Since the Jones era, most of the game's best players had followed the path of Von Elm from the amateur ranks to the pros. Ted Bishop was an exception, a pro golfer for several years who had his amateur status reinstated by the USGA. He stood over six feet, was very slim and had a mild, gentle manner.

He also had a severe hearing problem that might have helped him win against Quick. His natural tendency was to hit the ball high, with a hook, but over time he learned to fade the ball. That controlled fade helped him at Baltusrol where he played his 3-wood off the tee with great accuracy, especially in the final.

### Smiley Quick

Smiley Quick entered the championship as the hot golfer. Along with the Public Links crown, he had tied with Bud Ward for low amateur in the U.S. Open. Throughout the championship, he displayed a putting mastery which was nothing short of sensational. The crowd during the final was pulling strongly for Smiley, who reportedly was tagged with his nickname because of his dour disposi-

tion. At one stage, according to Johnny Farrell, Quick demanded that newsreel cameras be stopped behind the fifth green, saying, "he (Bishop) can't hear them; he's deaf. But I can."

### The Final Confrontation

In the final match, Quick had the early lead going 2 up on Bishop after the first 18 holes. Bishop fought back to even the match after 27 holes. The match remained all square through 35 holes, after Bishop holed a 25-foot putt followed by a 10-footer by Quick.

Then something extraordinary happened on the last regulation green. The Rules official in charge of the match had taken enough of the gallery's blatantly partisan behavior. He halted the proceedings and announced, "if there's one further outburst in favor of

*Stanley (Ted) Bishop.*

Smiley L. Quick, I will forfeit the match in Bishop's favor."

Both players then missed their putts, sending the match into extra holes. On the 37th green Bishop won the match when he chipped up and sank a 4 foot putt while incredibly Quick missed from 2 and 1/2 feet.

*The gallery surrounds the eighteenth green while Bishop and Quick each miss putt to win.*

## Championship Notes

The field was replete with "name" amateurs, some with storied pasts and some future champions. There was Chick Evans, Jr., who had played in every U.S. Amateur since 1907—a span of 39 years. Evans had won the 1916 and 1920 Amateurs and been runner-up in three others along with winning the 1916 U.S. Open. Other noted players included John W. Fisher, the 1936 Amateur champion; Johnny Goodman, 1937 Amateur champion and the 1933 U.S. Open winner—the fifth and probably last amateur to capture the crown; Willie Turnesa, 1938 and 1948 Amateur champion; Bud Ward, 1939 and 1941 Amateur winner; and Dick Chapman, who won in 1940. Other players of note were Doug Ford and Frank Stranahan along with Robert H. (Skee) Riegel, who later won the 1947 Amateur, and Dick Mayer, who would win the 1957 Open.

Two of Baltusrol's own greats were also in the field—Max Marston, a former Baltusrol member and Baltusrol club champion in 1914, 1915 and 1916; he also won the U.S. Amateur in 1923 and was runner-up in 1936. The other was A.F. Kammer, Jr., who was Baltusrol club champion in 1930, 1936, and 1938. Kammer beat Cary Middlecoff in the quarterfinals but was eliminated in the semifinals by Smiley Quick.

*Skee Riegel waiting for Bob Babbish to put in first round. Riegel won 1 up on the eighteenth.*

*Bishop selects his weapon for the fourth hole.*

*Bishop on the fourth hole, a popular spot for the gallery.*

*The Havemeyer Trophy.*

131

# 1954

*Furgol
Wins Open
on Lower
But
Upper Plays
Decisive Role*

The 1954 U.S. Open highlighted what absolute dedication and sheer drive can do. The field was crammed with the greatest players in the game— defending champion Ben Hogan was shooting for a record fifth Open. Other greats included Sam Snead, Bobby Locke, Cary Middlecoff, Lloyd Mangrum, Julius Boros, Doug Ford, Jackie Burke, and Jimmy Demaret. But none were to win. Instead a lame-armed journeyman pro, who only shortly before had settled down as a club pro after ten years on the PGA Tour, would make Open history. He was Ed Furgol, who for three days was the greatest player in the world.

### Ed Furgol
Coming to Baltusrol in 1954, Ed Furgol was given no chance to win, but people took notice of him because of his "broken wing"—his left arm was permanently damaged in a fall from playground cross-bars when he was twelve years old. That arm was permanently bent and six inches shorter than his right. It was remarkable that he could play golf at all. At the time, Furgol was considered a good tournament player, but he only had one big tournament win under his belt—the Phoenix Open earlier that year. The best he had ever done in the

Open was finish fifth in 1946 and seventh the following year. There was one man, though, who believed the 37 year old broken-winged pro could win, and that man was Ed Furgol himself. He said:

"When I teed it up at Baltusrol in 1954, I was a club professional from Westwood Country Club in St. Louis who, among the "name" players on hand naturally had to be given little chance, if any. And yet, like some current unknown heading for Baltusrol, in my own mind I knew I had a chance. I had worked hard getting ready for the Open, hitting as many as 400 practice balls every evening after my teaching duties were ended. Also I had led the field in the sectional qualifying round. So it was that, on the day before the tournament opened, when someone in the grill room asked for peanuts I put a towel over my arm and served the peanuts as if I was a waiter. 'What are you so happy about?' one of my friends asked me. 'You'll know in a few days' I grinned. Then sportswriter Oscar Fraley approached me and asked 'Who do you like?' 'I like Ed Furgol to win,' I said dead-panned. 'Are you kidding?' he asked, looking at me as if I was slightly demented. 'Why should I be kidding?' I asked him, and he just shook his head and walked away in a kind of daze."

### The Lower Takes its Toll

Baltusrol's Lower Course had been strengthened for the 1954 Open by Robert Trent Jones. At 7,060 yards, it was the longest par 70 in Open history, and the course quickly took its toll. Slammin' Sam Snead had no trouble with the length, but the greens, with their tricky weaves and shimmers, gave him fits. Hogan, that relentless splitter of fairways, was spraying the ball all over the course. In the first round, the only player to break par was Billy Joe Patton, the powerful, ebullient amateur, who had come so close to nipping Snead and Hogan at the Masters. He shot a 69.

The lowest round of the tournament was shot by 1940 Amateur champion, Dick Chapman. He combined an ace on the 204-yard ninth with two chip in birdies for a 67, two strokes lower than any other round posted. All told, there were only seven sub par rounds during the tournament.

The leader at the halfway mark was 23-year-old Gene Littler, the reigning U.S. Amateur Champion, who had turned pro only a few weeks earlier. At 139, he was two strokes ahead of Hogan and Furgol.

### The Final Day

In the first round of the final day – the format of the Open still called for 36 holes on the last day of competition – Furgol surprised everyone with a steady 71 while the two champions, Hogan and Littler, drifted back with identical 76s. Furgol now led the championship after three rounds at 212. Numerous players were easily within striking distance, but even with all the pressure that goes with the final round, the Clayton,

*Gene Littler blasting from the trap on sixteen. He lost his one under par advantage on this hole.*

*Mayer teeing off on seventeen. At this point he was even with Furgol. Inset: Hagen and Barnes.*

Missouri native played steady golf as his competitors wilted. The men in closest pursuit were Dick Mayer, a slim, stylish, cocky golfer who kept the heat on throughout the final round, and Gene Littler.

Furgol played ironclad golf from tee to green. On the greens, however, he was shaky, missing at least eight birdie putts of less than 15 feet. Determined not to let his putting undermine his confidence, Furgol gave himself a stern talking-to as he made the turn. He received another mental lift as he walked off the eleventh green:

"Strange the thoughts which occur to you, because as I walked off the green I saw two of my idols in the rather small gallery. They were Walter Hagen and Jim Barnes and, I thought, if they were impressed enough to watch me I owed them my best shot, too. The mere fact they were there gave me another big lift."

On the 620 yard seventeenth, Furgol faded his drive to escape the bunkers on the left but caught the rough to the right behind the fifteenth tee. It was a bad lie in heavy grass; ahead of him were the Sahara cross bunkers that he needed to carry to avoid a sure bogey. Furgol then pulled off one of his most important shots of the tournament; he dug the ball out with a 4-iron, cleared the bunkers and hit a 5-iron to the green and made his par.

### The Upper Gets the Nod

Dead even with Mayer, and playing two groups behind him, Furgol went to the eighteenth and was stunned to find the group ahead waiting on the tee. The delay was caused by Mayer,

*Top and bottom: Furgol's famous escape to eighteen Upper.*

who had sliced his tee shot deep into the woods. Mayer had to play a second ball and made a double-bogey seven. As he watched his opponent come to grief on the finishing hole, Furgol paced up and down the tee, trying to keep his inner turmoil in check. Then after a wait of over 20 minutes, it was his turn to hit. After considering a 1-iron, he instead went with the driver. He would remark later that "as I swung my left side gave out, simply collapsing, and I watched helplessly as the ball sailed to the left, into the trees that separated the Lower from the Upper." When he reached the ball, Furgol saw at once that he had no play back to the fairway. His only out was in the other direction, onto the Upper Course. In fact, he remembered seeing Hogan make the same play during an earlier round. He decid-

ed to take Hogan's route, and played a crisp, decisive 8-iron that sailed cleanly through the trees onto the eighteenth fairway of the Upper. After a 7-iron to the front of the green, Furgol then hit a 5-iron chip that looked like it might go in but slid six feet past the hole.

### The Winning Putt

Now he faced a slick right-to-left putt and, as he lined it up, Cary Middlecoff said "Don't worry about it, Ed. A six will win it for you." Although Mayer was in the locker room with 286 and Furgol was putting for 284, what Cary didn't know was that Littler was still on the course and making a run that would bring him home in 285. But Furgol's balky putter came through and he sank the six footer.

That scrambling, zigzag par won the Open for Ed Furgol. He posted scores of 71-70-71-72 for a total of 284, one better than Littler, whose eight foot birdie putt to tie Furgol at the eighteenth somehow stayed out. In some ways Furgol was the most deserving golfer in Open annals, and his victory would go into the books as the biggest upset since Manero on the Upper in '36.

### Open Notes

Low amateur honors were won by Billy Joe Patton, from Morgantown, North Carolina, who finished with a 289 to tie for sixth. Upon being presented his medal as low amateur by USGA president Ike Grainger of Montclair, he sent a glow through the massed thousands when he declared, "Everyone up here in Yankee land has been so nice. I almost forgot my

Grandpappy fought at Gettysburg."

The USGA estimated a record gallery of 39,600 for the three days of the tournament. Millions more watched the event on national television for the first time. Oldtimers were there in droves. Walter Hagen held court on the balcony overlooking the eigh-teenth green. The Haig walked 15 holes with Hogan one day and nearly as many with Snead another day. Johnny McDermott, Open champion in 1911 and 1912 was there, as was Fred McLeod, 1908 Open title holder. And Chick Evans, the veteran amateur from Chicago, was playing.

*More than 250 members of the press covered the event.*

*Ed Furgol with Ben Hogan and USGA President Ike Grainger.*

*Ben Hogan lines up a putt on the fourth green .*

*Sam Snead hitting out of the rough.*

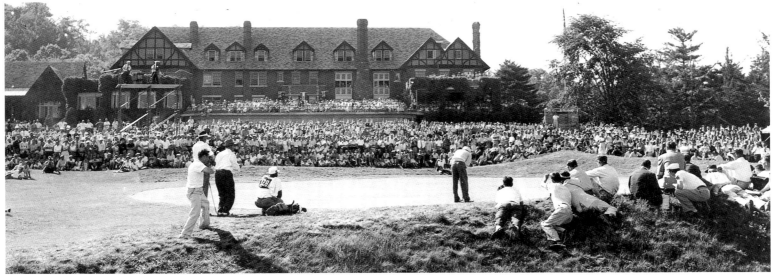

*Furgol prepares to stroke the winning putt.*

135

*Mickey Wright
Elevates
Women's Golf*

⚜

*Her Play on
Lower Simply
Marvelous*

# 1961
# U.S. Women's Open

The 1961 U.S. Women's Open showcased the talents of a sweet swinging Californian from San Diego—Mickey Wright. Coming into the championship, Wright had already won the Women's Open in 1958 and 1959, breaking tournament scoring records each time. This young woman, who had been national junior champion in 1952, was being hailed as the successor to the fabulous Babe Didrikson Zaharias, whose early death had left a large void in the golf world.

***The Lower Set Up Tough***
Coming to Baltusrol, Mickey's mind was not on the present Open, but the Open of the previous year. In 1960, she led going into the last round. "I played the double round with Betsy Rawls." she recalled, "I shot 82 and lost. Whenever something like that happened, it would just haunt me. That tournament haunted me longer than any other."

Playing at 6,372 yards, the Lower Course was extremely long for nearly all the players in the championship. With this length, narrow fairways and greens faster and tougher than normal, this Open was set up to Wright's advantage. During the championship, the entire field of 82 players

*Mickey Wright accepts the Open Cup from Mrs. Henri Prunaret, Chair of the USGA Women's Committee and USGA Vice President Clarence W. Benedict.*

produced only four rounds of par or better, and Wright had three of them!

After round one, Mickey and JoAnn Prentice were tied for the lead at even par 72. The length of the course intimidated most of the players, though it was no problem for Wright. For instance, on the par 5, 461 yard first hole, she was home with a drive and a 3-iron. In many cases, second shots with a 5-iron were enough for her on holes of around 400 yards. And on the 140 yard fourth over the water, she used a 7-iron,

while most of the women used 6-iron or stronger clubs.

At the halfway point, Prentice and Ruth Jessen shared the lead at 148. Mickey putted poorly in the second round and shot an 80. Facing a four stroke deficit, she had a restless night before Sunday's double round. She would later recount how she solved her putting problems that night:

"I was staying at a Howard Johnson's, and before they put in shag carpeting they used to have those blue and green rugs you could putt

on. At about 11 or 12 o'clock, I woke up and thought I'd figured out some little thing. I putted, putted, putted in the middle of the night. I went out to the course Sunday thinking that I had it solved. I had it! I think that gave me the momentum, because I just hit the ball so well and without any comparison, it was probably the best two rounds of striking the ball I ever had."

*Mickey Wright awaiting the presentation of the cup.*

*Mickey Wright stroked putting on the fourth green. Louise Suggs is on her left.*

### The Final Day

Mickey was paired with her good friend Betsy Rawls for the final. She put the ghosts of the previous Open to rest, firing a spectacular 69 in the morning round to take a two stroke lead over Rawls. She then added a solid 72 for a total of 293, finishing six strokes ahead of Rawls. Her play, throughout a long day of pressure, lifted women's golf to a new plateau. On hole after hole, swinging as fluidly as if she were on a practice tee, she laced one long drive after another down the narrow fairways. Her approaches to the green were pure, as she repeatedly put the ball within 20 feet of the pin. Noted golf historian, Herbert Warren Wind, gave this glowing assessment:

"En route to her 69, she had no fewer than six birdies, but in a way, her closing 72 was every bit as brilliant, for she was on every green except two in the regulation stroke. The difference was that she needed only twenty-eight putts in the morning and took two putts on every green in the afternoon. Had she been sinking her putts in the afternoon, she could easily have been around in 66. It is hard to think of a comparable exhibit of beautifully sustained golf over 36 holes in a national championship, unless it be Ben Hogan's last two rounds at Oakland Hills in the 1951 Open. These figures, eloquent as they are, do not begin to suggest the near perfection of Wright's play on the double-round. I believed that no other woman has ever played a long, exacting course quite as magnificently as Miss Wright did that last day at Baltusrol."

### Open Notes

Mickey considered the 1961 Open to be one of her most satisfying victories, particularly, because it was played on "such a marvelous test of golf." One of the most prolific winners on the LPGA tour, she won her fourth Women's Open in 1964. Betsy Rawls is the only other woman to win the Open four times.

Commenting on Mickey Wright's play at the closing presentation, Mr. Joseph C. Dey, Jr., USGA Executive Director, exclaimed, "It was tremendous!" The USGA also said the same about the attendance, which was the largest ever for a Women's U.S. Open. Almost 10,000 came out each day on Thursday, Friday and Saturday, an increase of 2,000 over the previous high.

137

# 1967 U.S. Open

## Nicklaus Finds White Fang

## Sets Open Record on Lower

When the Open rolled around in 1967, Jack Nicklaus honestly believed that any one of 30 players could win. At the head of his list was Arnold Palmer, who had already won two tournaments that year, and who would also be eager to wipe the slate clean after his collapse at Olympic in the 1966 Open.

### An Early Premonition

Jack may have had a feeling that something special was going to happen at Baltusrol, for he wrote in a preview to the Open:

"Whoever the winner is, given reasonably normal playing conditions, he will probably shoot somewhere around the Lower Course's 72-hole par of 280, which would be four strokes better than Ed Furgol's winning total in 1954.

And I have one last thought. There is a chance that in spite of its length—7,015 yards—someone could shoot a very, very low score at Baltusrol, well below what anyone might expect. If this happens, it won't be because the course is easy; it will be because it is in fine condition and completely fair. A record score would be a fitting compliment to Baltusrol. It is a superb 18 holes."

Off the record, Nicklaus

*Arnold Palmer congratulates Jack Nicklaus on winning the 1967 US Open Championship.*

had told a hometown friend, Bob Hoag, "If I win the Open, I'll break the record."

### White Fang

On Wednesday, Nicklaus fashioned an incredible 62 in a tune-up round in the company of Palmer that quieted some critics' carping about his allegedly crumbling game. Palmer, who lost $15 to Nicklaus in a friendly Nassau, didn't seem worried, "I can't imagine a round like that shaking anybody up."

Nicklaus also dismissed the tune-up round as nothing to get excited about,

though he sang the praises of a new putter acquired from his friend and rival, Deane Beman. Nicklaus had had nine one-putt greens, and he promptly dubbed the putter, a Bull's eye with its head painted white, "White Fang." He needled Palmer by reminding him playfully, "That's the lowest score I ever shot in the U.S., but I did shoot another 62 the day before the Australian Open of 1964 —which I won."

### Amateur Steals Show

On the first day of competition a long-hitting amateur named Marty Fleckman

stole the show. He shot a 67, two better than Palmer and Casper, and four better than Nicklaus. Jack was not unhappy with his 71, even though USGA watchdogs, who the year before at Olympic had warned him for slow play, now dogged his every step. He played with Bob Goalby and Mason Rudolph in 4 hours and 35 minutes and he announced on finishing, "We waited every single shot."

### Palmer vs. Nicklaus

On the second day, Palmer and Nicklaus asserted themselves. Palmer hit 17 greens to shoot a comfortable 68,

*In the final round Marty Fleckman loses his one shot advantage after pushing his tee shot into the trees on the first hole.*

and Nicklaus rolled in key putts on the way to his best Open scoring round ever, a 67. At the midpoint of the tournament, they had stuck their noses out in front.

It was probably too early to dismiss the golfers bunched behind them. Billy Casper, Deane Beman, and Don January were playing solid golf, and Fleckman had hung in with a 73. An unknown from El Paso, a fellow by the name of Lee Trevino, was breezing along nicely in his first Open, not the least bit daunted by his first taste of the big time (he would finish fifth).

It was also a memorable day for Rives McBee. Although he would exit after rounds of 76 and 72, he had the distinction of having six different caddies—one a newsman, one who worked on his grips in an ornery way, one who sassed back, one who fainted, and one the USGA ruled ineligible because he had caddied for another golfer in the morning.

To the gallery, this Open had defined itself as a head-to-head match, another chapter in the most dramat-ic rivalry of the decade. On Saturday, huge, boisterous throngs greeted Nicklaus and Palmer at the first tee, and charged through the rough to follow them the entire round. They were pulling for Arnie, but neither man played well. Palmer finished with a 73, Nicklaus with a 72. Mediocre golf, but they got off lightly, for the men behind them hadn't been able to make up much ground. Casper shot a 71 to tie them, and Fleckman, with a 69, had retaken the lead.

### The Final Duel
On the last day, Fleckman shot 80 and disappeared from contention in one of the all time great Open collapses. Nicklaus and Palmer, paired together, played just behind Casper and Fleckman. They saw those two falter on the opening holes, and – just for a moment – it looked as if Nicklaus might falter, too. He bogeyed the second hole and was lucky to lose only one shot, for Palmer let his birdie putt slither past the cup.

Over the next six holes the Open was decided. The key hole was the seventh, a monster par 4, 470-yard dog-leg right with bunkers threatening both the drive and the approach. After a good drive, Palmer came through with the kind of rousing shot that was his trademark, a low, laser-like 1-iron that was dead on line. Nicklaus saw it finish close to the hole and played his own approach, a higher, softer 3-iron that left him more than 20 feet away. At this point, Nicklaus was only one stroke ahead. If he missed and Palmer made it, which seemed likely, the match would be all even. It was just the kind of swing that could set off an inspirational player like Arnie.

By his own calculations, then, Nicklaus needed his long putt. He knocked it firmly into the back of the hole. The crowd was stunned, Palmer missed, and instead of being tied, Nicklaus was two strokes ahead.

### Jack's Perfect 1-Iron
Jack kept pouring it on, and when they reached the final hole the Golden Bear was four strokes ahead.

*Arnie reacts to missed putt.*

*Jack helps his putt in the hole.*

139

Knowing what had happened to Dick Mayer on this same hole in the 1954 Open, Nicklaus elected to hit a 1-iron off the tee. (In the third round, Nicklaus was home in two with the driver and a 4-iron.) He would remark later that "I had two things on my mind. I had a 4-shot lead, and the only way I could be tied was for Arnold to make three and me make seven."

Jack pushed the 1-iron shot into the right rough. It snuggled under a TV cable and two free drops later he hit a fat 8-iron leaving him 238 yards uphill to the green.

Jack then played one of the finest 1-iron shots in the history of the game. The ball bored through the air and nestled on the green approximately 22 feet from the pin, setting up a putt for a record Open score. With a thunderstorm looming overhead, Jack sank the putt, setting off a thunderclap and a downpour. That putt gave him a 65 for the final round, tying Arnie's Open record for the lowest final round, but more importantly, it set a new aggregate record total of 275, bettering Ben Hogan's previous mark of 276 set in 1948 at Riviera. Jack's play over the final round had been a spine-tingling display of power and precision. The pro-Palmer crowds had not just been silenced; they had been won over by golf of a rare high order. To this day, Nicklaus believes this 1-iron to be among his two or three best career shots.

Jack attributed much of his success on the greens to White Fang. His tee-to-green game had also been awesome throughout the week as he reached 61 greens in regulation.

*Gallery applauds Nicklaus as he approaches the eighteenth.*

### Trevino's Start
This Open also marked the advent of an assistant pro playing out of Horizon Hills golf course and driving range in El Paso, Texas—Lee Trevino. Lee finished fifth and won $6,000. He was the quintessential unknown player who every so often lends a special meaning to the Open. Trevino was not a tour "rabbit" in 1967. He had never played on the Tour. He was a guy from Texas with a strange swing and an appealing manner. With $6,000 in his pocket, Lee decided not go back to El Paso but to try the PGA Tour instead. A year later, he broke 70 in every round to win the Open at Oak Hill in Rochester, New York, and

*Lee Trevino's career started at Baltusrol.*

tie Nicklaus' 72-hole record of 275. Over his career he has been one of the most prolific winners on the PGA and Senior Tours, having won every major at least once, with the exception of the Masters. Looking back on his magnificent career prior to the 1980 Open, Trevino recalled fondly that "it all started at Baltusrol really. I'd never seen a place like that. Jeez, that clubhouse—I was nervous just about going inside. I didn't think I had any business in there... I got to feeling more comfortable one afternoon early in the week when I met a guy – he was married to one of the McGuire sisters – named Chuck Smith. He was sitting on the porch outside the clubhouse and asked me

if I wanted a beer. It was hot as hell and one thing I could do very well back then was drink beer. I said certainly. And I had a beer and one led to another. And he said, 'as long as you drink 'em, I buy 'em,' and when we finished up that week he said, 'I never saw a man who could consume as much beer as you can.' I was there seven days and I drank at least 10 to 12 a day with him."

### Beman's Record
Lee's 283 to tie for fifth in 1967 was a shot ahead of Deane Beman, who later became PGA Tour commissioner. Beman, the two-time U.S. Amateur Champion (1960 and 1963), had turned pro in the spring of 1967 at the relatively ripe old age of 29. The Open was only his second event as a professional. Beman, whose pinpoint accuracy made him a factor in a number of Opens, did something that does not happen very often. He played the first hole in a total of 12 strokes over the four rounds. The first hole is a par 4 of 465 yards. Beman was not a long driver, so he needed a wood for his second shot. On the first day Beman holed his second shot (about 230

*Deane Beman set a unique record on the first hole.*

yards) for an eagle two. In both the second and third rounds he made birdies. And in the fourth round he made a routine par 4.

### Hogan's Final Open
This Open marked the last Open appearance for Ben Hogan. Incidentally, his first Open appearance had been at Baltusrol in 1936. After the 54 year old Hogan shot 72-72-76-72 for 292 and thirty-forth money of $940, he insisted, "Hell can't be any hotter than this."

There was a poignant incident involving Hogan on Thursday. Play had been interrupted by a thunderstorm while Hogan was playing the eighteenth hole. A spectator, Norb Anderson of St. Paul, Minnesota, ducked under the ropes and shared his umbrella with Hogan. Anderson, who had slipped off from a business meeting to see his idol Hogan for the first time, was enchanted. Play resumed when the rain abated. Anderson moved to the side but stayed in the fairway as Hogan played the eighteenth. He then returned to Hogan's side, covered him with the umbrella and up the hill to the eighteenth

*The par 3 fourth was a favorite viewing spot for the gallery.*

green they went, Ben Hogan and a public links golfer from St. Paul.

### Open Notes
An amusing incident occurred on Monday, the first practice day. A spectator with a bag of clubs over his shoulder approached an entrance gate. Matt Glennon, one of the Baltusrol officials, inquired as to the man's purpose. The man said that he had been given a ticket to a practice day of a golf tournament and that he therefore had come to play his practice round. It said "Practice Day" right on his ticket.

The other big winner at

the Open was the Lower Course. Alfred Wright wrote in Sports Illustrated that the Open had gone off "without – for the first time in living memory – a cacophony of complaints about a U.S. Open layout." In a preview article on the Open, Jack Nicklaus wrote:

"Next week's U.S. Open is going to be different. It is being held on a course that is marvelously fair and yet exceptionally challenging. The Lower Course at Baltusrol is a pure test of golf. It is one of the finest courses we have played the Open on in years, and I think both the field and the spectators will enjoy it very

much."

Joseph C. Dey, Jr., the executive Director of the USGA, summed the Lower up as follows:

"The Lower Course at Baltusrol is always a Championship test, and this time it was absolutely prime —wonderful lies in close-cropped fairways, putting greens that were keen and firm and a thorough gauge of trueness of stroke. It tried practically every club in the bag in a round, even for one as long as Jack Nicklaus. Jack carried irons 1 through 9, a pitching wedge, a sand wedge, a putter, a driver and a three wood. Baltusrol's rough in some places was not as heavy as usual in the Open, due to a cold spring, but it was testing if one strayed. There were some wonderful individual rounds, and they only confirmed the truth that great and fair courses yield to great play."

The USGA also was delighted from another perspective. The four day estimated attendance of 88,414 was the largest on record, smashing the previous record of 65,262 set at Bellerive C. C. in 1965.

*This was Hogan's last appearance in the Open.*

*Mr. and Mrs. Nicklaus hold the massive trophy.*

# 1980

## U.S. Open

*Throughout the 70's, Jack Nicklaus went imperturbably about the business of building the most monumental record in golf. In 1979, however, he failed for the first time in his career to win a single tournament, finishing 71st on the money list. It appeared that, at age 40, he might at last be prepared to give way to the younger golfers who had already proven their ability to take on the Golden Bear.*

### A Record Day

The opening day at Baltusrol was one of the most explosive in the history of the Open. Heavy spring rains had softened the Lower Course; the greens were receptive, and they were putting at something less than breakneck speed. No fewer than 19 players broke par in that first round, and by early afternoon Tom Weiskopf had tied Johnny Miller's single-round Open record of 63 set at Oakmont.

Nicklaus, playing a few groups behind Weiskopf, was well aware that the Lower was there for the taking. After saving his par on the first hole, and making bogey at the second, he went on a spree of his own, making the turn in 32. Adding five more birdies on the back nine, he came to the par-5 eighteenth need-

*Jack Is Back!*

*Lower Course Scene of Epic Open*

ing one last birdie for 62. With a big drive, a 3-wood, and a deft pitch, Nicklaus left himself a little three-footer, and the new record seemed to be in the bag. Virtually everyone on the course was gathered around the eighteenth green to be in on this historic moment; no one had ever shot 62 in a major championship. Nicklaus missed. His putt started right and stayed right.

### Aoki Masters the Greens

As the tournament progressed, the Lower got tougher and the Open pressure mounted. On the following day, when Nicklaus might have frittered away strokes after such a tremendous opening round, he shot a respectable 71 contrasting with Weiskoph's 75. That was good enough for a two-day total of 134, an Open record, and he was two strokes ahead of Isao Aoki, of Japan, the nearest pursuer.

Aoki moved into position to challenge Nicklaus, who was his playing partner all four days, with only 23 putts and a second straight 68. Aoki had one-putted eight of the last nine greens, and for 36 holes had only 50 putts. Weiskopf had 71 putts for the same 36 holes.

At the age of 37, Aoki was a savvy campaigner, an unorthodox swinger – a puncher, really – who made up for the defects of his long game with wizardry around the greens. His style of putting was uniquely his own, a sweeping, slicing motion with his hands held low and the toe of the putter pointing skyward. His style sometimes inspired snickers, but they quickly died when the ball dropped into the hole from anywhere

*Lon Hinkle.*

on the green.

So, going into the third round, Aoki and Nicklaus, threatened to run away with the championship. Although Aoki's putting slipped on the third day, as he used 31 puts, he still shot a 68 to Nicklaus 70, and they shared the lead, one stroke ahead of Lon Hinkle. Their three-round total of 204 was yet another record. The Open seemed to belong to one of them, although Tom Watson had come alive in the third round with five birdies in a stretch of six holes, shooting a 67 to get within two.

### Duel to the Finish
In the final round, Nicklaus and Aoki gradually pulled away from their challengers. The contest quickly became a match-play situation. Nicklaus boomed one long tee shot after another and deftly landed his approach shots close to the flag. For many players, being out driven by nearly 20 to 30 yards on each hole can be unnerving, but Aoki repeatedly holed putts to stay close.

Nicklaus, out in 35, had a two-stroke lead at the turn, and then both men hit their

*Tom Weiskopf and Jack Nicklaus.*

*Nicklaus and Aoki on the eighteenth green.*

stride. Nicklaus stuck a 7-iron close to the pin at the tenth hole for a sure birdie. Aoki answered by chipping in for his birdie. The game was on, and though Nicklaus hit one flawless shot after another, he couldn't shake his opponent.

Nicklaus' final nine holes were as close to perfection

as we are likely to see in a lifetime. Any spectator could sense that these two veterans were pouring absolutely everything they had - all their experience, resolution, and pride - into this championship.

The turning point came at the seventeenth hole, at 630 yards the longest par five on

any Open course. Aoki played it ideally, pitching his third shot to five feet. Nicklaus, still with two strokes in hand, played a safer pitch, and found himself looking at a 20-foot birdie putt to match what would certainly be an Aoki birdie. Jack knew that his putt was crucial, and when it tumbled into the hole, the enormous crowd following the two players roared wildly. Jack's face broke into the jubilant grin that would stand as the lasting image of his sweetest Open victory.

Epic. That's the only way to describe the last hole of this championship. As Nicklaus and Aoki walked to the eighteenth green the tremendous gallery broke the ropes and followed the pair to the green. Someone in the gallery started a chant, "Jack is Back." The chant quickly grew, sweeping through the gallery, reverberating against the stately clubhouse and booming across Baltusrol Mountain—Jack is Back! Jack is Back! Jack is Back! For those in the gallery, the moment was choked with emotion and joy.

### The Record Falls Twice
Yet this Open was not quite over. To have any chance at all, Aoki would need an eagle 3 at the home hole—and he nearly got it. His pitch missed the hole by inches. Nicklaus, too, pitched close, and closed out the tournament with a last birdie. As spectators surged forward, Nicklaus raised his hand, palm toward the gallery, stopping the massive crowd in their tracks—Aoki had still to putt out. It was a wonderfully thoughtful, sportsmanlike gesture. Nicklaus had finished his tournament, set-

ting a new Open record of 272; but before savoring his victory, he wanted to make sure that his opponent had a chance to finish and break the old Open record of 275. Aoki made the birdie for 274, and he too had broken the old record. Then the crowd let loose again, roaring their approval, and chanting, Jack! Jack! Jack!

In case anyone needed to have the significance of the moment spelled out, the big scoreboard carried a message: JACK IS BACK. It hardly seemed that he had been away.

### Open Notes

This was Jack's fourth Open victory, matching the record shared by Ben Hogan, Bobby Jones, and Willie Anderson. When asked how he felt about this victory, Nicklaus replied, "You'll never know how sweet it is!" For the four rounds, Jack excelled from tee-to-green by hitting 59 greens in regulation. Aoki had come two shots short with the finest putting exhibition in the history of the Open—a total of only 112 putts.

Tom Watson, who scored a hole-in-one on the fourth hole during the championship, finished in a tie for fourth with Lon Hinkle and Keith Fergus at 276—a score that would have won or at least gained a playoff in all but two of the previous 79 Opens.

The 1980 Open was also a tremendous financial success for the USGA, reflecting the new age of commercialism in professional golf. This Open marked the first large scale marketing of corporate tents; over 20 were sold. The galleries were among the largest, if not the largest, in the history of the Open. Over 102,000

spectators attended over the four tournament days. This does not include those that attended the practice rounds over the first three days. There were over 29,000 for the third round alone.

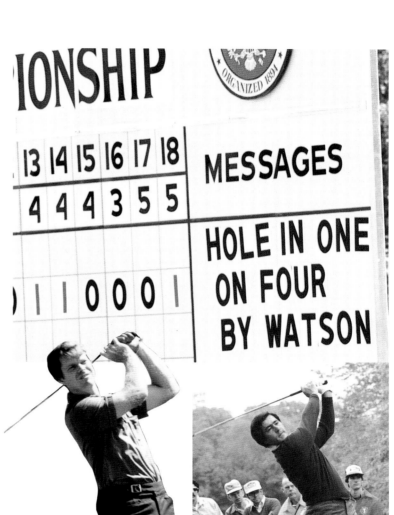

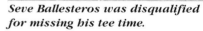

*Keith Fergus.*

*Arnie's escort.*

*Larry Nelson, Johnny Miller and Ed Snead.*

*Seve Ballesteros was disqualified for missing his tee time.*

*Ray Floyd makes his putt.*

# 1985 U.S. Women's Open

*Kathy Baker accepts the Open trophy from Judy Bell.*

*Judy Clark*

Twenty-five years after Mickey Wright's superlative victory, the women returned to Baltusrol for their 40th Open Championship. Long before play began on the Upper Course, Nancy Lopez – one of the most popular, charismatic, and successful women players in the history of the game – was clearly everyone's favorite to win. Lopez was then at the peak of her powers, with 32 tournament victories, though she had not yet succeeded in winning the Open.

Other name players in the field included Betsy King, Amy Alcott, and three-time Open champion Hollis Stacy. Over shadowed and nearly overlooked was Kathy Baker, a 24-year old from Clover, South Carolina, who had established solid amateur credentials. In 1982 she won the NCAA Women's Championship, and later that year she represented the United States in both the Curtis Cup and Women's World Amateur Team Championship. Obviously, she could play the game—but no one expected her to hold up under the pressure of a national championship.

### Lopez Favored to Win

Most of the media attention focused on Nancy Lopez, the darling of the press and

146

gallaries. When she shot a 70 in the first round, and shared the lead with Baker and Janet Anderson, she completely justified the expectation that this was to be her Open. With another 70 in the second round, she was the undisputed leader at the halfway mark. She was playing steady golf, and added a 71 in the third round, for a three-round total of 211.

However, she had lost the lead by one to Kathy Baker, who birdied the final hole to finish with a 68 and a total of 210. Judy Clark also was one behind Baker, having vaulted into contention with a blistering 65, matching the single round Open scoring record set by Sally Little in 1978 at the Indianapolis CC. Lurking two stokes back were Vicki Alvarez and Janet Coles, who each shot 71.

### The Final Day
With the five leaders grouped within two strokes, the stage was set for the finale. Although public sen-timent favored Lopez, she dashed her fans' hopes early, starting out weakly en route to a 77, a score that would only be good enough for fourth place.

As she faded, it became clear that the women playing the best golf were Kathy Baker and Judy Clark. Paired together in the final round, Baker and Clark dueled for the title as the rest of the field fell behind. As they began the back nine, Baker was in charge with a two-stroke lead. Clark gained a stroke when Baker bogeyed the fourteenth, but Baker rallied with a birdie at the fifteenth. The decisive hole proved to be the sixteenth, where Baker got a miraculous bounce. She fully understood its significance:

"It was one of those little things—just the right bounce at the right time—that often wins a champi-onship. The sixteenth has a little dip right in front and if you don't carry that, your ball will roll down to the front, or off the front of the green. I missed my shot a little, but my ball happened to bounce just right and settled near the hole. Judy hit the same kind of shot and she got the type of bounce you expect. My ball shouldn't have, but did, bounce forward."

Baker made her birdie and parred the last two holes for a two under-par 70—one of only four sub-par rounds on the final day. Baker's four round score of 280 eight under par was a marvelous feat over the demanding par 72 Upper Course. For the tournament, only Baker, Clark and Vicki Alvarez finished under par. The Upper had proved its mettle as a championship course, rewarding only excellent play.

### Open Notes
This was Baker's first pro win, making the tenth time the Women's Open was a player's first win. Baker's quiet, calm demeanor throughout the tournament was testimony to her religious beliefs and her inner strength. When asked after the championship if winning the Open had been a lifetime dream, Baker remarked philosophically, "It is a thrill, but I don't need to win the Open to be happy."

By retaining her composure and refusing to falter even though the large crowds (47,300 fans were on hand during the four days) preferred Lopez, Kathy Baker clearly deserved her victory and a place on Baltusrol's roster of dark horse champions.

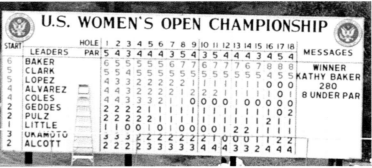

**U.S. WOMEN'S OPEN CHAMPIONSHIP**

| START | LEADERS | PAR | 1 | 2 | 3 | 4 | 5 | 6 | 7 | 8 | 9 | 10 | 11 | 12 | 13 | 14 | 15 | 16 | 17 | 18 | MESSAGES |
|---|---|---|---|---|---|---|---|---|---|---|---|---|---|---|---|---|---|---|---|---|---|
| | | 5 | 4 | 3 | 4 | 4 | 4 | 3 | 5 | 4 | 3 | 5 | 4 | 4 | 4 | 3 | 4 | 5 | 4 | |
| 6 | BAKER | 6 | 5 | 5 | 5 | 5 | 5 | 6 | 7 | 7 | | 6 | 7 | 7 | 7 | 6 | 7 | 8 | 8 | 8 | WINNER KATHY BAKER 280 8 UNDER PAR |
| 5 | CLARK | 5 | 5 | 4 | 5 | 5 | 5 | 5 | 5 | 5 | | 5 | 5 | 5 | 5 | 4 | 5 | 5 | | | |
| 5 | LOPEZ | 4 | 3 | 3 | 2 | 2 | 2 | 2 | 1 | | 1 | 1 | 1 | 1 | 1 | | 0 | 0 | 0 | | |
| 4 | ALVAREZ | 4 | 4 | 3 | 2 | 2 | 2 | 1 | 2 | | 2 | 2 | 1 | 1 | 1 | 1 | 0 | 1 | | | |
| 4 | COLES | 4 | 4 | 3 | 3 | 2 | 1 | | 0 | 0 | 0 | 0 | 0 | 0 | 0 | 0 | 0 | 1 | | | |
| 2 | GEDDES | 2 | 2 | 2 | 1 | 1 | 1 | 1 | 1 | | 1 | 1 | 1 | 1 | 1 | 1 | 0 | 2 | | | |
| 2 | PULZ | 2 | 2 | 2 | 2 | 1 | 1 | 1 | 1 | | 1 | 1 | 1 | 1 | 1 | 2 | 1 | 1 | | | |
| 1 | LITTLE | 1 | 1 | 0 | 0 | 1 | 0 | 1 | 0 | 0 | 0 | 0 | 1 | 2 | 2 | 1 | 1 | | | | |
| 3 | OKAMOTO | 3 | 3 | 3 | 2 | 2 | 2 | 2 | 2 | 2 | T | 0 | 0 | 1 | 2 | 2 | | | | | |
| 2 | ALCOTT | 2 | 2 | 2 | 3 | 3 | 3 | 3 | 3 | 3 | 4 | 4 | 3 | 3 | 2 | 4 | 4 | 4 | | | |

*Leader board with final results.*

*Janet Coles.*

*Vicki Alvarez.*

*Ayako Okamoto.*

*Danielle Ammaccapane, top, tied for Low Amateur with Kathleen McCarthy bottom.*

*Clockwise: Amy Alcott,Sally Little and Nancy Lopez.*

# 1993 U.S. Open

When the 93rd U.S. Open came to Baltusrol, no one was sure what to expect. There were no clear favorites. The hero of prior Opens, Jack Nicklaus only arrived at Baltusrol through a special exemption from the USGA, as did Tom Watson. Another great Open player, Lee Trevino wasn't in the field at all.

Most of the attention focused on the the foreign contingent, led by Englishman Nick Faldo, Australia's Greg Norman, Germany's Bernhard Langer, and Zimbabwe's Nick Price. America's favorites included Payne Stewart, Fred Couples, Paul Azinger and defending champion Tom Kite.

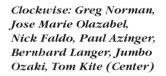

*Clockwise: Greg Norman, Jose Marie Olazabel, Nick Faldo, Paul Azinger, Bernhard Langer, Jumbo Ozaki, Tom Kite (Center)*

### Players Love the Lower

The USGA had set up the Lower course in a way to put the driver back in the players hands, a club that had been missing in recent Opens. The pros were ecstatic. Corey Pavin, a player not noted for his length to begin with, remarked, "In past Opens you might as well have left your driver in the trunk of the car." Mark McCumber said, "I'll use driver all week. They've set it up so you can drive the golf ball. They've put the club back in play." The players also raved about how most of the Tillinghast greens were open in the front,

149

allowing for a run-up shot; rather than the common forced carry that marks the modern penal style of green architecture generally found on the Tour. This provided the player several options to reach the green —and returned shot making to the Open. The overall course condition and set up was why not one disparaging word about the Lower course was heard.

The landing areas in most fairways were 35 yards across, although a few of the short par 4's did narrow to 28 yards. An unseasonably dry and hot spring had left the rough sparse in many areas. The USGA prescribes a half shot as the penalty for a drive in the rough. The actual penalty was calculated to be a third of a shot, on average. Even though the rough was thin, hot and humid weather throughout the week left the Lower Course playing hard and fast, the way the USGA likes it.

### The First Round
In the first round, the players took advantage of the perfect playing conditions. By the end of the day, the average score was 72.282, smashing the prior record low of 73.402 set at Oak Hill in Rochester. Three unlikely players, Scott Hoch, Joey Sindelar and Craig Parry each shot 4-under par 66's for a share of the lead. After his round, Joey Sindelar said "The scoring conditions were as good as you could have for a U.S. Open Championship and that has to do with the course setup and the weather. For a classic, tough, great test of golf on a nice golf day, this is as good as it gets."

With little fanfare, a 28 year old, curly haired blond

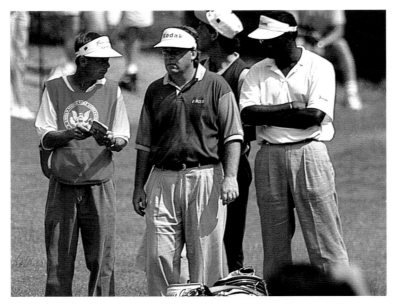

*Joey Sindelar, the first round leader, and Vijay Singh.*

from Kissimee, Florida posted a 67, one shot off the pace. His name was Lee Janzen. Lee had joined the PGA Tour in the fall of 1989 and made considerable progress. He came to Baltusrol a two-time winner on the Tour, having won the 1992 Northern Telecom and the 1993 Phoenix Open. His ability to play well on classic courses was already known after he shot a course record 61 at Colonial during the Southwestern Bell tournament, and finished third at Westchester the week before the Open. After his first round he said,

*Sixteen year old Ted Oh.*

"Last week was similar to U.S. Open conditions, with high rough and hard, fast greens. I don't want to say that because of last week that I have to play well here, but there could be something to that."

A lot of attention in the first round was also focused on a 16 year old from California named Ted Oh. He was the youngest to qualify for the Open since Tyrell Garth, Jr. did it at 14 in 1941. Despite a triple bogey seven on the tenth hole, Oh shot a respectable 76. With a 79 in the second round, he missed the cut.

### Janzen Sets the Pace
In the second round, Lee Janzen found himself in the lead on the eighteenth hole, putting for birdie and in the enviable position of deciding the cut line and the fate of several notable players. The cut was limited to the low 60 players or those within ten shots of the lead. Janzen made his birdie for another 67 and a total of 134. This tied the 36 hole Open record set by Jack Nicklaus at Baltusrol thirteen years before. That birdie also knocked out two

*Nick Price shot a 66 along with Watson and Stewart in the second round.*

big name players—defending Open champion Tom Kite, and Masters champion Bernhard Langer. Joey Sindelar, who had ballooned to a 79 in the second round, was also eliminated, marking the first time a first round leader had failed to make the cut. Despite Janzen's record tying pace, a record 88 players made the cut. This would cost the USGA an additional $143,964 in prize money, for the additional 28 spots.

Janzen still had a name field in close pursuit. Tom Watson and Payne Stewart each shot 66 and trailed by two. Three shots back were Nick Price and Corey Pavin.

### The Unreachable Falls
Something extraordinary also occurred in the second round. The 630 yard seventeenth, the longest hole in Open competition, was reached in two for the first time ever. The man was

150

*John Daly winds up on seventeenth tee. Inset: Daly is greeted with a standing ovation on the green.*

John Daly. At the seventeenth tee, the spectators in the gallery and the marshals shouted "You're going to do it!" John replied "I'm going to try." He wound up and boomed his drive 325 yards down the left side of the fairway leaving him a perfect angle and 290 yards uphill to the green. He took his 1-iron and swung as hard as he could, nearly coming out of his shoes and falling forward as he hit the ball. The ball rocketed towards the green, landing hot in the rough, bounding through a bunker, and rolling at last onto the green. The crowd erupted. As described by Dave Anderson of the New York Times, the sound was "like the roars that once responded to a moonshot home run by Mickey Mantle or Reggie Jackson."

### The Field Fades
In the third round, Janzen, paired with Tom Watson, shot a 69, finishing 7-under and tying the 54-hole Open record at 203. But the Lower Course and the subtle greens were taking their toll, as the rest of the field fell behind. Watson missed a number of short putts and fell from contention with a 73. When the day was over, only four players were in realistic striking distance. Nick Price was 3-under par and three behind, and Paul Azinger and David Edwards were five behind at 2-under par. The fourth player, Payne Stewart, broke from the pack with a 68, finishing one behind Janzen, and setting up one of the greatest duels in Open history.

### A Classic Duel
The championship had boiled down to Janzen and Stewart, paired together for the final round. Neither

*Payne Stewart and Lee Janzen battled during the final round.*

player was solid from tee-to-green in the last round, hitting only six of 14 fairways, but the sparse rough wasn't making them pay for their mistakes. Janzen made the turn with Stewart still one behind.

On the tenth, Janzen faltered and pushed his drive into the right rough. He was blocked out by a stand of large oak trees. When he tried to carry the trees with a 5-iron, the ball flew low out of the rough and went dead center into the crown of one of the largest oak trees. Janzen reacted with doom on his face. "I'm

thinking, 'Well, that's probably going to bounce deeper into the trees and I'm going to make double bogey."

Miraculously, the ball sailed through unscathed and bounced onto the green. Janzen made his par, which probably jolted Stewart, who was looking at a two shot swing his way.

The duel continued. On the twelfth, Janzen missed a five footer and the Open was tied. He birdied the fourteenth to regain a one shot lead. Stewart tried to counter on the fifteenth, but his birdie putt barely missed. Then on the par 3 sixteenth, Janzen made the shot of the Open. After missing the green, he faced a slick downhill chip on the short side of the hole. It was a shot reminiscent of Tom Watson at Pebble Beach, and like Watson, Janzen holed the chip. He now had a two shot lead with two holes to play.

### Two Records Are Tied
The tournament was not over, though. Janzen got another break on the seventeenth; he pushed his drive into a large linden tree which kicked the ball back into the fairway. On the par 5 eighteenth, Janzen again pushed his drive, finding the right rough. Stewart, still two behind, needed to make an eagle for a chance for the title. His drive found the fairway, and he went for the green in two with a 3-iron. His shot was almost there, but the ball hit the bank in front of the green and bounced back into the front bunker.

Janzen knew a par would probably win the title. From his lie, he had no chance of reaching the green and a good chance of dumping the ball in the

*The 1992 U.S. Amateur Champion Justin Leonard.*

*Fred Couples and Ian Baker-Fitch leave the first tee.*

with Lee and our mutual friend, Rocco Mediate. That was just two weeks before the Open.

In any event I was not surprised, and I was very pleased, when Lee played so well at Baltusrol and that he held the lead in the closing rounds against some very strong opponents."

Once again the galleries were one of the largest in Open history over the seven day event. In addition, 46 corporate tents were sold, illuminating the corporate popularity of professional golf.

This Open was conducted under the USGA's revised contract with the USGA and the host club. Under this contract, the USGA assumed much more of the operational and financial responsibility for the tournament, representing a bold experiment for the USGA.

At the award ceremony on the eighteenth green, Mr. Stuart Bloch, President of the USGA, praised the support of the Baltusrol members and its tournament committees, the condition of the golf course, the conduct of the tournament, and the financial results. He concluded by saying, "this Open was the most successful yet!" A fitting close to a historic tournament.

creek. He played safe with a sand wedge, then hit a 4-iron eight feet from the hole. The Open was his. After the fact, Stewart pitched to the green and made his birdie. Then Janzen calmly holed his eight foot birdie for a 69. That birdie tied both Jack Nicklaus' four-round Open record of 272 and Lee Trevino's 1968 Open record of four consecutive rounds in the 60's.

### Open Notes
Janzen was modest in his analysis of his achievement. "Some of the things that happened out there, I felt

like somehow I was just destined, because I got some of the greatest breaks you could ever get," he said. "There's a lot of guys who I feel have better games than I do, and for me to come through like this, it might be the over achievement of my life."

After the Open, Arnold Palmer wrote:

"I was impressed by Lee Janzen long before he won the U.S. Open – and I might even claim a little credit for his victory. Perhaps Jack Nicklaus and I tuned him up a bit when we played a practice round prior to this year's Memorial tournament

*Lee Janzen proudly holds up the championship trophy.*
*Inset: His chip shot on sixteen won the tournament.*

153

# Other Tournaments at Baltusrol

*Marc Michael.*

### 1903 New Jersey Amateur

Marc Michael of Yountakah won the championship over N.B. Cole of the Englewood G. C. James Tyng of Baltusrol won the second cup. The medal score was won by F. Murray Olyphant, the young Princetonian, with a 79.

*A*mateur and professional golf at all levels has been well served by Baltusrol. Over its 100 year history, Baltusrol has hosted dozens of regional championships of note. Most of them are listed below:

The 1900 East Jersey League
The 1902 and 1909 Griscom Cup
Two Metropolitan Open Championships (1908 & 1988)
Two Metropolitan Amateurs (1908 & 1912)
The 1914 Lesley Cup Matches
The 1917 PGA War Memorial Tournament
Six New Jersey State Amateurs
(1903, 1907, 1913, 1925, 1941 & 1979)
The 1983 New Jersey State Open
The 1935 New Jersey PGA
The 1930 New Jersey Junior Championship
Five Women's Metropolitan Championships
(1905, 1916, 1925, 1964 & 1983)
Five Women's New Jersey Championships
(1949, 1953, 1958, 1973, & 1983)
Twenty Baltusrol Invitationals (1975 to present)

Several Baltusrol members distinguished themselves in many of these events, particularly in the early years. Their names were James Tyng, Max Behr, Wallace Sinclair, C. G. Sullivan, Max Marston, Augie Kammer and E.M. Wild. The highlights of many of these events follow.

### 1907 New Jersey Amateur

Jerry Travers of Montclair beat Max Behr of Baltusrol and Morris County 7 & 6 to take the championship. Two other Baltusrol members qualified—Howard Giffin and James Tyng. Behr would later defeat Travers for the 1910 New Jersey Amateur title at Essex County.

---

NEW YORK HEARLD TRIBUNE, SUNDAY JUNE 9, 1907

#### J.D. Travers Wins New Jersey State Golf Title

Metropolitan Champion Defeats Max Behr, of Morris County by 7 Up and 6 to Play in Thirty-Six Hole final for Chief Honors over the Difficult Baltusrol Links, Completing Both Rounds Inside Eighty, with a Total of 157.

---

### 1908 Metropolitan Amateur

Charles H. Seely of Wee Burn deprived Montclair's Jerry Travers of the title. Those who watched the 36-hole final saw one of the greatest matches ever played. After being 6 down to Travers after the first 18 holes, Seely came back to tie the match on the 35th hole and sank a 15 foot putt on the thirty-eighth hole to win the title. The medal was won by Walter Travis from Garden City with a 159.

A class field of Amateurs participated in the championship including Findlay Douglas, C.B. Macdonald, and H.J. Whigham. Also of note, three Baltusrol members qualified for the match play rounds, Walter Kobbe, C. J. Sullivan, and C.F. Watson, Sr.

*Left: Walter Kobbe.*

*Right: C.H. Seely.*

## 1908 Metropolitan Open

*John Hobens.*

After a one year hiatus, the Metropolitan Open was held at Baltusrol in 1908. John Hobens from Englewood won the title, and Alex Campbell from Brookline finished second. In 1906 George Low won the Metropolitan Open at Hollywood. In 1907, no club could be induced to host the event, so Low retained the title for two years. At Baltusrol, Low finished 12th.

## 1912 Metropolitan Amateur

Jerry Travers of Upper Montclair defeated Oswald Kirkby of Englewood in the 36-hole final, 9 & 8. Travers had beaten Kirkby for the same title the year before at Garden City. The 36 hole qualifying medal was won by Kirkby with 163. Kirkby also defeated the great, but now aging, Walter Travis in the quarterfinals, 1 up. The tournament was of special interest because six Baltusrol members qualified for the match play rounds, Wallace Sinclair, C.J. Sullivan, Max Behr, C.E. Van Vleck, Jr., William Watson and James

*Travers and Kirkby.*

Tyng. Sinclair advanced the farthest, losing to Kirkby 2 & 1 in the quarterfinals.

## 1913 New Jersey Amateur

In a rematch of the prior year's final at Atlantic City, Jerry Travers defeated Oswald Kirkby to win the title. In the final 36-hole match, Travers came from 3 back after the morning 18 to win the match 3 & 1. The last three holes were played in a torrential thunderstorm that turned the course into a lake. The greens were impossible to putt and on the final hole of the match, with lightning bolts striking nearby, Travers jumped the ball into the hole with a mid-iron. Baltusrol was well represented with seven members making the championship matches, C.E. Van Vleck, Jr., Howard Giffin, Max Behr, William Watson, Max Marston, E.B. Schley, and Wallace Sinclair. Giffin and Behr made it the farthest, losing to Travers and Kirkby, respectively, in the semifinals.

## The 1914 Lesley Cup Matches

This celebrated event in honor of Robert W. Lesley featured the prominent amateur players of the day representing teams from the Metropolitan area, Massachusetts and Pennsylvania. In the featured match, Francis Ouimet defeated Jerry Travers 2 & 1. However, this was not enough for the Massachusetts team, as the Lesley Cup was won by the Metropolitan team. The Metropolitan team was well represented with three Baltusrol members, Max Marston, C.J. Sullivan and Augie Kammer.

*J. Anderson in the ditch on the first hole in his Lesley Cup match.*

## 1916 Women's Metropolitan Championship

Baltusrol was awarded this championship at the 11th hour, after losing its bid for the USGA Women's Amateur. Since Baltusrol did not have a big attraction for the coming season, the club petitioned the WMGA for this event. Mrs. Quentin F. Feitner (formerly Miss Lillian B. Hyde) from South Shore defeated Miss Georgianna Bishop from Brooklawn to win her fifth Metropolitan championship. Her win surpassed the four titles held by Miss Genevieve Hecker. Three Baltusrol members qualified for the championship matches, Miss Pauline Starrett, Mrs. Stephen P. Nash, Mrs. C.J.S. Fraser and Mrs. F. Pruyn.

155

*Standing:* (L-R) Norman Maxwell, Perry Adair, Oswald Kirkby, Grantland Rice, C.E. Van Vleck, Jr., D.E. Sawyer. *Sitting:* J.S. Worthington, Bobby Jones, J.D. Travers, Gilman Tiffany and Robert Gwathmey *Missing:* J.G. Anderson.

*Standing:* (L-R) Frank Belwood, Arthur Reid, A.J. Sanderson, J.M. Barnes, George Sargent, Wilfrid Reid. *Sitting:* Gordon Smith, James West, Cyril Walker, Gilbert Nicholls, Harrry Harris and Herbert Strong.

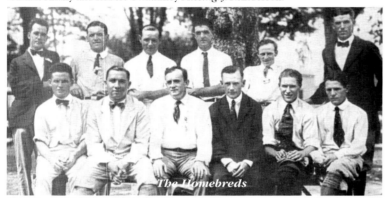

*Standing:* (L-R) H. Lagerblade, Tom Kerrigan, Mac Brady, E. French, J. Dowling, O. Hackbarth. *Sitting:* Jack Burke, Walter Hagen, Tom McNamara, W. McLean, E. Loos, and Chas Hoffner.

*Standing:* (L-R) Alex Cunningham, George Fotheringham, Jock Hutchison, Willie Macfarlane, Isaac Mackie. *Sitting:* George O. Simpson, Alex Campbell, George Low, Fred McLeod and Jack Hobens. *Missing:* Alex Smith and James Maiden.

## The 1917 P.G.A. War Relief Tournament

Organized on short notice by the fledgling Professional Golfers Association, this charity event raised thousands of dollars for the Red Cross Society and was hailed as a tremendous triumph. This was a team event played over four Metropolitan courses: Englewood, Baltusrol, Siwanoy and Garden City. There were four teams: the leading Amateurs of the day, the Americans or Homebreds, the English and the Scots. A star studded field of amateurs and professionals competed included Jerry Travers, Bobby Jones, Walter Hagen, Willie MacFarlane, Gilbert Nichols, Jim Barnes, Tom MacNamara and others. On the first day a mixed foursome event was played which included Mrs. William A. Gavin and Miss Violet Miller from Baltusrol. The Homebreds were the ultimate winners.

### 1925 New Jersey Amateur

Baltusrol's own Augie Kammer beat Bill Reekie of Upper Montclair in the final, 2 & 1. Kammer was the defending champion, having won the 1924 title at Shackamaxon, but he barely made it in this tournament, after shooting an 80 in the qualifying round. The medal was won by Jack Sharkey with a 71. Kammer bested Sharkey in the second round with a gallant come from behind rally. Fellow Baltusrol member, Edwin M. Wild fell to Kammer 3 and 2, in the semifinals. Kammer went on to suc-

*Augie Kammer*

cessfully defended his title in 1925 at Deal, becoming the first player to win the state crown three times.

### 1925 Women's Metropolitan Championship

Miss Marie R. Jenny from Hudson River defeated Mrs. Joseph Davis of Piping Rock to win the crown.

*Miss Jenny and Mrs. Davis.*

*A unique shot was made during the Championship. Seitz ricocheted her ball across the pond and on to the green for an ace.*

### 1935 New Jersey PGA

Maurrie O'Connor of Branch Brook won the championship by defeating Byron Nelson of Ridgewood G. C. in the longest state PGA on record—108 holes. Nelson was in his first year as assistant pro to George Jacobus, then PGA president. O'Connor and Nelson tied after 72 holes at 291. They played 18 holes the following day and were still tied at 75. O'Connor won the last 18 holes with a 71 to Nelson's 73.

### 1941 New Jersey Amateur

Charles Whitehead of Plainfield overwhelmed Karl Kellerman of Rock Spring by a record 14 & 12 to win his fourth consecutive New Jersey Amateur title, breaking Auggie Kammer's record of three in a row. Whitehead went on to win an unmatched fifth straight the following year at Montclair.

### 1979 New Jersey Amateur

George E. Haines, Jr. of Somerset Hills took the title and the emblematic Edwin M. Wild trophy with a four round total of 297 over the Lower. The format had been changed from match-play to stroke play. Runner-up honors were shared by Howard Pierson and Kenneth Hardwick.

### 1983 New Jersey Open

Jack Kiefer won the title over the Upper with a four round total of 286. His closest challenger, Steve Sieg from Montammy C.C, finished second six shots back at 292.

*Jack Keifer (L) receives trophy from Russ Helwig, defending Champion, Arthur Lynch (C), Chairman. looks on.*

### 1988 Metropolitan Open

After 90 years, the Metropolitan Open returned to Baltusrol. Bobby Hines won the crown over the Lower after a close challenge from Tom Joyce and Jim Albus.

## The Baltusrol Invitational

The concept of a Fall amateur tournament by invitation had been considered by the Baltusrol Golf Committee for a number of years in the early 1970's. Competitive amateur golf having a great tradition at Baltusrol, it was decided that the Club should continue its position of leadership and initiate an annual amateur event for representatives of local clubs to compete. The collateral benefit of showcasing the Club and its golf courses was almost certainly an element of the decision. A Committee made up of a number of Baltusrol members, including Robert A. Potter, John J. Farrell, Jr., Douglas H. Barden, Charles H. Simpson, James B. Collins and Allen E. Grogan, Chairman, was organized and the initial tournament was held in the Fall of 1975. Terry Sawyer and Bobby Kotz, Jr., representing the Trenton Country Club, won the first Baltusrol Invitational.

For its first eight years, the tournament was held as a one day, 36 hole two man team event using a Ryder Cup format. In 1982 the format was changed to a 54 hole event.

The most successful pairing has been the team of Duke Delcher and Blaise Giroso of Stone Harbor (NJ) Golf Club, wining in 1992, 1993 and 1994. Certainly not far behind in terms of competitiveness was the team of Mike Bodney and David Eger (1988 USGA Mid Amateur Champion) who, representing the Tournament Players Club at Sawgrass, finished second in 1987 and 1988, and won the tournament in 1989 and 1990. To date only one Baltusrol team has won—Richard Shea and John Lewis in 1988.

The tournament is now conducted annually on the Wednesday and Thursday prior to Labor Day, the field being made up of 50 teams representing some of the finest domestic and international clubs. In 1994, the Invitational celebrated its 20th anniversary, the tournament by then having developed into a nationally recognized amateur event. The Albert W. Tillinghast trophy was dedicated the evening of August 31, 1994, and is permanently maintained in the Baltusrol Club House. In 1989, Red Hoffman writing in the Met Golfer described the Baltusrol Invitational as "having been conceived in the best tradition of Baltusrol; to afford outstanding amateur golfers the opportunity to compete on two of the finest golf courses in the nation under true championship circumstances."

# Women's Golf
# &
# Baltusrol

*Top: Miss Beatrix Hoyt and Miss Eunice Terry.*
*Bottom: Miss Marion Oliver and Miss Griscom.*

𝒻rom Baltusrol's very beginning, women have played a key role. Louis Keller enjoyed the company of women, and he recognized the importance of women in recruiting members, promoting social events and staging tournaments. Several women played on Baltusrol's opening day in October, 1895; and the afternoon tea held following the golf was hosted by a number of prominent ladies from New York and New Jersey social circles.

### The Early Days
Many of Baltusrol's early members were women. Some had joined on their own while others inherited membership from their fathers.

The women's golf program in the early years was built around the lifestyle of Baltusrol's first members. Many would spend the hot months – July and August – at summer homes in the Berkshires or Adirondacks

or in similar spots. The consequence was a split golfing schedule. There was a series of seven weekly "cup matches" that began in late May. The woman with the most points after the seven events won the Spring Cup. Beginning in September a series of mixed fourball, women's four ball and two ball matches were featured in a schedule that lasted until the end of October or even later.

Around the turn of the century, amateur golf was much more publicized than it is today. And women's golfing events at the club level were widely reported in all the newspapers of the day. All the major metropolitan clubs sponsored interclub events that were highlights of their annual calendars. At Baltusrol, Louis Keller sponsored a Women's Open Championship (open to members of clubs that

belonged to the USGA) that attracted the best women golfers in the Northeast and also from points as far west as Pittsburgh and Chicago. The event was held in October, a week or so after the U.S. Women's Amateur Championship, then called the National Women's Championship, and most of the entrants in the National Championship also entered the "Open" at Baltusrol. A number of papers stated that the event was as important as the National Championship, and was a better test of golf, since the original course at Baltusrol had by 1897 been lengthened and improved to the point where it was considered one of the longest and severest courses in the country.

Baltusrol's first Women's Open was played on October 14, 1897, and was covered at great length by *The New York Herald* and other papers. Over fifty women entered—by far, it was reported, the largest field in women's golfing history. The entrants included players from Shinnecock Hills, Albany, Westchester, Montclair, Ardsley, Tuxedo, and Morris County. Mrs. Arthur Turnere of Shinnecock, a former champion of that club and runner-up at the U.S. Women's Amateur of 1896, probably was the best known of the entrants.

The format was usual for the time—a morning round of 18 holes at stroke play was followed by lunch and a putting contest. The players all possessed handicaps, and the low net prize was won by Miss Bessie Pitcher of Baltusrol, a 40 handicapper, who shot a gross score of 141, and thereby became the first winner of a women's interclub event at Baltusrol. The four players who had scored the lowest gross scores in the morning round played nine hole matches for the open championship in the afternoon. The winner of those matches was Miss Helen Shelton, the Morris County champion. Miss Shelton had made a gross score of 110 in her morning round and 112 in her afternoon round, which was concluded in the dark.

It should be noted, for purposes of comparison, the men's course record at the time was 82. A large crowd, by the standards of the day, of over 500 attended the event.

In the next year, the Baltusrol Women's Open was held as a two day event. Owing to a driving rain and high winds the tournament committee attempted to postpone the second day's rounds, but the women, led by the Morris County contingent, insisted that the golf proceed, and teed off almost on schedule over the objections of the committee.

This event continued annually until 1901, when Baltusrol hosted its first national championship—the U.S. Women's Amateur. Curiously, the Baltusrol Women's Open, that had been so successful prior to the 1901 National Championship, was not resumed in the following years. This may have been because Baltusrol's stature had now developed to the point where it was in position to request the regional and national men's and women's events sponsored by the USGA, MGA, WMGA and the NJGA—organizations in which Baltusrol members had attained positions of leadership. In effect then, the Baltusrol Women's Open had been the stepping stones for the club's launch into the national spotlight. For in 1903, Baltusrol hosted its first U.S. Open and in the following year, its first U.S. Amateur.

### Baltusrol and the Met

The Woman's Metropolitan Golf Association (WMGA or also known as the "Met") was formed in 1899 to promote interclub women's competition. Philadelphia is credited with the first organization for women's golf—the Women's Golf Association of Philadelphia, formed in 1897. The Met was second, followed by Boston with its own organization. By 1900, the Met had outstripped Philadelphia and Boston in point of size and activity. Today the Met represents around 1,850 members from the 150 clubs in the Metropolitan area.

Baltusrol was one of the Met's founding clubs and Baltusrol women have been active in the Met throughout its history. Credit for form-

*Miss Griscom and Miss Oliver.*

*The gallery at the 1900 women's tournament.*

*Mrs. William Fellowes Morgan.*

ing the Met goes to five active golfers of the day—Mrs. W. Fellowes Morgan, a founding patroness of Baltusrol, Mrs. A. deWitte Cochrane of Ardsley, Mrs. William Shippen of Morris County, Miss Beatrix Hoyt of Shinnecock and Miss Ruth Underhill of Nassau. Mrs. W. Fellowes Morgan was the Met's first president and

*Mrs. Edward Manice.*

served for four years.

In all, six Baltusrol women have presided over the Met. Mrs. Morgan was followed by another Baltusrol member, Mrs. Edward Manice, who also was the Met Champion for three years running, beginning in 1902.

Mrs. Myra Patterson served as president for several terms while representing a number of clubs. She was President of the Met for four years beginning in 1910 during her time at Baltusrol. Mrs. Patterson was a fine golfer. She was the champion at Baltusrol and Englewood, runner-up in the 1904 Met championship, captain of many Baltusrol and Met teams, first winner of the North and South at Pinehurst in 1903 and again in 1904 and 1905, and a qualifier for the 1905 Women's National. At some time after her term as President of the Met she moved to Westchester, where she continued her active interest in women's golf. The Met's Myra D. Patterson Trophy, donated in 1925, is played for by teams representing Westchester, Long Island and New Jersey.

Two other Baltusrol members who were Met Presidents were Mrs. Frederick B. Ryan, who served from 1930 to 1933, and Mrs. Wright Goss, Jr., who served from 1942-1945.

Helen Hawes was the latest Baltusrol member to serve as Met President from 1955-1956. In addition, she also was president of the New Jersey Women's Golf Association and a member of the Women's Committee of the USGA. She was rewarded for her contributions to golf in 1967 when she was appointed nonplaying Captain of the Curtis Cup Team.

In addition to the Met, Baltusrol women have also been active and have held leadership positions with the Women's New Jersey Golf Association and the Garden State Women's Golf Association. These organizations serve similar roles to the Met in the Garden State.

### Margaret Gavin

Mrs. William A. (Margaret) Gavin, a noted Baltusrol champion, was one of the most accomplished players of her day. She came to the United States from England in 1915 and is also known as the first woman to cross the English Channel in an airplane.

**Mrs. Gavin Will Tour West in Golf Benefits**

Baltusrol Woman to Continue Red Cross Exhibitions Against Men.

She won the Met Championship in 1917 and 1921, the Eastern Championship in 1916 and finished second in the U.S. Women's Amateur in 1915

*Mrs. Gavin.*

*Mrs. Gavin in her much publicized match with George Low.*

and 1919. She often teamed up with George Low, the Baltusrol pro, in many of the interclub team tournaments of the day. Mrs. Gavin received tremendous notoriety when she played a series of exhibition matches against men professionals. The proceeds from the matches went to the Red Cross to fund ambulances as part of the World War I relief effort. Mrs. Gavin was given nine strokes and played from the same teeing areas as the professionals. Her matches in the metropolitan area were so successful that a tour of the western United States was organized under the auspices of the Western Golf Association. On every course over which she played, Mrs. Gavin succeeded in breaking the woman's record by not less than six strokes. When Mrs. Gavin returned, she decided to go to France to drive an ambulance that she herself had donated.

After the war in 1921, Mrs. Gavin teamed up with Miss Marion Hollis, the national champion, to defeat the Leitch sisters in an exhibition match at Baltusrol, sponsored by the Metropolitan Women's Golf Association. Miss Cecil Leitch, the famous British Women's Champion had the low round with 85. Her sister, Edith, though, found the going much rockier.

**Eighteen Golf Matches Carded for Mrs. Gavin**

Baltusrol Woman Player to Start Western Round of Competition Today at St. Paul Minn.

Plays Well-Known Professionals

### Baltusrol Champions

While it is clear that club championships were played in the early years of the club, as newspapers spoke from time to time of Baltusrol women champions, including Mrs. Morgan, Mrs. Manice, Mrs. Patterson and Mrs. Gavin, club records of these event have not survived. The first club champion listed in the record is in 1916, and there are several gaps in the record between that year and 1929. These championships were always played at match play, so we don't know just how well the various champions played and there are no reports of medal play scores.

Baltusrol women champions also won ten New Jersey State Championships. Helen Hockenjos won six, Mrs. Sherbourne (Harriet) Hart two, and Miss Gail Wild and Mrs. Wright Goss, Jr., one each. Gail was the daughter of E.M. Wild, a nine-time Baltusrol club champion.

The dominant story of the Baltusrol women's' championship revolves around Helen Hockenjos, who won 13 club championships from 1948 to 1968. She was one of the best woman golfers ever to play at Baltusrol, and in addition to her six New Jersey State Championships, she was runner-up in the Met Championship on one occasion. She also presided over the Met during the 1948-1950 term, when she represented Lake Hopatcong.

Mrs. Hockenjos and Charlotte De Cozen, who herself won the championship five times, won all the championships in the ten year period between 1948 to 1959. Helen Hawes won in 1947 and in 1960. So it could also be said that these three women dominated the event over a twelve year period. Helen Hawes also won the Met Seniors Championship in 1959 and the prestigious U.S. Senior Women's Golf Association Championship in 1961.

*Harriet Hart.*

Harriet (Hatsy) Hart won the Met Championship in 1970 and went on to play on the LPGA tour. She learned to play golf at age 24 and won the New Jersey State Championship in 1969 and 1970. She was club champion of Baltusrol in 1973 and reached the quarter finals of the U. S. Open in

*Lee Steffens.*

1974 when it was played at Montclair. During the next two years, she qualified for membership in the LPGA (she was age 40 at the time) and played in ten LPGA tournaments, all of which were located in the Northeast, and made several cuts. When the LPGA instituted a rule requiring more travel away from family and home than Mrs. Hart felt was warranted, she retired and was reinstated as an amateur.

More recently, Lee Steffens had a banner year in 1984 when she won the Met Championship, the Garden State Woman's Golf Association Championship and the Baltusrol Championship.

### Women's Records

All the women who have played at Baltusrol, from Bessie Shelton, whose gross 141 was good enough to win a prize back in 1897, to the most recent club champion, have recognized and perhaps enjoyed the fact that they were playing courses designed and built for championship play. Except for the "Short Course," which was only in use for a few years prior to 1900, the women's tees have been either played from the forward portion of the men's tees or a smaller teeing ground just forward of the men's tees.

Consequently, women's records for the Old Course and the Upper and Lower courses are relatively high. Miss Marion Hollis

of the West Brook Club made an 83 during the 1916 Met and this score stands as the record for the Old course. Mickey Wright's brilliant 69 is the women's record for the Lower, while Marlene Streit's 74, also set during the 1961 Open is the women's amateur record for that Course. The brilliant 65 shot by Judy Clark (Dickinson) during the 1985 Open is the women's record for the Upper, while the amateur record for the Upper is 71 shot by Danielle Ammacapane also in the 1985 Open.

*Woman's Championship Trophy.*

*Mrs Helen Hockenjos.*

161

# Distinguished Baltusrol Men Golfers

*J*ust as Baltusrol itself has been in the mainstream of American golf since 1895, so have its golfers. Their names are found on Baltusrol's roster of Presidents, Governors and club champions; and from Baltusrol they ventured forth to distinguish themselves in the organizations that shaped golf in America and the Metropolitan area.

### The Presidents
Over the last 100 years, a long line of Baltusrol members have provided distinguished service to the United States Golf Association (USGA), The Metropolitan Golf Association(MGA), and the New Jersey State Golf Association (NJSGA). They have served as officers and committee members and some have been leaders. William Fellowes Morgan, a founding member of Baltusrol, was the MGA's first president. He was also an early secretary and treasurer of the USGA. Lionel Graham was the first President of the NJSGA. The MGA and NJSGA Presidents that have represented Baltusrol are shown in the box.

### The First Champions
James Tyng was among the first converts from baseball and general athletics to gain prominence in metropolitan golf and until beaten by Archibald Graham in the first New Jersey Amateur in 1900 he had been the "uncrowned king" in New Jersey Golf. Tyng played for both Morris County G. C. and Baltusrol. He was

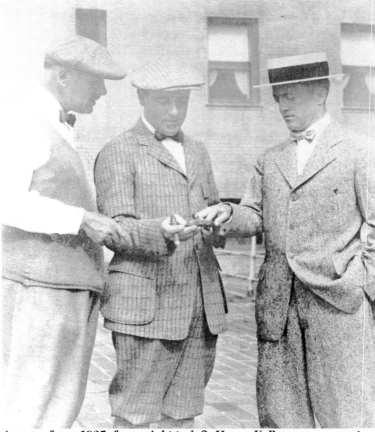
*A scene from 1925: from right to left, Harry Y. Barrow, current MGA President, discussing the slotted clubs recently barred, with Findlay Douglas, former MGA President and Bill Reekie, the MGA Amateur Champion.*

Baltusrol's first club champion in 1899. He also won the U.S. Seniors Championship in 1912 and 1915. According to Fifty Years of American Golf,

Tyng made baseball history as well as golf history, having been both a catcher and a pitcher while at Harvard in 1896. He is said to have been the first catcher to don

a catcher's mask.

Next in fame to Tyng was Henry Pennington Toler, who often joined Tyng in foursomes and four ball matches to uphold the colors of New Jersey against the best amateurs of that decade. The Baltusrol Club Championship was originally known as the Toler Cup. Toler donated the cup for Baltusrol's first championship in January 1896, which was won by Tyng. The Toler Cup was lost in the clubhouse fire of 1909, and ironically, Toler never won the club championship.

In September 1896, Tyng and Toler were red-hot favorites to win the final at an amateur foursome competition staged at the Newport Golf Club. But they were beaten by Fred Havemeyer, age 16, and Harry Havemeyer, age 18, sons of "Sugar King" Theodore Havemeyer, who was the first president of the USGA.

Louis Bayard, Jr., Hugh K. Toler, and Craig Hamilton were also noted Baltusrol players of the time. In the

*Early instructional photographs (circa 1897) show Tyng demonstrating the proper golf swing.*

many interclub events, they would often round out the Baltusrol team headed by Tyng and H.P. Toler. Bayard, Jr., who won the club championship in 1904, initially made his mark as a collegiate player for Princeton University and then Baltusrol. His father served the longest term as club president of Baltusrol—from 1898 to 1919. Hugh Toler would also distinguish himself as the hero of the 1909 Baltusrol clubhouse fire by "swinging the women out the windows of the burning building." Craig Hamilton, who won the club championship in the Fall of 1899 and Spring of 1900, was most noted for his stunning victories over the great Amateur champions, Findlay Douglas and Walter Travis in invitational events at Lakewood in the spring and fall of 1900, respectively.

Tyng, Bayard, Jr., and H. P. Toler also qualified for the 1896 U.S. Amateur at Shinnecock Hills, but they were eliminated before the semifinals. The Amateur champion was H. J. Whigham of Chicago, a son-in-law of the defending champion, Charles B. Macdonald.

### Max Behr
Behr was a top amateur in the first decade of the century, playing for Morris County and then Baltusrol. He was the runner-up to the great Jerry Travers in the 1908 U.S. Amateur and the 1907 and 1908 New Jersey Amateurs. He finally beat Travers for the New Jersey Amateur title at Essex County in 1910. He also won the New Jersey Amateur the year before at Montclair defeating M.K. Smith. Behr was also a noted golf architect and was

*Behr (L) at St. Andrews with Alister MacKenzie.*

the publisher of Golf Illustrated. A protege of Alister MacKenzie, he remodeled the Lake and Ocean Courses at the Olympic Club in the 1920's. He won the Baltusrol Club Championship in 1909.

### Max Marston
Marston was a contemporary and worthy competitor of Bobby Jones, George Von Elm, and Chick Evans in the middle 1920's. He had won the Baltusrol club championship 1914-15 and the New Jersey Amateur in 1915 and 1919. He resigned from Baltusrol in 1918 to move to Philadelphia, and there won three Pennsylvania Amateurs. Marston defeated Francis Ouimet in the semifinals of the 1923 U.S. Amateur Championship, and then beat the great Jess W. Sweetser to win tournament. Sweetser had beaten Chick Evans to win the Amateur the preceding year. Both Marston and Sweetser were members of the 1922 U.S. Walker Cup team. According to Who's Who in Golf, Marston, like Mac Smith, "never took a divot." In 1923, Marston was made an honorary lifetime member of Baltusrol.

### Wild and Kammer
They were outstanding rivals at Baltusrol for years. Edwin M. Wild was of slight build, weighing only 135 pounds, and was handicapped by a left arm that had been injured in an ice boating accident. Nevertheless, he won the Baltusrol Club Championship eight times in a row, 1922-1929, and again in 1931. While Wild had the upper hand on Augie Kammer in the Club Championship, he could not beat Kammer in the New Jersey Amateur. Wild made it to the finals in the New Jersey Amateur on five occasions only to lose each time; three of those losses were to fellow members: Kammer in 1924 and 1926 and Max Marston in 1919. Although he never won the Amateur, in later years his contributions to golf were recognized when the New Jersey Amateur trophy was donated in his honor by a fellow Baltusrol member.

Kammer was the first player to win three consecutive New Jersey Amateur titles in 1924, 1925, and 1926. In the 1924 Amateur at the Shackamaxon C. C. Kammer beat Wild, 1 up. Incidentally, Wild tied for the medal with two others, but lost it on a coin toss. In

*Wild (R) with Travis.*

*Augie Jr. and Sr., 1926 NJSGA Father and Son champions.*

the 1925 Amateur at Baltusrol, Kammer defeated Wild, 3 and 2, in the semifinals and then beat Bill Reekie of Upper Montclair in the final, 2 and 1. In the 1926 Amateur at the Deal C. C., Kammer again beat Wild, 5 and 4. Commenting on his victory The New York Times said "Deadly putting was Kammer's forte and today he was almost uncanny." An Augie Kammer putting contest is held annually at Baltusrol on Labor Day weekend.

Wild and Kammer's children were chips of the old blocks. Wild's daughter, Gail, won the New Jersey Women's Championship in 1937 and the Baltusrol Women's Club Championship in 1939, 1940, and 1942. Kammer's son, Augie Jr. (Fred), won the Baltusrol club championship four times, the New Jersey Junior Championship in 1928 and 1929, and in 1946 he reached the semifinals of the U.S. Amateur at Baltusrol. In the following year he was named to represent the Unites States in the Walker Cup matches.

### R. C. James

The Baltusrol Seniors tournament was virtually dominated by R. C. James. He won the championship in ten successive years from 1923-1932. He and his son R.C. James, Jr. won the New Jersey Father and Son in 1930. James occupied the house that was formerly located in the triangle at the right of the first, second, and third Lower fairways. There were a few such houses on the land that Louis Keller had acquired in the 1890s, and the club apparently rented them. The house has long since been razed.

### Colonel Lindgrove

Colonel Martin S Lindgrove was Club Champion four times and Seniors Champion six times. He also won the New Jersey Seniors Championship eight times: 1947 - 1950, 1952 - 1954, and in 1957; and he won the U. S. Seniors Championship in 1947, the International Seniors Championship in 1951, and captained the U.S. Seniors Golf teams to Great Britain and Europe in 1954 and to Africa in 1955.

### Baldwin and Carpenter

Lifelong competitors, Dave Baldwin and Larry Carpenter met at a junior golf tournament when they were 15 and became close friends. They went to Lehigh together and were co-captains of the golf team. At Baltusrol, Carpenter won the club championship eight times between 1948 and 1973—a remarkable span of 25 years. In 1954, he distin-

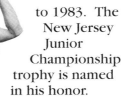

guished himself internationally reaching the quarter-finals in the British Amateur Championship and the semi-finals in the French Amateur, and winning the German Open Championship in Nuremberg. He also won the Baltusrol Seniors Championship four times and won the New Jersey Seniors Championship in 1986.

Baldwin, a former Baltusrol President, was also a Baltusrol Club Champion and Senior Champion. In 1954, he stunned the New Jersey professional golf scene by becoming the second amateur to win the New Jersey Open Championship, which was held at Essex County. In that same year, he was runner-up in the National Left Hander's Tournament, in which he won the long-driving contest. Baldwin and Carpenter also teamed up to win the New Jersey Scotch Foursome Championship three times.

*Larry Carpenter.*

### Lichtenwalter

Homer O. Lichtenwalter, Jr. was a four time Baltusrol Club Champion. He played in the U.S. Amateur

Championship in 1952 and 1953 and was a medalist in the New York sectional qualifier in 1953. He was considered a statesman of golf. He served as president of the New Jersey State Golf Association from 1981

*Dave Baldwin.*

to 1983. The New Jersey Junior Championship trophy is named in his honor.

### Billy Dear

William "Billy" Dear, Jr. Dear played championship golf for over 40 years despite 42 surgical operations, including a complete shoulder replacement, 2 chrome knees, 4 fused vertebrae, and 5 plastic fingers. He won the New Jersey Amateur Championship in 1951 and was runner-up in 1941, 1946, 1953, and 1957. He also was runner-up in the New Jersey Open in 1951. He won the New Jersey Seniors championship in 1976 and the Metropolitan Seniors Championship in 1971. A former president and tournament chairman of the Metropolitan Golf Association, the New Jersey Boys Championship and Pre-Senior Championship trophies are named in his honor.

### Other Champions

A past Club Champion, John Poinier won the New Jersey Golf Association Seniors Championship in 1971, and

the New Jersey Seniors Championship in 1970. He also was president of both the New Jersey and the Eastern Seniors Golf Association. A Baltusrol Seniors Champion, Thorwald "Tom" Larson won the New Jersey Seniors Championship in 1967, while Richard A. Henry, a three time Baltusrol Club Champion, won it in 1969.

John Farrell, Jr., the son of the celebrated father, won the New Jersey Junior

*Dick Henry.*

Championship in 1950 and the Korean Airforce Championship in 1956. He won the Club Championship four times.

In recent years, a new breed of Baltusrol Club Champions have ably represented Baltusrol in outside events. They include Bobby Gaertner, Gil Zimmerman, Jeff Kiley and Rick Shea.

| MGA Presidents | |
|---|---|
| 1901-1908 | William Fellowes Morgan |
| 1925-1926 | Harry Y. Barrow |
| 1948-1949 | Sheppard Barnes |

| NJSGA Presidents | |
|---|---|
| 1900, 1903-1904 | L.H. Graham |
| 1915-1916 | William Watson |
| 1924-1925 | Harry Y. Barrow |
| 1935-1936 | Curtis W. McGraw |
| 1970-1971 | Joseph H. McCabe, Jr. |
| 1982-1983 | Homer O. Lichtenwalter, Jr. |
| 1994-1995 | Thomas Paluck |

# APPENDIX

## Presidents

| | |
|---|---|
| 1895-1898 | Arthur D. Weeks |
| 1898-1919 | Louis P. Bayard |
| 1919-1926 | Robert S. Sinclair |
| 1926-1929 | W. G. McKnight |
| 1929-1938 | Stewart Baker |
| 1938-1943 | Caxton Brown |
| 1943-1945 | Walter R. Hine |
| 1945-1947 | Maurice N. Trainer |
| 1947-1952 | Stoddard M. Stevens |
| 1952-1955 | Hobart C. Ramsey |
| 1955-1958 | Monroe J. Rathbone |
| 1958-1961 | John C. Smaltz |
| 1961-1964 | W. H. Feldmann |
| 1964-1967 | William M. Walther |
| 1967-1970 | Robert Finney |
| 1970-1973 | Matthew J. Glennon |
| 1973-1976 | John S. Roberts |
| 1976-1979 | B. P. Russell |
| 1979-1982 | Robert J. Boutillier |
| 1982-1985 | Paul J. Hanna |
| 1985-1987 | Robert A. Potter |
| 1987-1989 | Kenneth C. Nichols |
| 1989-1991 | David M. Baldwin |
| 1991-1993 | Alan L. Reed, Jr. |
| 1993- | F. D. Meyercord |

## Club Champions

| | |
|---|---|
| 1899 Spring | James A. Tyng |
| 1899 Fall | Craig Hamilton |
| 1900 Sping | Craig Hamilton |
| 1900 Fall | James A. Tyng |
| 1901-1902 | R. E. DeRaismes |
| 1903 | F. C. Reinhart |
| 1904 | L. P. Bayard, Jr. |
| 1905 | A. S. Morrow |
| 1906 | Walter Kobbe |
| 1907-1908 | C. J. Sullivan |
| 1909 | Max H. Behr |
| 1910 | Oscar Woodward |
| 1911 | C. J. Sullivan |
| 1912 | C. E. Vanvleck, Jr. |
| 1913 | W. F. Morgan, Jr. |
| 1914-1916 | Max Marston |
| 1917 | Stephen P. Nash |
| 1918 | R. H. Gwaltney |
| 1919 | A. F. Kammer |
| 1920 | S. Van Vechten |
| 1921 | A. F. Kammer |
| 1922-1929 | E. M. Wild |
| 1930 | A. F. Kammer, Jr. |
| 1931 | E. M. Wild |
| 1932 | F. Jefferson, Jr. |
| 1933 | Robert Finney |
| 1934-1935 | M. S. Lindgrove |
| 1936-1938 | A. F. Kammer, Jr. |
| 1939-1940 | M. S. Lindgrove |
| 1941 | H. S. Hall |
| 1942 | Rollin P. Taylor |
| 1943 | P. H. Hartung |
| 1944 | Richard A. Henry |
| 1945 | Eugene F. Krautter |
| 1946 | Richard A. Henry |
| 1947 | W. G. Johnston |
| 1948-1949 | L. E. Carpenter, Jr. |
| 1950 | H. Lichtenwalter, Jr. |
| 1951 | George H. Frey |
| 1952 | W. G. Johnston |
| 1953 | Stephen G. Lee |
| 1954 | L. E. Carpenter, Jr. |
| 1955 | Richard A. Henry |
| 1956 | L. E. Carpenter, Jr. |
| 1957 | H. Lichtenwalter, Jr. |
| 1958-1960 | L. E. Carpenter, Jr. |
| 1961-1962 | H. Lichtenwalter, Jr. |

| | |
|---|---|
| 1963 | David Baldwin |
| 1964 | John Farrell, Jr. |
| 1965 | John Poinier |
| 1966 | Oliver H. Havens |
| 1967-1968 | Ed Crosland, Jr. |
| 1969 | John Farrell, Jr. |
| 1970-1971 | J. Schermerhorn, Jr. |
| 1972 | John Farrell, Jr. |
| 1973 | L. E. Carpenter, Jr. |
| 1974 | Robert T. Gaertner |
| 1975 | Jerry Swon |
| 1976-1977 | Robert T. Gaertner |
| 1978 | Christopher B. Scott |
| 1979 | Eric J. Gleacher |
| 1980 | L. Randy Riley |
| 1981 | John Farrell, Jr. |
| 1982-1983 | G. A. Zimmerman, Jr. |
| 1984-1985 | Bryan Burke |
| 1986 | Richard W. Shea, Jr. |
| 1987 | Jeffrey T. Kiley |
| 1988 | Richard W. Shea, Jr. |
| 1989 | John Lewis, Jr. |
| 1990-1991 | Richard W. Shea, Jr. |
| 1992 | Robert T. Gaertner |
| 1993 | Richard W. Shea, Jr. |
| 1994 | Stephen F. Boyd |

## Seniors Association Champions

| | |
|---|---|
| 1922 | Robert Sinclair |
| 1923-1932 | R. C. James |
| 1933 | C. N. Fowler |
| 1934 | J. R. Monroe |
| 1935 | A. F. Kammer |
| 1936 | H. N. Balch |
| 1937 | John F. Duffey |
| 1938 | Caxton Brown |
| 1939 | H. N. Balch |
| 1940-1941 | M. S. Lindgrove |
| 1942 | C. E. Dwyer |
| 1943 | W. P. Conway |
| 1944 | Arthur E. Jones |
| 1945 | E. J. Ogden |
| 1946 | M. S. Lindgrove |
| 1947 | W. P. Conway |
| 1948 | W. V. Cadmus |
| 1949 | E. F. Krautter |
| 1950 | S. R. Williams |
| 1951-1953 | M. S. Lindgrove |
| 1954 | S. R. Williams |
| 1955 | W. W. Krautter |
| 1956 | R. A. Henry |
| 1957 | George H. Frey |
| 1958 | George A. Murray |
| 1959 | George H. Frey |
| 1960-1961 | Robert Finney |
| 1962 | R. A. Henry |
| 1963 | A. Konkle |
| 1964-1965 | Robert Finney |
| 1966 | Thorwald Larson |
| 1967 | R. A. Henry |
| 1968 | Robert Finney |
| 1969-1970 | William Y. Dear, Jr. |
| 1971 | John Roberts |
| 1972-1973 | John Poinier |
| 1974 | Thorwald Larson |
| 1975 | John A. Deitrich |
| 1976 | W. W. Reinhard |
| 1977 | John A. Deitrich |
| 1978 | Thorwald Larson |
| 1979-1980 | John A. Deitrich |
| 1981 | Arthur R. Paterson |
| 1982-1983 | John A. Deitrich |
| 1984-1986 | L. E. Carpenter, Jr. |
| 1987 | David M. Baldwin |
| 1988 | L. E. Carpenter, Jr. |
| 1989 | Richard T. Miller |
| 1990 | James E. Rutter |

| | |
|---|---|
| 1991 | Daniel A. McMillan |
| 1992 | James E. Rutter |
| 1993 | L. E. Carpenter, Jr. |
| 1994 | David O. Zenker |

## USGA Tournament Chairmen

| | |
|---|---|
| 1901 | Louis Keller |
| 1903 | Louis Keller |
| 1904 | Louis Keller |
| 1911 | Louis Keller |
| 1915 | Louis Keller |
| 1926 | Jay R. Monroe |
| 1936 | Jay R. Monroe |
| 1946 | Charles P. Burgess |
| 1954 | Charles P. Burgess |
| 1961 | Frank W. Boyd |
| 1967 | Bob Finney |
| 1980 | Chuck Simpson |
| 1985 | Bob Potter |
| 1993 | Dick Miller |

## Women Champions

| | |
|---|---|
| 1916 | Mrs. S. P. Nash |
| 1919 | Elizabeth A. Hardin |
| 1920-1921 | Mrs. S. F. Dubois |
| 1922-1923 | Elizabeth A. Hardin |
| 1929 | Mrs. R. F. Decker |
| 1930 | Mrs. C. L. Voorhees |
| 1931 | Charlotte E. Clutting |
| 1932-1933 | Mrs. C. L. Voorhees |
| 1934 | Mrs. C. H. Donner |
| 1935 | Alice Rutherford |
| 1936 | Mrs. W. D. Goss, Jr. |
| 1937-1938 | Alice Rutherford |
| 1939-1940 | Gail Wild |
| 1941 | Mrs. Bruce Ryan |
| 1942 | Gail Wild |
| 1943-1946 | Mrs. H. C. Ramsey |
| 1947 | Helen R. Hawes |
| 1948 | C. Helen Hockenjos |
| 1949-1950 | Charlotte DeCozen |
| 1951-1952 | C. Helen Hockenjos |
| 1953 | Charlotte DeCozen |
| 1954 | C. Helen Hockenjos |
| 1955 | Charlotte DeCozen |
| 1956 | C. Helen Hockenjos |
| 1957 | Charlotte DeCozen |
| 1958-1959 | C. Helen Hockenjos |
| 1960 | Helen R. Hawes |
| 1961 | Essene D. Baldwin |
| 1962 | Lucille Hickman |

| | |
|---|---|
| 1963-1968 | C. Helen Hockenjos |
| 1969 | Lucille Hickman |
| 1970-1971 | Isabel Mercer |
| 1972 | Brita Blauvelt |
| 1973 | Harriet Hart |
| 1974 | Ruth Swart |
| 1975 | Isabel Mercer |
| 1976 | Nancy Rogers |
| 1977 | Betty Lou McCabe |
| 1978 | Dorothy Paluck |
| 1979 | Ruth Swart |
| 1980 | Janet Wilcox |
| 1981 | Dorothy Paluck |
| 1982-1983 | Robin Jervey |
| 1984-1985 | Lee Steffens |
| 1986 | Nancy Rogers |
| 1987-1988 | Robin Jervey |
| 1989 | Maria Busch |
| 1990 | Mariko Bridgewater |
| 1991 | Lyn McCarthy |
| 1992 | Mariko Bridgewater |
| 1993 | Lyn McCarthy |
| 1994 | Susan Penny |

## Women's Golf Chairpersons

| | |
|---|---|
| 1945-1946 | Mae Rummel |
| 1947-1948 | Ruth Evers |
| 1949-1950 | Helen Hawes |
| 1951-1952 | Peg Pelletier |
| 1953-1954 | Claire Beckett |
| 1955-1956 | Jessie Hassell |
| 1957-1958 | Janice Vilett |
| 1959-1960 | Ernestine Murray |
| 1961-1962 | Ruth Lichtenwalter |
| 1963-1964 | Elizabeth Johnston |
| 1965-1966 | Helen Kalchthaler |
| 1967-1968 | Mary Lou Hodge |
| 1969-1970 | Marie Tansey |
| 1971-1972 | Ruth Swart |
| 1973-1974 | Bette Gaertner |
| 1975-1976 | Kay Ellison |
| 1977-1978 | Nancy Rogers |
| 1979-1980 | Carmen Mumma |
| 1981-1982 | Isabel Mercer |
| 1983-1984 | Janet Talbot |
| 1985-1986 | Marjorie Reinhard |
| 1987-1988 | C. Wigton & B. Wolff |
| 1989-1990 | J. Byrne & A. Reed |
| 1991-1992 | Julie Meyerholtz |
| 1993-1994 | Dale Feeney |
| 1995-1996 | Anne Lyon |

## Baltusrol Invitational

| | Players | Representing |
|---|---|---|
| 1975 | Terry Sawyer & Bobby Kotz, Jr. | Trenton CC |
| 1976 | Steve Dropkin & Howard Pierson | River Vale CC |
| 1977 | Bob Housen & Vic Gerard, Jr. | Woodlake G&CC |
| 1978 | Jimmy Dee & Lee Martinson | Ridgewood CC |
| 1979 | Jay Blumenfeld & Ned Steiner | Mountain Ridge CC |
| 1980 | Ben Brundred & Brad Prichard | Congressional CC |
| 1981 | Terry Sawyer & Tom Bartolacci | Copper Hill GC |
| 1982 | Terry Sawyer & Tom Bartolacci | Copper Hill GC |
| 1983 | Bucky Erhardt & Pete Green | Fox Fire Club |
| 1984 | Tom Hamilton & Jon Saxton | Greenwich CC |
| 1985 | Tom Hamilton & Jon Saxton | Greenwich CC |
| 1986 | Randy Sonier & Bill Pelham | Champions GC |
| 1987 | Jonny Doppek & Ron Springer | Brae Burn CC |
| 1988 | John Lewis & Rick Shea | Baltusrol GC |
| 1989 | Mike Bodney & David Eger | TPC at Sawgrass |
| 1990 | Mike Bodney & David Eger | TPC at Sawgrass |
| 1991 | Duke Delcher & Tom Carter | Sandy Run CC |
| 1992 | Duke Delcher & Blaise Giroso | Stone Harbor GC |
| 1993 | Duke Delcher & Blaise Giroso | Stone Harbor GC |
| 1994 | Duke Delcher & Blaise Giroso | Stone Harbor GC |

# INDEX